THE HIDDEN CODE OF REVELATION

The Soul's Journey to Awakening and Atonement

VOLUME II

NICHOLAS C. DEMETRY, M.D.

Copyright ©2015 Nicholas C. Demetry, M.D.
All Rights Reserved
No part of this book may be reproduced, stored in a retrieval system, or transmitted by any means, electronic, mechanical, photocopying, recording, or otherwise without written permission from the author.

ISBN 13: 978-0-9792961-3-0
ISBN 10: 0-9792961-3-7

Library of Congress Control Number: 2014944286

Editing
Diane Kistner
dkistner@futurecycle.org

Book Design
Donna Overall
donnaoverall@bellsouth.net

Original Graphics, Diagrams, Charts, and Tables
©2015 Donna Overall
donnaoverall@bellsouth.net

Cover Image
St. John's Vision of the New Jerusalem
Courtesy of St. Takla Haymanout Coptic Orthodox Website

www.etherikos.com

Table of Contents

Table of Contents i
Diagrams, Charts, and Tables iv
About the Author v
Acknowledgments vi
Foreword vii
Introduction 1
Understanding an Ancient Text in a Modern Light 1
Archetypal Psychology and How We View the Revelation ... 3
Kabbalah, Initiation, and Revelation 7
The Secret Sephirah of Da'at and Human Consciousness 8
Revelation and the Turning of the Ages 9
The Age of Pisces and Aquarius 9

Chapter 12 of Revelation 13
The Heart's Purification 13
The Emergence of the Divine Feminine 14
The Red Dragon 16
The Sexual/Relational/One-to-One Instinct 17
Wounded Expressions of the Sexual, One-to-One Instinct
 ("The Dragon") 18
The Flight into Egypt—An Instruction for the Sexual/
 One-to-One Instinct 19

Chapter 13 of Revelation 23
The Beast 23
The Social Instinct 24
Wounded Expressions of the Social Instinct ("The Beast") ... 25
The Good Samaritan—An Instruction for the Social Instinct
 Given by the Christ 25
The Pseudo-Lamb 27
The Self-Preservation Instinct 29
The Feeding of Four Thousand—An Instruction for the
 Self-Preservation Instinct Given by the Christ 30
Self-Introspection and Healing Practice for All Three Types
 of Instinctual Wounding (Relational/Sexual, Social, and Self-Preservation) .. 31
The Secret Meaning of the Number 666 33

Chapter 14 of Revelation 35
Spiritual Instruction to Awaken the Heart 35
The Harvesting—Revelation 14:6-20 38

    The First Harvesting, the Angel—The Holy Idea of Love 38
        The Malkut Type *39*
        Awakening Holy Love in the Heart *39*
    The Second Harvesting, the Angel—The Holy Idea of Truth 41
        The Yesod Type. *41*
        Awakening Divine Truth in the Heart *42*
    The Third Harvesting, the Angel—The Holy Ideas of Strength
        and Holy Work. 44
        The Hod Type. *45*
        Awakening the Sanctity of Work in the Heart. *45*
        The Netzach Type. *47*
        Awakening Strength and Faith in the Heart *47*
    The Fourth Harvesting, the Angel—The Holy Idea of Origin. 49
        The Tiferet Type. *50*
        Awakening an Awareness of the Divine Origins of the Soul in the Heart *50*
    The Fifth Harvesting, the Angel—The Holy Ideas of Omniscience
        or Transparency and Holy Law. 53
        The Din Type. *54*
        Awakening the Awareness of Omniscience in the Heart. *54*
        The Hesed Type *57*
        Awakening the Awareness of the Divine Plan in the Heart. *57*
    The Sixth Harvesting, the Angel—the Holy Ideas of Will, Freedom,
        and Perfection. 60
        The Binah Type *61*
        Awakening Freedom and Divine Will in the Heart. *61*
        The Chokmah Type. *64*
        Awakening Divine Perfection in the Heart *65*
    The Seventh Harvesting—The Winepress 66
        Awakening the Divine Light of the Heart *67*
        The Movement from Crucifixion to Resurrection—The Dawning of Atzilut *70*
        Ascension Through Adult Spiritual Development *71*

Chapter 15 of Revelation. **75**
Seven Divinities in the Kabbalah. 75

Chapter 16 of Revelation. **81**
Outpouring of the Vials—The Cleansing of the Etheric Veil
    of the Mind 81

Chapter 17 of Revelation. **97**
Transformation of the Whore of Babylon 97

Chapter 18 of Revelation. **105**
The Process of Ego-Death and Spiritual Awakening 105
The Egoless Life 110

Chapter 19 of Revelation **115**
The Dawning of Self-Realization and the Seventh Chorus 115

Chapter 20 of Revelation **121**
The Threefold Domains of Consciousness................................. 121

Chapter 21 of Revelation **133**
Resurrection, Ascension, and Unification 133
The Precious Stones of the Apocalypse 138
    1. *Opal — New Awakening* 139
    2. *Lapis Lazuli — Power of Discernment* 140
    3. *Chalcedony — Developing Faith and Humility in God* 142
    4. *Aquamarine — Healing Grief, Developing Communication Skills*. 144
    5. *Sardonyx — Overcoming Laziness, Taking Right Action*. 145
    6. *Carnelian — Developing Courage and Overcoming Challenges* ... 146
    7. *Topaz — Surrendering to Divine Will* 148
    8. *Beryl — Accepting Spiritual Authority and Clarity*........... 149
    9. *Chrysolith — Developing Prosperity and Well-Being*. 151
    10. *Chrysoprase — Connecting with Divine Love and Mother Earth* . 152
    11. *Hyacinth (Zircon) — Actualizing Spiritual Ideals and Purpose* 154
    12. *Amethyst — Spiritual Purification and Awakening Higher Truth*. 155
The Unfolding of the Seventh Initiation — Awakening Divine Love 159

Chapter 22 of Revelation **163**
From Spiritual Realization to God-Realization and Beyond................ 163
The Nine Qualities of the Soul's Essence 163
    1. *Beingness* 164
    2. *Power* 165
    3. *Emptiness*.. 167
    4. *Absorption* 168
    5. *Joy*... 170
    6. *Love*.. 171
    7. *Peace*... 172
    8. *Purity*.. 173
    9. *Kindness*.. 174
The Twelve Fruits of the Tree of Life................................... 177

Annotated Bibliography **183**

Appendix I **A1-1**

Appendix II **A2-1**

Appendix III **A3-1**

Diagrams, Charts, and Tables

Diagram 1	Sephiroth, Archangels, and Planets	x
Diagram 2	Piscean Wounding and Aquarian Ideals	12
Diagram 3	Kabbalah of the Beatitudes and the Harvesting	37
Diagram 4	Three Versions of the Transformation Journey	70
Diagram 5	Movement of Ascension through the Five Universes	72
Diagram 6	Kabbalah with Qualities of Essences	74
Diagram 7	Auric Colors and Mantra Sounds	78
Diagram 8	The Three Frogs as They Manifest in The Nine Sephiroth or Enneagram Types	86-87
Diagram 9	Resurrection, Ascension, Unification	132
Diagram 10	The Twelve Spiritual Gemstones of the Tree of Life	158
Diagram 11	The Symbolic Journey of Transformation	A1-9
Diagram 12	Composite Tree of Life (Jacob's Ladder)	A3-2
Chart 1	Beriyah–Higher Mental Body–4th Initiation–Approaching Crucifixion–The Last Supper	69
Chart 2	Atzilut–Spiritual–Movement from 4th Initiation (Crucifixion) To 5th Initiation (Resurrection)	131
Table 1	Realm of the Dragon	18
Table 2	Realm of the Beast	25
Table 3	Realm of the Pseudo-Lamb	30
Poem	Understanding Zorba by Donna Overall	104
Painting	Jacob's Dream by William Blake	A3-3

About the Author

Nicholas C. Demetry, M.D., is a holistic psychiatrist. He received his medical degree from Emory University School of Medicine. After completing his medical training, he continued his studies at the University of Hawaii, specializing in general psychiatry and transcultural studies.

He is a graduate of Delphi University and previously taught Ro-hun Therapy and Transpersonal Psychology there. He studied the Enneagram with Helen Palmer.

Dr. Demetry has been an avid student of many wisdom traditions. He visited with the Christian mystic Dr. Stylianos Atteshlis (better known as Daskalos) numerous times between 1991-1994, attending lectures and receiving personal instruction in spiritual healing, meditation, Esoteric Christianity, and Theosis.

Dr. Demetry is Director of the Etherikos International School of Energy Healing and Spiritual Development headquartered in Atlanta, Georgia. The school has offered programs and classes in the United States and more than a dozen other countries. He is Director of the Institute for Spiritual Health, a non-profit organization that promotes peace through spiritual health and education, and is also a Founding Diplomate of the American Board of Holistic Medicine. Dr. Demetry is currently in private practice in Atlanta.

Acknowledgments

My love and gratitude go out to all the individuals and teachers of various wisdom traditions who have contributed to my spiritual education, inspiration, and experience.

To my beloved students who humble me and teach me about Divine Love. To my mother's family, especially my grandmother and the three generations of clergy in my father's family.

Grateful thanks to my wife, Maria, and the Etherikos support team for their dedication and love. Special thanks go to Diane Kistner for her masterful editing of the manuscript and to Donna Overall for her creative guidance and wonderful graphic creations.

Finally, my gratitude and love go out to all Researchers of the Truth the world over who have dedicated themselves to the pursuit of sharing and spreading unity, love, peace, and harmony to better the world and humanity.

"We are Many, yet we are One," and, "We are One in the Many."

Foreword

This book, in two volumes, serves three major purposes for the reader who is on an inner quest to awaken deeper realities and transformation in their lives.

(1) The book is a modern-day interpretation of an ancient text and can bring the reader a greater understanding of the symbology and spiritual meaning of Revelation. In this manner, the book can be utilized as a contemplative journey to better elucidate the mystical teachings within it.

(2) The book is a Kabbalistic journey through Revelation revealing the nature of spiritual and psychological growth stages, inner initiations of the Soul, and personal milestones of maturation.

(3) The book contains a formatted program to prepare oneself for self-realization through a series of exercises to carry the practitioner through various levels of consciousness.

The first two purposes of the text have, in part, been dealt with in numerous writings on Kabbalah, Esoteric Christianity, spiritual study of the Enneagram, ascension principles, and both exoteric and esoteric biblical interpretations of Revelation. *(See the Annotated Bibliography for references and discussion.)* I have attempted to broaden, synthesize, and add a greater overview to the present knowledge base of these topic areas with an emphasis on the Kabbalistic roots of Revelation.

The third purpose outlined above, I believe, contains the most original and important part of the program. The healing exercises were developed over the past 12 years during seminar programs in Patmos, Greece, and were inspired by the teachings of Saint John, Jesus, Daskalos,[1] and others of the mystical lineage. They can, by practice, activate the Christ Consciousness within the student of spirituality on the path to Theosis.

Once you step into this process, your spiritual evolution will accelerate; then your inner guidance, intuition, creativity, and understanding can blossom. You may well come to recognize that the Book of Revelation is written in the recesses of your heart and the inner knowledge will reveal itself to you as your own book, for this is the Aquarian spirit of individualized spiritual understanding.

In Volume I, which covers chapters 1 through 11 of Revelation, the reader is introduced to the spiritual journey and esoteric instruction given by Saint John for the initiate's ascension through the physical, astral, and lower mental (causal) bodies. It includes the following periods of the Christ story: birth (the first initiation), baptism (the second initiation), and transfiguration (the third initiation). Each initiation contains corresponding exercises and meditations to enhance personal and planetary healing and transformation. Included are descriptions of the personality changes that take place as the student grows toward Christ Consciousness as well as detailed information about the Kabbalah at the level of Asiyah, Yetzirah, and Beriyah. The nature of vice and mental fixation and how to awaken virtue and holy ideas within one's personality are explored for each Sephirah.

In Volume II, we continue the ascension journey through the mental and instinctual levels and Soul, coursing through the mission years of Jesus and the crucifixion (the fourth initiation), resurrection (the fifth initiation), ascension (the sixth and seventh initiations), and unification (the eighth through the twelfth initiations). Chapters 12 through 22 of Revelation are explored with corresponding exercises and meditations to enhance personal and planetary healing and transformation. Descriptions of the personality changes that take place in those higher states on the journey to self- and God-realization plus detailed information on the Kabbalah at the level of Beriyah and Atzilut are included. The nature of holy ideas as expressed through the Beatitudes of Jesus, the awakening of the heart, the transformation of instincts, and the qualities of the Soul's nine essences for each Sephirah are described with an emphasis on how to awaken the direct experience of holy ideas and essence within oneself. Volume II, Appendix II includes an interview with Daskalos on Divine Love.

In addition to several lengthy meditations at the end of certain chapters—also available through the Etherikos website, www.etherikos.com—the following essential meditation practices are included in this book to accompany your daily practice program, and most can be downloaded in mp3 format from our website at **www.etherikos.com/meditation2**.

- Seven exercises for the churches.....................................Volume I
- One introspective exercise...Volume I
- Nine exercises for the seals ....Volume I
- Thirty-six exercises for the trumpets ....Volume I
- Nine exercises for the harvesting ....Volume II
- One meditation exercise for the vials ....Volume II
- Twenty-seven exercises for the instincts, of which three will be particularly relevant for the participant depending on their Enneagram type and corresponding three instinctual subtypes ....Volume II
- Twelve exercises for the twelve gemstones of John's Vision of the New Jerusalem..Volume II
- Nine exercises for the essences ....Volume II
- Five meditation journeys...Volume II

The number 3 represents an ego function of thesis, antithesis, and synthesis. Synthesis brings the union and neutralization of polar opposites, allowing the student practicing these exercises to advance to the next stage of their growth process. By doing each of these meditation exercises three days in a row (a cycle of three days for each), one will advance on a course of study that will take approximately 9-12 months to complete.

—Nicholas C. Demetry, M.D.

The Love Religion

The inner space inside
that we call the heart
has become many different
living scenes and stories.

A pasture for sleek gazelles,
a monastery for Christian monks,

A temple with Shiva dancing,
a Kaaba for pilgrimage.

The tablets of Moses are there,
the Qur'an, the Vedas,
the sutras, and the gospels.

Love is the religion in me.
Whichever way love's camel goes,
that way becomes my faith,
the source of beauty and a
light of sacredness over everything.

—*Ibn Arabi*

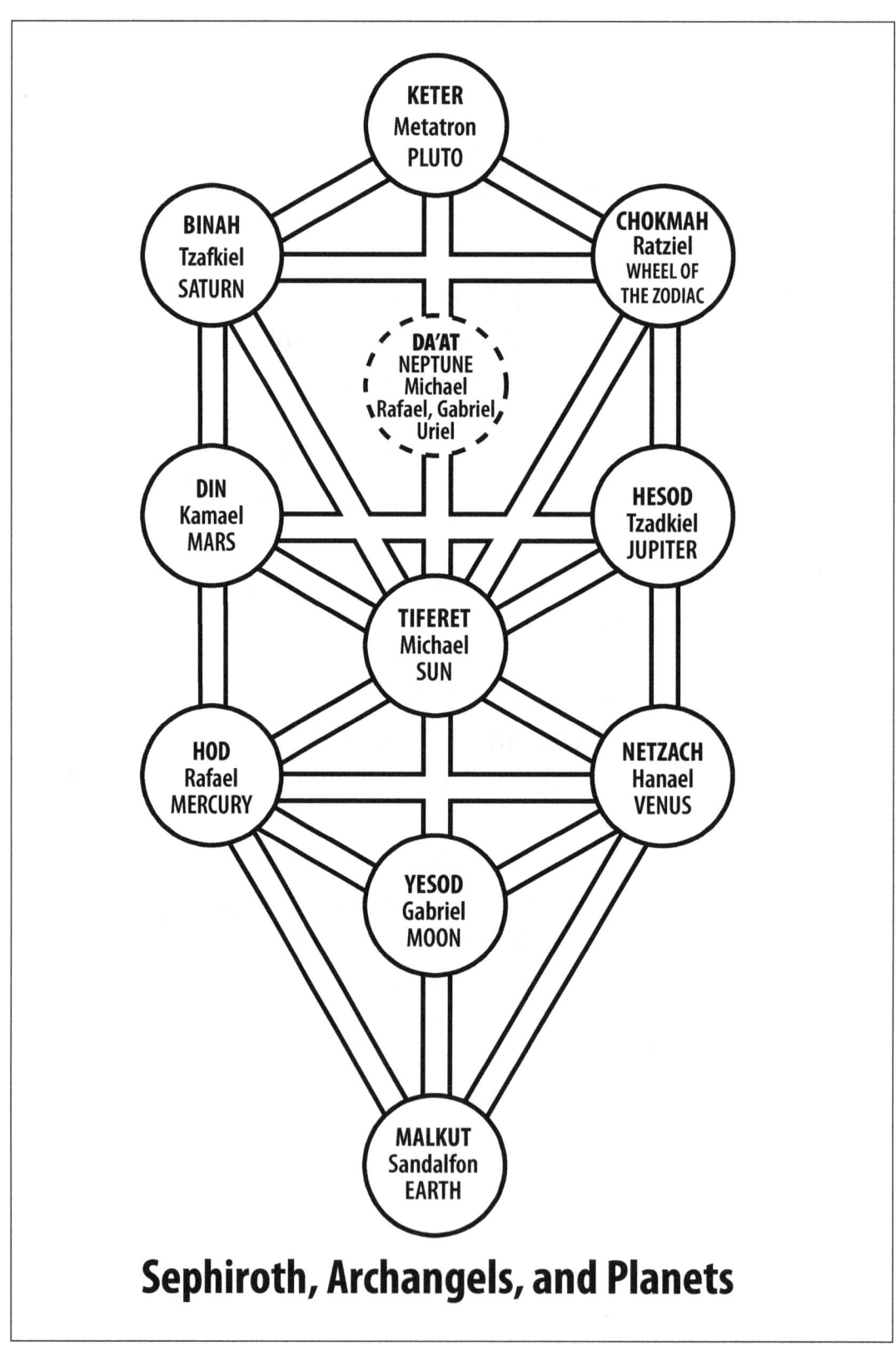

Sephiroth, Archangels, and Planets

Introduction

Understanding an Ancient Text in a Modern Light

I have been fascinated with Saint John's Book of Revelation for many years. Over the past 12 years, I've led spiritual retreats for students of depth psychology and spirituality who seek awareness for dealing with their life challenges. Many are members of the health field—doctors, social workers, and healers—all who believe that spiritual and psychological dimensions of life are important to their well-being. The island of Patmos, where Saint John received the vision for the Book of Revelation, has been a frequent setting of the retreats. Patmos is a beautiful, sun-drenched island, surrounded by an aquamarine blue sea, beautiful flowers, and mountains with far-reaching views that inspire the heart to seek a deeper understanding of life. The villagers are friendly, open, and welcoming. The center point of attraction on Patmos that brings visitors from worldwide is the famous cave of Saint John the Divine, located on a hillside above the main city of Skala. Over the years my retreats have been offered twice yearly, and I often had the opportunity to meditate in the cave and in the beautiful surroundings of nature on the island.

In 1994, I was visiting one of my spiritual teachers on the island of Cyprus, named Stylianos Atteshlis, better known as Daskalos ("teacher" in Greek). I shared with him my desire to visit Patmos and my intention to write a book about spirituality and medicine. He looked at me with a smile and said "Father Yiohannan, or Saint John, will be with you from now on." It is to this day I remember his words and feel the ever-present love of Saint John and the inner peace of heart that visiting Patmos brings me. Saint John's presence permeates the island and motivates one to travel to a place of sanctity, a holy place within the heart and soul.

As we turn to the biblical account of the Book of Revelation, I have researched a number of interpretations—exoteric, prophetic, apocalyptic, and esoteric—about the true meaning of the book. I would like to begin by clarifying that every account has some relative truth to it. In fact, one can read it from just about any perspective and find meaning. Having been a psychiatrist for 35 years, and an avid student of spirituality for just about as many, I've studied many viewpoints on religion and wisdom traditions the world over. I am constantly amazed that all these viewpoints reflect some relative truth about God. This also holds true for Saint John's Book of Revelation.

Working as a psychiatrist, I have witnessed many, many different viewpoints of individuals, different belief systems, attitudes, and behaviors that can either support a patient's healing and recovery from mental illness or not. I have observed that attitudes and beliefs give one a perspective of the world. A change of attitude, especially from the negative to positive viewpoint, can promote recovery and actual advancement in that person's life over what they had been living before. In spirituality, we call this a change in consciousness for the better, sometimes even leading an individual to miraculous healing and positive lifestyle changes.

This can also hold true in the arena of collective beliefs that humanity holds at a given period of history. Every age is dominated by crystallized or consensus beliefs about life. And yet, these beliefs change and the world changes with them, sometimes dramatically. For example, scientific thinking and belief has had a powerful impact on how we see and experience the world. This is in extreme contrast to the perspectives and perceptions that people held, for example, in the Renaissance, the Middle Ages, or in more ancient times. In addition, there are many examples throughout history of how pioneering individuals in all fields of life can impart change in the world for collective benefits. There have been great artists, musicians, scientists, avatars, philosophers, military geniuses, and actors that have contributed. The fresh and new perspective they held brought new stimulus to human evolution and cultural and ethical change.

At the same time, the gift of free will to choose our beliefs and life actions has cultivated both positive life-affirming contributions to society and negative destructive contributions. For example, some people are in power to choose success in physical life, accumulating wealth to help the poor and better the material side of life for themselves and others. Others are capable of great physical feats, and others, on the other hand, are focused on the negative results such as domination, destruction, cruelty, and violence. Some people are in power to improve and demonstrate their emotional values, improving humanity's capacity for social communication, bonding, improving their ethical values, and so on. On the other hand, other individuals are focused on negative emotional results, such as destroying human values, creating anarchy, destructive emotions, racism, prejudice, and bigotry.

Some people are in power to support and uphold valuable contributions of the past—the champions of institutions, of achievement, of history, works of art—the archival keepers of all we value in our cultural roots, the positive foundations that enrich the heritage of our nations and values in humanity. Other individuals focused on the negative stream are driven to destroy the past, disregard human achievement, and set up repressive systems of government and hardship in their own quest for power. Some individuals are empowered for higher thinking, abstract thought, for research, promoting new discoveries in science, physics, biology, and medicine. Others on the negative thought stream wish to hold all progress back, even denying scientific discoveries as sound.

Some people are empowered to awaken new, more evolved understanding of the psyche and God, of principles of spiritual development, and the inner life. Others are motivated to create unhealthy and self-destructive cults and movements in the name of someone or something of their choosing, perpetuating repression, slavery in their followers, and justification for destructive behaviors. All these examples result in how we identify as Soul (our spiritual nature), either positively or negatively with our various bodies of perceptive consciousness—Physical, Emotional (Astral), Causal (Memory Body), and Mental (Intellect, Reason).

All wisdom traditions, regardless of religious origin, teach that the way to return to our holiness and purity of Being is to free ourselves from positive and negative enslavement of each of these bodies and turn our attention fully toward our spiritual nature, filling each of these bodies of consciousness that we inhabit with love and reverence for life and our planet earth. We are reminded here of the words of Jesus Christ: And he said, "Truly I say to you, unless you change and become like little children, you shall not enter into the kingdom of heaven." (Matthew 18:3—*Peshitta*)[2]

One individual that has shown the way toward more freedom and liberation, and the meaning of why we are here and where we are going, is Saint John the Divine. His Book of Revelation holds an endless energy and understanding of spiritual transformation. I believe humanity could benefit from an understanding of this book in a modern way for the emerging Aquarian age we are entering. It is for this reason I have pursued an interpretation of Revelation in the spirit of archetypal psychology, Kabbalah, and the understanding of spiritual initiation and ascension.

Archetypal Psychology and How We View the Revelation

How can it be that we can coexist in such a diverse world of beliefs, acting them out on a grand scale of drama either as positive or negative expressions of our thought, feelings, and action? Clearly free will is in operation here, but how and why? The best explanation for this, from a psychological viewpoint I believe, comes from an understanding of the nature of universal blueprints in our psyches called *archetypes*. An archetype, simply stated, is a living thought pattern that occupies the collective unconscious mind of humanity.

Psychiatrist and psychotherapist Carl Jung and others have identified many such archetypes, and they influence us all unconsciously to a greater or lesser extent. Archetypes can be seen as divine gifts, serving as links between the unreachable mystery of Spirit and the concrete reality of our everyday lives. An archetype often expresses itself in our awareness through dreams, symbols, myths, and emotions. Though the essence of a given archetype is the same all over the world, its particular form may vary from culture to culture. It is for this reason that spiritual writings must often be interpreted symbolically to understand their spiritual content. In the same way, dreams have symbolic meaning as well. Yet each individual, as each culture, sees the archetype expression from their own kaleidoscope of beliefs and expressions.

When we as individuals, or the collective of humanity, are wounded in our relationship to a given archetype, we essentially express three dysfunctional roles—we take the role of victim, abuser or rescuer. All three roles are unhealthy and a result of a wounded relationship to the archetype. When our ego is disconnected from the archetypal energy in an unhealthy way, these above roles exist, and we therefore see the world through the kaleidoscope of these unhealthy or wounded patterns. The abuser would believe that it is necessary to take domination and control through force and destructive measures to control the fragile ego. The victim may feel deflated, helpless, powerless, depressed, fearful, and unable to activate his or her own power for life. The rescuer witnesses the relationship between the abuser's energies and victim and decides to take charge for God and to change things for the positive. Each of these expressions reflects a different viewpoint.

This also holds true for those reading the Book of Revelation. If one sees it literally, concretely, using a sectarian interpretation alone, one is likely to miss the universal spiritual content altogether and its deeper message to humanity. When we view the book from the standpoint of the rescuer, we believe if we do good acts in life and uphold the higher values, then we will reach heaven. If we take the viewpoint of the abuser, we see that the book is a book of wrath, that we should condemn others for not being of God. If we are victims, we may understand it from the standpoint of fear and so on. When we view the Book of Revelation from a healthy perspective, we can begin to see that it is a book that can guide us to our spiritual freedom and to the expression of true power, love, and wisdom of the Soul.

Revelation is a book of self-awakening spiritually. Jungian psychologist Edward Edinger sees the book as one particular presentation of the Archetype of the Apocalypse.[3] He has identified four basic features of such apocalyptic literature: (1) revelation, (2) judgment, (3) destruction and punishment, and (4) renewal and a new world. Psychologically, Edinger explains that these features actually describe the universal but poorly understood process of the coming of the higher Spirit-Self into conscious realization. Uncovering that which has been hidden, whenever the ego is unwilling to bend to the higher authority of the Spirit, this process becomes a world-shattering experience. If the ego won't break, it *must* break. The personality, nation, or planet that is bound up by materialistic and egotistic desires simply cannot stay organized around the illusions of the ego when the reality of Spirit enters awareness. If the spiritual forces act upon our lives without our conscious understanding and cooperation, it must by necessity appear that disaster is being thrust upon us from without. It appears that we are judged and punished by God.

It could be said, therefore, that the world's apocalyptic literature presents the shadow (collective unconscious) side of the Archetype of the Apocalypse.

The Archetype of the Apocalypse can give us insight into the phenomenon of terrorism. Terrorism is disrupting and destabilizing nations worldwide, bringing unspeakable tragedies and threatening still much more. Terrorists are often portrayed as either insane or criminal, and so it seems. Edinger believes, however, that terrorists are better understood as zealots—driven by fanatical resentment and possessed by the dark face or the shadow side of collective archetypal forces such as the Archetype of the Apocalypse. These zealots are willing to sacrifice their lives for a perceived collective gain and often have expectation of personal reward in heaven as well. They have convinced themselves that they are agents of divine justice and punishment, and they believe they are bringing in a new and better world order.

The phenomenon of terrorism itself should be enough for us to call into question the common assumption that God's justice is a matter of wrath and punishment. Humankind has always projected its own nature onto its creator, usually unconsciously. We see that we as creatures become angry and full of revenge, believing the one that created us must posses these same traits. Vivid and familiar examples of such projection are seen in the character traits of the ancient Greek or Roman gods and goddesses. Zeus, Hera, and their fellow Olympians never hesitated to lash out in jealousy or vengeance at god or man whenever their grandiose egos were insulted. The mythological deities of the ancients demonstrated both archetypal qualities and humanity's collective ego projections. These humanized gods and goddesses therefore reveal both the divine and human nature within us.

Modern-day psychologists in turn have profitably used this wealth of ancient mythology to better understand the human mind. On the other hand, no one claims to better understand God from this study of Greek or Roman mythology, and yet our image of God more often resembles Zeus than the loving merciful father revealed by Jesus and Isaiah. The ancient Greeks and Romans did not generally challenge the validity of their projections. Their factual scientific understanding of the Cosmos was minimal, and they did not have our modern-day understanding of the unconscious mind in its defenses. Psychology as a discipline did not emerge until nearly 2,000 years later.

Unfortunately, despite our increased understanding, we challenge the validity of our projections about as often as the ancients did. Psychologists are well aware that we project outside ourselves those traits that we dislike in ourselves as a means of protecting our fragile egos. Projection is in fact one of the most common psychological defense mechanisms. If we can project wrath and vengeance onto God, does it not make it much easier to justify these vices inside ourselves and resist the love and forgiveness that great teachers such as Jesus and Buddha practiced? Projection is clearly not a useful way to get to know God, others, or oneself. In fact it is the major obstacle to that process.

Clearly we must interpret the Book of Revelation in accordance with the advanced wisdom of our age so that our spiritual insight and experience may grow proportionally. Ancient writers, such as the Apostle John, could only express the inspiration they were given by God in the light of concepts in language of their own era. They are not responsible for our misuse and overly literal interpretation of their writing. A literal, dogmatic, non-spiritual fixation on the words themselves may not take us to the source of light we seek, but rather to our separated, fearful human egos. If we wish to understand Revelation (*The Holy Bible*, KJV) we must read it with an appreciation of its source:

> *1: The Revelation of Jesus Christ, which God gave unto him, to shew unto his servants things which must shortly come to pass; and he sent and signified it by his angel unto his servant John:*

Jesus, clearly identified as the source, said during his earthly life, "I and my Father are one" (John 10:30). As discussed in some depth in *Awakening Love*,[4] Jesus built upon the highest God concepts of the Hebrew prophets, most notably Isaiah, to reveal a God of love and mercy. Not only his words but also his very life and ministry were a revelation of the same loving and merciful attitudes towards all. If we accept his revelation of God as true, consistency demands that any apocalyptic destruction cannot be a consequence of God's wrath, but rather a natural consequence of human ignorance. The thesis that God is merciful and non-punitive, therefore, does not lessen the gravity of prophecies concerned with global disaster. The dark and unconscious and disowned forces that operate on the human psyche provide more than enough hazard.

The Book of Revelation is full of rich symbolism that portrays these forces operating in the unconscious mind. The imagery is derived in large part from the Old Testament. Whether interested in prophecy or not, many millions are feeling a vague sense of impending doom. Not knowing how to respond, or even where the problem lies, millions are using psychological defense mechanisms to create a false sense of security. Projection of human passions onto God, as discussed previously, makes it seem unnecessary to deal with those passions (vices) that are actually inside us. We can let God be the angry, vengeful one, follow a simple formula to appease his rage, and sit back complacently and wait for salvation by "Rapture into the clouds."

On the other hand, millions prefer to numb their fear through the uncomplicated escapes of self-absorption, isolation, and addictions, while others flee to the god of human reason and openly deny any reality beyond material existence. Logic, unfortunately, is a whimsical god; the mind can easily convince itself of whatever it wants to believe. Some of us may want to avoid the change by holding onto the false security of the status quo and outer authority, whether this authority is social, political, or religious. In this manner we can avoid thinking or making decisions for ourselves, leaving open the option of blaming outer figures of authority and feeling like victims when things go wrong. We may hide behind combinations of these defense mechanisms. All the while we remain asleep in the materialism and egotism, inviting global disaster.

So where does the hope lie? It lies in the same place as the hopelessness. It lies in our free-will choice, as human spirits, either to wake up consciously and do what needs to be done, or to stay spiritually asleep—only to be awakened by a global nightmare of our own making. Despite its alarming connotations, the Archetype of the Apocalypse is ultimately no more than the process of awakening the life of Spirit, our Higher Self in our hearts. The end result of apocalyptic breakdown is the growth of the group harmony derived from the common planetary experience of spiritual brotherhood. Those who wake up consciously and by choice to the spiritual self within will experience this awakening in the true sense of the word. The modern-day hero is one who experiences this inner awakening and then returns to the world on the mission of love and service to light the way for others. It is from the inner temple of the holy stillness that we can join together with our source to create the new heaven and the new earth described in the Book of Revelation, a home that will pay tribute to the glory of God and mirror the beauty of our own divine nature. Therefore, archetypes are like multifaceted diamonds that reflect many viewpoints of the relative truth, depending on the ego consciousness, its level of wounding, and the biases of the onlooker, positive or negative.

Kabbalah, Initiation, and Revelation

Turning from archetypal psychology to some of the origins of the Book of Revelation in Jewish mysticism and Gnostic Greek thought—that of Plato for example—one can follow the progression of John's vision and journey as a Kabbalistic journey of spiritual ascension along the middle pillar of the Kabbalah that proceeds in seven sequential steps that parallel the life stages of Jesus Christ from the Bible and the journey of the Prodigal Son. The Kabbalah (Tree of Life) is a cosmological symbol originating in Egypt, and adapted to Jewish mysticism and to Esoteric Christianity. The word *Kabbalah* means "to impart or reveal"—in this case, something of God or of the Divine. The Kabbalah is an instruction in the ascension journey to self-realization and God-realization.

The word *apocalypse* in Greek means "something that is hidden and later revealed or unveiled." "Apocalypse" is substituted for the original Greek written word *epopteia*, meaning "initiation into seership." In early Greek times, initiates were called *epoptai*—"those having super sight" or seers. Therefore once the Book of Revelation (the Apocalypse of Saint John) is understood from this viewpoint, it becomes obvious that it describes an inner psychological process of spiritual growth, initiation, self-conquest, and maturation—or what Jung would refer to as growth into psychological wholeness and spiritual mastership. This occurs through the four stages outlined by Edinger discussed earlier. The Kabbalistic journey of the initiate represents this psychospiritual journey as well: a process of ascending consciousness that brings one closer to God, the return of the Prodigal Son to heaven, the ascension and unification of Christ in the Bible account.

The Secret Sephirah of Da'at and Human Consciousness

In Kabbalah, this process of ascension takes place through ten gateways or emanations of higher consciousness (Sephiroth). The Sephiroth can also be understood as sacred discs that are anatomically arranged along the body in the same location as the wheels of energy described as chakras in Eastern spirituality. In the Kabbalah, these ten individual Sephirah, which represent doorways to higher consciousness, each represent a part of the spiritual journey and a particular expression of God's imparted wisdom to mankind. The Gnostic Christian teacher Tau Malachi[5] suggested Saint John's Apocalypse, or Revelation, can best be understood by taking into account the nature and meaning of the Kabbalah's secret Sephirah, known as Da'at, anatomically located at the level of the throat chakra in our neck area. Da'at, which means "that which is secret or hidden," reveals itself as the combination of both divine knowledge and cosmic ignorance. The planet Neptune, associated in Gnostic teachings with the Sephirah of Da'at, often symbolizes, in astrological thinking, the source of transcendental cosmic consciousness and unity and holds at the same time in itself its shadow form as illusion, false emotions, addiction, and cosmic distortion of the truth. It is said that Da'at (originating in the mind of the great archetypal energies of life) is where the great light of unity splits through the prism into seven rays, or qualities, that also represent seven perceptions of reality.

The message of Da'at, or the mental forces of polarity, is that how you perceive and believe things to be is how they become. Do we perceive life through the eyes of the victim, the abuser, the rescuer—or through the eyes of the compassionate and loving self, empowerment, and wisdom? It may sound magical but, simply stated, it means that what we believe forms the kaleidoscope through which we view life and how we experience it and how we choose to act. We all live by the relative truths of our minds, and the Sephirah of Da'at colors our reality for better or for worse. If we perceive beauty or ugliness, it is our choice. We can choose to live with love and respect for all life or with hate and vengeance. It is our choice, our schoolhouse of learning and, of course, our responsibility to choose the higher path of consciousness, which is our ultimate destiny as a human race. Saint John's Revelation journey expresses just that, whereas the choice to remain complacent and resistant could well lead to the extinction of our species.

Revelation and the Turning of the Ages

Some individuals and religious groups consider the Apocalypse of John to relate to events leading to the end of the world, the second coming of Christ, and the "rapture" in which the chosen ones will be liberated and those others less fortunate will perish in a great catastrophe. They look for signs of the impending battle of Armageddon. Historically, while this remains a possibility, as change is always possible for better or worse in the world, already many periods and events of human catastrophe have occurred, from natural disasters to plagues, to the cruel persecution of various religious groups, ethnic cleansing and, most recently, terrorism. The dynamics of the Archetype of the Apocalypse are timeless in nature and could relate to any of these events. However, at present, it is interesting to note that several prophecies point to the time we live in now as one of great spiritual challenge and change in our worldview. The Archetype of the Apocalypse, we could say, exists in the secret Sephirah of Da'at and gives the relative truth to all our human experience.

We can also speak of the cyclic shift of time into the present Aquarian age, an astrological fact. Some astrologers indicate the Aquarian age began in the year 2000. Others indicate that we are still in the foothills of this change, and the true blossoming and expression of the Aquarian age will not occur until 2500 AD or so. However, the shift appears to be upon us already as the beliefs and values of the Piscean age of the last 2,000 years are coming to a close rapidly.

The Age of Pisces and Aquarius

The following is the outline of the difference: for about 2,000 years, we have been in the emotional, psychic, spiritual, idealistic, Soul-developing sign of Pisces, motivated by ideals of self-sacrifice, glamour, compassion, and duality. The Piscean age gave birth to many of the world's greatest religions and philosophies, to the arts, music, the love of nature, and great architecture; yet it also produced devastating wars, extremes of cruelty, poverty, self-glorification, excessive materialism, and a belief in a punitive God demanding suffering and hardship and high emotional drama to reach heaven. The focus of one's relationship to God, especially in the

Western religious traditions, became devotion, austerity, separation of heaven and earth, and the mediation of one's relationship to God through the priesthood and through ritual practice.

The Piscean shadow-self created a deceptive prison of the Victim, Abuser, and Rescuer roles. One can think of these as a triangle, containing three different identities. Heaven was bounded by the Rescuer, who held the Piscean ideal of suffering: the ideal of the Hero Savior. This is an inflated, positive ego response to the Archetype of the Apocalypse. The second role, the Abuser, is a negative ego inflated response. The Abuser felt abandoned by God, angry, and identified itself as God. This is a negative inflated expression of the wounding of the Archetype of the Apocalypse. Then the third position, the deflated ego position, is called the Victim—a kind of hell. The Victim felt abandoned by God, vulnerable and afraid, and felt deserving of punishment. This is the negative deflated position of the wounding of our ego with the Archetype of the Apocalypse.

On the other hand, when we look at the Aquarian age that is now emerging, it brings the hope that the positive virtues of this star sign will influence humanity favorably and align us in a healthy way with the Archetype of the Apocalypse. Aquarius is a sign of altruism, invention, universality, equality, spiritual ideals, compassion, and the individual contributions to group consciousness, independence, and social responsibility toward humanity. Aquarian ideals emphasize recognizing ourselves as co-creators with God, respect and love for all life, awareness of God in everything great and small, our capacity to create our own reality, to share and extend compassion, and impersonal love to all beings.

The goal is to bring heavenly ideals into practical application on earth and developing resources for the common good of humanity; learning to be heart-centered, open in relationship, seeking win-win situations and emphasizing independence, autonomy, equality, freedom and individualism; learning self responsibility for one's own consciousness. The Aquarian ideals emphasize our learning to follow the spiritual laws of life, simplifying our technologies, and acting ethically toward the planet and humanity.

The new triangle of the Aquarian Age, emphasizing spiritual freedom and self-responsibility, would be (1) the wisdom to walk the path of non-attachment and neutrality and to learn to let go and surrender all to a higher, Divine Plan (2) the attribute of love—the capacity to form community and care, acceptance, and tolerance for each other, and a willingness to work together for that Divine Plan, and (3) empowerment—the respect and honoring of everyone's life space and boundaries and the ability to recognize the uniqueness and contribution of all individuals, thereby supporting each other in win-win situations.

Pisces was focused on development of exoteric forms of worship, religious development, and monastic spirituality. The Piscean preoccupation was with money, control, and power. The Aquarian spirit is focused on love toward oneself and others and the realization that everyone is a mirror of oneself in a similar way; to learn to love oneself is to love others. One's state of consciousness attracts the same outer conditions, what one experiences internally by co-vibration. Therefore self-responsibility for one's thoughts, feelings, actions, and deeds becomes essential to the right way to live. Aquarian spirituality recognizes that God is within and can be known only through inner reflection and inner states of subjective reality as they relate to the outer world. Aquarian thinking asserts that learning is a continual process and that flexibility and creativity are paramount in overcoming adversity and challenges. Therefore, once again, the Aquarian triangle of freedom is (1) wisdom, showing flexibility, surrender to a creative flow of truth, and non-attachment to results, (2) love, cooperation, and individual cooperation in community and with each other, and (3) power, peaceful use of the will to progress humanity, all bringing freedom.

Saint John's book of the Apocalypse, the unveiling of the Soul, is a pioneering Aquarian approach to the future of spirituality. It is a journey of self-realization. It emphasizes that the way to God and to heaven on earth is through an inner process of transformation and self-responsibility for one's consciousness—not simply blind, external worship. It reveals the great depth of the disowned shadow of the collective unconscious of humanity and a need for individual effort and trust in God and discipline and a spiritual viewpoint on life to overcome the lower human desires and outer trap of life's illusions.

Saint John shows us that the Soul is destined to return home to God within itself, and that the unveiling of the illusions of the physical, emotional, and mental life must give way to the ever-present, eternal life of the Soul and spiritual truth. The Soul is free and has always been so. However, once identified and attached with the thoughts and beliefs of its mental body, positive or negative, the past images of experience of its causal or memory body, positive or negative, the sea of changing passions and emotions of its astral body, positive or negative, or the sensory impressions of its physical body, positive or negative, the Soul loses touch with its essential nature as freedom itself.

The unveiling process, which is the journey of the Apocalypse of Saint John, is the falling away of false identity and attachment of the Soul from each body of illusion to eventually reveal itself to itself as freedom itself. The Soul, as the image of New Jerusalem, experiences its return home to its core being. The optimistic message of John's text is that we have always been free and that the journey of life is the journey of initiation into deeper realization of truth. Like the prodigal sons and daughters of God in the Bible, we recognize that we are destined to eternal life.

The great abiding truth of the Aquarian spirit is that all the virtues and qualities, such as wisdom, the mental freedom to explore and express the truth, love, the emotional freedom to discover, feel, and act with compassion and power, the physical freedom to enact our highest values in life ethically and without harm to anyone, in an empowered way, are all the effect of the realization of the Soul of its true nature and divinity. From the outset of the Apocalypse, through the sequence of initiations and trials and tribulations, we are eventually led back home to a world that reflects the Divine Plan of Spirit for humanity.

MEDITATION

As Daskalos once shared in a meditation process, "Feel yourself in your physical body, your life in your body. Study yourself, your senses. Study your senses. Who are you? You have a physical body, but you are not your physical body. Now feel yourself in your emotional body, the flow of feelings within you. Study your emotions. Who are you? You have an emotional body, but you are not the emotional body. Now feel yourself in your thoughts, your mental body. Study your thoughts. From where do these thoughts arise? Who are you? You have a mental body, but you are not your thoughts, your mental body. Then who are you now? *Ehyeh Asher Ehyeh* [Aramaic for "I Am that I Am"]. *Ehyeh Asher Ehyeh*, I Am that I Am. *Ehyeh Asher Ehyeh*, I Am that I Am."

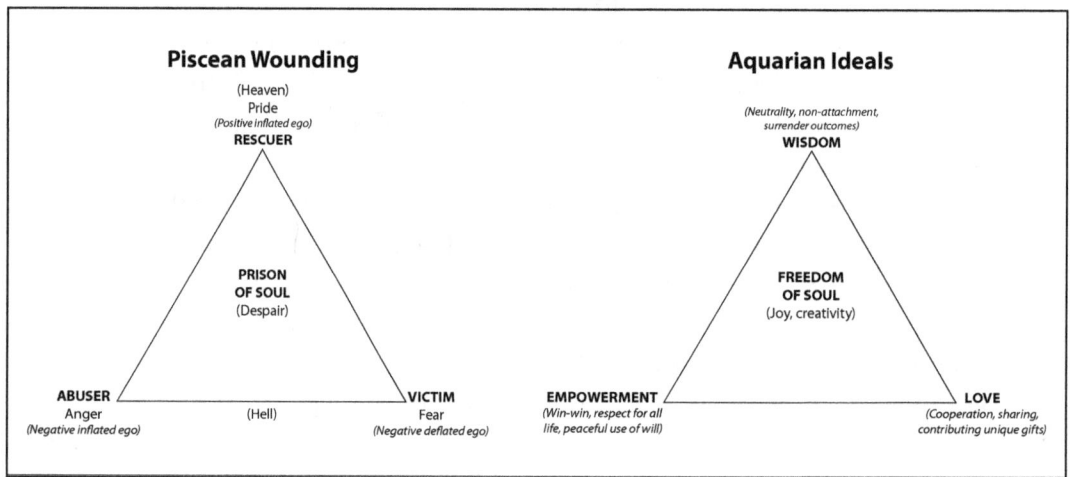

Volume II, Diagram 2

Chapter 12 of Revelation

The Heart's Purification

The war in heaven, or the awakening of the divine feminine, represents the connectedness to Tiferet. The fourth initiation begins with the establishment of Tiferet—corresponding to the mission years of Jesus—the balancing of mind and heart and obedience to the spiritual laws of life, thereby leading the initiate to the harvesting—the heart's purification and awakening of essence. This represents the movement of the initiate from Tiferet to Din and Hesed (the moral triad) and, finally, to the outpoured vials and the final judgment, the mastery of instinctual urges. All of this takes place in the fourth initiation with its completion in crucifixion. This is the ascension process through Hesed and Din through Da'at, into the fifth initiation, Resurrection, in Binah and Chokmah. The Soul moves through Beriyah into ego death and emerges into Atzilut, self-realization.

Chapters 12 through 15 relay the message of the heart's purification, the deeper understanding of the nature of the illusion of form and how to deal with it, and the three instincts represented by the beast, the dragon, and the pseudo-lamb as separated aspects in our consciousness that are perverted into the destructive tendencies now present in our world. The Mother God brings the powerful image of the mandala of healing for our world today, which leads to the purification and restoration of these three instincts, located in the first three chakras: (1) the beast in the solar plexus of Hod and Netzach, (2) the dragon in the sacral center of Yesod, and (3) the false lamb or pseudo-lamb in Malkut, or the root center. When the Spirit of Christ awakened on our planet 2,000 years ago, it incarnated at a time when an unimaginable deprecation and debauchery of instincts accompanied the decadence of the ancient world. This debauchery of pain and suffering was mostly associated with matter, body, and emotions.

These debauched aspects of life were originally identified with the feminine side of our nature, and we became cut off from the divine feminine. Venus was at one time a carrier of sacred life energies. For example, to Lucretius, as he writes and celebrates his homage to the Divine Mother of Aeneas, founder of Rome, or to Solomon in his praise of Sophia, the feminine Spirit was and is a sacred expression of God and life. The Seal of Solomon is a six-pointed star. Two interlocking triangles embody the integration of heaven and earth; the upward-pointing triangle represents the fire element and the downward-pointing triangle represents the water element. When the fire element becomes separated and disconnected from the water element—the divine feminine—the downward-pointing triangle loses its connection to the Divine Plan and its unity with Spirit, and the upward-pointing triangle becomes disconnected from life, abstract and lifeless. Because water represents desire in its three forms—thought, emotion, and sensation—these three arenas become separated and reflect illusionary desires like cancerous elements of chaos.

The sixth commandment of Moses is "thou shall not kill." The number 6 esoterically represents Spirit moving from the higher consciousness and Divine Plan of evolution into matter, into more perfect manifestations to eventually bring about the realization of the Soul. The only way a man can kill is to separate any form from the life pulse of its connecting Spirit. Whenever we separate, disconnect, or deny Spirit, we are killing our own spiritual evolution within ourselves and on the earth. By reuniting with the Divine Spirit symbolized by the six-pointed star and the number 6—which also represents community, creativity, harmony, beauty, compassionate service, devotion, manifestation of expansive vision, artistry, and justice—we reunite the ascending and descending energies, the masculine and feminine, the sun and the moon, and the Soul in its journey to Spirit both on earth as well as in heaven. Without including and allowing the divine feminine energies to flourish, we condemn our planet and our spiritual evolution to death through extinction of the earth and our species. Either we choose to affirm life, or we choose to follow destruction. At this time (and, as we will see, for some time), the battle goes on as new changes in consciousness give us the opportunity to change our ways and direction. The choice is ours to make—or not to make.

The Emergence of the Divine Feminine

> *1: And there appeared a great wonder in heaven; a woman clothed with the sun, and the moon under her feet, and upon her head a crown of twelve stars:*

To continue our discussion of the divine feminine, let us look at a Kabbalistic interpretation of this powerful image. The Divine Mother has many faces depending on from which perspective she is viewed on the Tree of Life. As the supernal mother "in Heaven" she is Binah, the Divine Mother. Along with Chokmah, the Divine Father, she is inseparable and in unity, love, and wisdom in perfect union and divine bliss in Atzilut. In the worlds of duality, Beriyah, she is the divine presence within all forms, within all creatures and creation. She is the Holy Spirit, dwelling in all. The sacred marriage brings the unification of divine male and female and the divine joy and bliss of creation. When we meditate, pray, and desire union with the Holy Spirit, we are participating in this sacred marriage process.

In Atzilut, the Divine Mother is the formless, all-powerful creative presence that gives birth to form in Beriyah, Yetzirah, and Asiyah. In Beriyah, she is the bright mother and dark mother, the bright mother of positive enlightened thinking (the holy ideas) and the dark mother of mental fixations and negative cosmic ignorance or illusionary mental fixations of thought. At the level of Yetzirah, she is enlightened virtues and cosmic illusionary vices. In Asiyah, she is sensory material refinement and creativity, mirroring, reflecting, divine truth in matter, or cosmic illusion as sensory deprivation and indulgence. She is therefore God's mercy or God's judgment. When we feel our union with her, she is God's mercy, the virginal female. When separated, she becomes judgment, the whore of Babylon. The holy emergence or the holy expression of the divine feminine, the Virgin Mary is the incarnation of Mother God. Her impure or separated expression—the mother of abomination and ruination—is the whore of Babylon. The negative or dark expression is selfishness, envy, greed, fear, gluttony, anger, lust, apathy, arrogance, deceit—all the nine vices and passions described in Volume I, Chapter 4 (pp. 115-116) in our discussion of the seals of Yetzirah.

The biblical story of Mary Magdalene spans the whole continuum of her expression from darkness to eventual light and holiness. She expresses herself in the whole spectrum of consciousness. In the vision of Saint John, she is truly the woman of light—the Divine Mother. She is a visual image of God as the *Shekinah* or the feminine aspect of God, the *Alaha Ruha d'kudsha* in Aramaic, "God the Holy Spirit," or *Alaha Shekinah,* "God the Holy Spirit." In her healed unity as Binah, Hesed, Din, Tiferet, Hod, Netzach, Yesod, and Malkut, she operates as the source of both light and dark. Malachi uses the various stages of the life of Christ to exemplify this polarity.[6] In birth, the mother gives life but also eventual suffering, the sorrow of death. In baptism, the Soul is reborn to Spirit but must face the temptations of the temporal world. In Transfiguration, the Divine Mother brings forth the blessings of divine power and awareness, but this is followed by the Passion and Crucifixion. Through this darkness, she brings rebirth as the redemption of Resurrection, Ascension, and Unification into the supernal consciousness of Realization. Whether she manifests as mercy or judgment, the Divine Mother is always pure, eternal, unchanging, formless light and sound, the all-pervasive cosmic intelligence of creation. She is like a mirror that reflects whatever one holds in their consciousness and, therefore, is the keeper of karma and the dispensation of truth, goodness, and dharma. This is why Mary Magdalene can be seen as both virgin and harlot. How she is viewed depends on whether we perceive her in separation or in union.

For example, in separation we will view ourselves as dark, unworthy, rejected, shamed, guilt-ridden, and so on. We cannot see our true goodness. We cannot consecrate our lives as holy. In the image of "a woman clothed with the sun" in

Revelation, Mother Mary embodies the healed union and energy of the Supernal Mother. She comes from "heaven," the supernal kingdom of Binah—the Divine Mother in union with the father—and she is "clothed," meaning her nature is "with the sun" in union with the supernal light of Chokmah—the Divine Father. The "sun" also refers to the Christ center of Tiferet, the heart, and "the moon under her feet" symbolizes the connecting link from Keter and Binah to Chokmah through Tiferet to Yesod. The moon and the astral plane are under her command. The once-present fragmentation of heaven and earth is being healed through her divine love and cosmic heart. Her feet, "earth," anchor her in Malkut. The crown, or divine authority, and the 12 stars, which represent the perfected, illuminated thought of the mental plane of Beriyah, suggests mastery and divine dispensation.

> *2: And she being with child cried, travailing in birth, and pained to be delivered.*

The conception of a divine child represents the reconnection of the triangles in the six-pointed star, the union of the divine feminine and divine masculine in sacred marriage as equal co-creators. The six-pointed star is the symbol of the heart center (Tiferet) in Daskalos' version of the Tree of Life. Within this center is the Christ Consciousness. The "child" in Revelation 12: 2 refers to the birth within each of us of the Christ Self of divine love and wisdom, the union of heart and mind. This birthing that is happening now is one of great labor and struggle. The birth of new consciousness in the heart center brings a resistant force that actually strengthens the new movement of evolution. The resistant force acts like an eggshell that must be broken through when the emerging infant is ready, in spiritual strength and form, to handle the outside world. If the infant is still in the yolk-stage, or early infancy, it is too vulnerable to withstand the forces of the world.

The Red Dragon

> *3: And there appeared another wonder in heaven; and behold a great red dragon, having seven heads and ten horns, and seven crowns upon his heads.*

The red dragon, located in Yesod or the sacral chakra, symbolizes perverted, externally motivated desire that intoxicates the Soul and enslaves it in outer form (illusion). This causes desire for satisfaction in the world and destructive astral emotions. The dragon represents the animal survival instinct, which is disconnected from higher understanding and purpose. In psychological terms, it represents the sexual/relational instinct that arises in the genitals and is driven by sexuality. It colors the way we act, think, feel, and express ourselves in partnership and relationship. It affects our capacity to bond intimately.

Whenever instinctual drive dominates or commands an undue amount of notice, it becomes overused and leads to the creation of strong elementals that demand more and more of our attention, taking us away from the essential task of transformation. The combination of instinctual drives and our unique human nature create a kind of relationship we call the personality, or the false self. The instinctual drive attempts to protect and insure the survival of the personality when it is stressed; this ultimately produces more stress and no protection. The "seven heads" of the dragon refer to the seven vices of the separated ego personality identified with the sexual/relational instinct that drives its behavior. The "seven crowns" represent the domination and authority this instinct holds over the unevolved personalities of the masses of humanity. The "ten horns" refer to the accumulated negative power over the ten Sephiroth that this instinctual force can generate.

The Sexual/Relational/One-to-One Instinct

Our survival involves pair bonds and primary one-to-one relationships. The one-to-one instinct governs our intimate relationships, our close friendships, and the intensity in our bodies of the energy of our life force. In development, this instinct develops as a growing awareness of self and other with our primary caregivers. The preoccupation of the one-to-one instinct is more with finding an ideal or perfect partner. Its focus is more on intimacy than on simply physical sexual gratification. It seeks to express intensity, attractiveness, and closeness in union with a mate. The difficulties that develop when this instinct is wounded or out of balance may involve playing out a victim, abuser/aggressor, or rescuer role with others.

In the rescuer role, one may attempt to rescue the partner by over-sacrificing and over-caring for them, leading to lack of focus on one's own priorities. In the victim role, one can lose one's self-worth and value and, through attachment and co-dependency, become submissive, fearful, helpless, masochistic, and tolerant of abusive or disrespectful behavior from the partner. Or, in the abuser or aggressor role, one can become obsessed with the partner, controlling and dominating and amping up emotional intensity through dramatic outbursts and sadistic behaviors. When wounded, the one-to-one instinctual type may exhibit one of two polarities of behavior: (1) a lack of focus, promiscuity, and acting-out behaviors to feel a sense of aliveness or (2) an intense aversion to and fear of sex and intimacy.

Wounded Expressions of the Sexual, One-to-One Instinct ("The Dragon")

The major wounded expressions of the one-to-one instinct that relate to each of the nine points of the Enneagram and their corresponding Sephirah are as follows:

Realm of the Dragon
Wounded Expressions for the Sexual, One-to-One Instinct for the Nine Sephiroth and Enneagram Personality Types

Sephiroth	Enneagram Point	Vice	Wounded Sexual Instinct	Description
Chokmah	1	Anger	Jealousy	The judging of one's partner in intimate situations
Binah	2	Pride	Seductive	Manipulative in intimate situations
Hesed	3	Deceit	Image	Striving to present oneself as an ideal image of male or female
Tiferet	4	Envy	Competition	Competing with a rival for a desirable partner to build a sense of self-value
Din	5	Greed	Keeping Confidences	Driven to exchange confidences and bond privately in intimate situations
Netzach	6	Fear	Strength and Beauty	Using strength and beauty to diffuse the fear of intimate situations
Hod	7	Gluttony	Being Suggestible	Using imagination and pleasant fantasies to engage a partner in intimate situations
Yesod	8	Lust	Possession	Dominating the heart and mind of the partner in order to feel safe and be able to surrender to intimacy
Malkut	9	Sloth	Seeking Union	Becoming totally identified and merged in all levels with relationship

Volume II, Table 1

All of these illusions act as the red dragon and kill the Christ Child of intimacy in relationship. An antidote to the perversion of the sexual/one-to-one instinct are the following positive affirmations: "I Am in union with God and seek to know God intimately"; "My desire is to know God within myself and others in an intimate connection."

> **4:** *And his tail drew the third part of the stars of heaven, and did cast them to the earth: and the dragon stood before the woman which was ready to be delivered, for to devour her child as soon as it was born.*

The instinctual desire of "the dragon" can pollute some of the mental ideas, the "stars" of holy ideas, and transform these pure energies that create intimacy

(Soul connectedness) into false presentations (illusions) that confuse, hurt and bring death to higher consciousness. The "child" (the young but awakened Christ Consciousness) can easily be lost if not protected or made strong enough to endure challenge.

The Flight into Egypt—An Instruction for the Sexual/One-to-One Instinct

In the gospel story of the birth of Christ, Mary and Joseph are told to flee Palestine with the newborn and go to Egypt, because the reaction of Herod—the negative force of cosmic ignorance—threatens them. Analogously, the new spiritual powers must remain hidden within for a while to work silently and secretly. In the gospel story, Mary and Joseph are persecuted. The young Christ-conscious child within the initiate or humanity also undergoes testing as the activation of new spiritual energy always brings a counterreaction. In relational bonding, every new advance of authentic intimacy between two people is often met with the energy of old woundings; intimacy becomes unsafe in some manner. The protecting defenses unique to the personality attempt to come into play and devour the renewed energy of Soul connectedness and the values of love, trust, and intimacy. Sometimes by avoiding conflict and drama, and remaining silent when triggered by past hurts, one is able to reclaim projected energies and heal old hurts—allowing new growth and energy for mutual transformation to take place.

> *5: And she brought forth a man child, who was to rule all nations with a rod of iron: and her child was caught up unto God, and to his throne.*

The "man child" here is the Soul, the Christ Consciousness in Tiferet that brings guidance and a cooperative Spirit to all aspects of the personality and rules with discernment and wisdom, "a rod of iron." The Christ Consciousness is connected to God in Keter; "her child was caught up unto God, and to his throne."

> *6: And the woman fled into the wilderness, where she hath a place prepared of God, that they should feed her there a thousand two hundred and threescore days.*

The initiate, "the woman," becomes inwardly receptive and meditates, introspects, prays, and contemplates to strengthen the inner connectedness, remaining in the inner sanctum until harmony and peace prevail. This period of introspection and testing lasts 1,260 days, or 3.5 years.

> *7: And there was war in heaven: Michael and his angels fought against the dragon; and the dragon fought and his angels,*

The introspective period is one of struggle between the higher mind and the clarity of truth that Archangel Michael brings. Archangel Michael represents the great guardian of the underworld. He enters darkness (illusion) with his solar power (intuition of the light of truth) and transforms the instinctual chthonic energies—the energies of the underworld, Behemoth and Leviathan—which are collective transpersonal animal drives that attempt to destroy higher consciousness. Michael is the embodiment in Beriyah of the Spirit-Soul and its power to overcome all sources of adversity in human consciousness.

> *8: And prevailed not; neither was their place found any more in heaven.*

Illumination dispels illusion.

> *9: And the great dragon was cast out, that old serpent, called the Devil, and Satan, which deceiveth the whole world: he was cast out into the earth, and his angels were cast out with him.*

The battle between Michael (the Creative Logos, the dragon of light) and Satan (the adversary, the dragon of darkness) results in the expulsion from the mind of all addictive instinctual yearnings and desires of the emotional body centered in Yesod (the second chakra)—particularly lust and passion for self-gratification or selfish desire.

> *10: And I heard a loud voice saying in heaven, Now is come salvation, and strength, and the kingdom of our God, and the power of his Christ: for the accuser of our brethren is cast down, which accused them before our God day and night.*

When we enter our authentic Christ Self, we have strength and freedom in the power of the eternal present. This awareness releases us from all illusions that bring judgment from the superego.

> *11: And they overcame him by the blood of the Lamb, and by the word of their testimony; and they loved not their lives unto the death.*

Through the love ("the blood") of the Spirit-Soul ("the Lamb") and the mind's intuitions ("the word of their testimony"), the initiate can still the obsessive, driven instincts of survival—socially, relationally, and physically—thereby avoiding "the death," or unconsciousness.

> **12:** *Therefore rejoice, ye heavens, and ye that dwell in them. Woe to the inhabiters of the earth and of the sea! for the devil is come down unto you, having great wrath, because he knoweth that he hath but a short time.*

When the initiate leaves Soul awareness—the eternal now, the I Am—and falls into identity with the psychic or physical bodies, he reactivates illusion.

> **13:** *And when the dragon saw that he was cast unto the earth, he persecuted the woman which brought forth the man child.*

When the initiate identifies with the illusions of the personality ("the earth"), he or she reactivates the suffering and pain of separation from his or her source.

> **14:** *And to the woman were given two wings of a great eagle, that she might fly into the wilderness, into her place, where she is nourished for a time, and times, and half a time, from the face of the serpent.*

The divine feminine ("the woman") is given "two wings of a great eagle"—spiritual power, inspiration, ascension, the energy of the Kundalini—to rejoin her origins in Binah, the supernal oneness, and overcome any tendency to become identified with the lower separated energies of the body and emotions.

> **15:** *And the serpent cast out of his mouth water as a flood after the woman, that he might cause her to be carried away of the flood.*

Strong emotional reactions can trap the initiate in the lower psychic instincts, causing forgetfulness and loss of self-identity.

> **16:** *And the earth helped the woman, and the earth opened her mouth, and swallowed up the flood which the dragon cast out of his mouth.*

When psychic or emotional disturbances threaten the equanimity of the initiate, focusing one's attention on the physical domain ("the earth") and one's human need for work, sleep, nutrition, exercise, and constructive activities, the renewed energy and grounding can bring balance once again.

> **17:** *And the dragon was wroth with the woman, and went to make war with the remnant of her seed, which keep the commandments of God, and have the testimony of Jesus Christ.*

As long as we are embodied in the physical world, we will be challenged by illusion and the instinctual desires (the dragon), to ignore our Soul essence and heart center, forgetting the teachings of wisdom and love, "the testimony of Jesus Christ." For there is always another step to take in our spiritual growth—and always another challenge to meet!

Chapter 13 of Revelation

The Beast

> 1: *And I stood upon the sand of the sea, and saw a beast rise up out of the sea, having seven heads and ten horns, and upon his horns ten crowns, and upon his heads the name of blasphemy.*
>
> 2: *And the beast which I saw was like unto a leopard, and his feet were as the feet of a bear, and his mouth as the mouth of a lion: and the dragon gave him his power, and his seat, and great authority.*
>
> 3: *And I saw one of his heads as it were wounded to death; and his deadly wound was healed: and all the world wondered after the beast.*
>
> 4: *And they worshipped the dragon which gave power unto the beast: and they worshipped the beast, saying, Who is like unto the beast? Who is able to make war with him?*

The beast represents the collective lower desire-mind and the perversion of the social instinct. The imagery, according to Pryse,[7] is consistent with the constellation called Cetus, named after a nondescript marine monster (Leviathan). Since this beast comes out of the sea, it is associated with the desire life. It is described as having the form of a leopard and sea-bear or as a hybrid of a lion and panther—a debased form of a lion (the true ruler of light and kingship, nobility). In this case, the higher mind (lion) is contaminated with lower desires: the feet of the monster or bear (heaviness and slothfulness), the mouth of a lion (unfulfilled appetites), the strength of a dragon (destructiveness and being poisonous). The seven heads are the seven deadly vices or passions, and the ten horns with crowns are the negative powers that dominate, or subjugate, the ten Sephiroth.

The "name of blasphemy" relates to polluted, shameless thoughts and emotions and the desecration of physical expressions of sanctity and holy ritual. The wounded head that becomes healed is the lust for power that comes when the solar plexus (center of the social instinct) has been wounded, sometimes developing hurt pride or humiliation. When this happens, the individual personality strives to make things right, to become the hero or a success, to right things, to become a so-called rescuer, to find outer redemption in society's eyes. Often deep feelings of resentment, vengeance, or inadequacy prompt the personality to gain outer confirmation and recognition of success from past failures and hurts. Sometimes this drive is positive, and at other times it is negative and destructive.

The beast is fueled by the dragon (emotional desire) and asserts itself through pomp and circumstance, enacting glamour, and boosting intellectual knowledge, rigid beliefs, and unreasonable attitudes dissociated from philosophical reason and the spiritual intuition of the higher mind. It seeks admiration in the world at all costs. In psychological terms, it represents the perverted or distorted social instinct that arises in the solar plexus and hooks into the heart chakra, ruling the personality, driven by the desire for power and control.

The Social Instinct

The social instinct developed in humans as a need to cooperate for purposes of survival and to make meaningful contributions for the progress of our species. The social instinct allows us an avenue to form friendships, participate in groups, form communities, and create our social identity—the face we present to the world. Balanced, healthy expressions of the social instinct occur when we are not wounded by life experiences that compromise our ability to naturally access the instinct's energy. The social instinct, when healthy, is connected through the body to the higher spheres—the transpersonal energies of the Holy Spirit and the holy archangels—and can ultimately be harnessed for spiritual development and service to humanity.

In group situations, the social instinct brings focus to social and collective activities and interactions with others. Some areas of activity include family, hobbies, work, and groups working toward a shared purpose. Finding one's position in the social group can lead to a desire to be recognized and appreciated, to build self-value and feelings of safety and belonging, to feel successful in one's contributions to society. Friendships and interactions with others is the primary focus, with intimacy being less important.

When the social instinct is wounded, it can lead to unhealthy social behaviors, attitudes, and emotions that embody what Saint John refers to as "the beast"— ego-based preoccupations that are separated from the natural transpersonal flow of these energies such as anti-social behavior, chronic resentments, social isolation, inflexible social dealings, vengefulness, and domination and persecution in social situations. In addition to wounds expressing as abuser behavior, one could take the position of victim in group situations, feeling blamed, shamed, persecuted, and unable to establish a viable position or make a contribution, therefore feeling helpless and rejected by society. Or one might take on the rescuer role, sacrificing everything for the welfare of others, assuming over-responsibility, and shouldering the burdens of others in social situations.

Wounded Expressions of the Social Instinct ("The Beast")

The major wounded expressions of the social instinct that relate to each of the nine points of the Enneagram and their corresponding Sephirah are as follows:

Realm of the Beast
Wounded Expressions for the Social Instinct for the Nine Sephiroth and Enneagram Personality Types

Sephiroth	Enneagram Point	Vice	Wounded Social Instinct	Description
Chokmah	1	Anger	Inadaptability	Rigid, uncompromising positions and behaviors in social settings
Binah	2	Pride	Ambition	Secures attention by being associated with people deemed important or powerful
Hesed	3	Deceit	Prestige	Pursues status and positions of power
Tiferet	4	Envy	Shame	Focuses on manners to cover up social inadequacy and maintain social position
Din	5	Greed	Totem	Offers specialized knowledge and expertise to maintain social standing in group
Netzach	6	Fear	Duty	Ensures loyalty to the group by sticking to its social rules and being the most reliable
Hod	7	Gluttony	Sacrifice	Resolves social insecurities by letting go of personal freedom in order to feel secure
Yesod	8	Lust	Friendship	Domineering and possessive in forming bonds with others to maintain social position
Malkut	9	Sloth	Participation	Motivated to belong and adapt to the social convention and traditions of the group to feel power and social acceptance

Volume II, Table 2

All of these illusions act as the beast and kill the Christ Child of contribution and selfless service to the world as a part of the Divine Plan.

The Good Samaritan—An Instruction for the Social Instinct Given by the Christ

On one occasion a lawyer came forward and put this test question to him: "Master, what must I do to inherit eternal life?" Jesus said, "What is written in the Law? What is your reading of it?" He replied, "Love the Lord your God with all your heart, with all your mind; and your neighbor as yourself." "That is the right answer," said Jesus; "do that and you will live."

But he wanted to vindicate himself, so he said to Jesus, "And who is my neighbor?" Jesus replied, "A man was on his way from Jerusalem to Jericho when he fell in with robbers, who stripped him, beat him, and went off leaving him half dead. It so happened that a priest was going down by the same road; but when he saw him, he went past on the other side. But a Samaritan who was making the journey came upon him, and when he saw him was moved to pity. He went up and bandaged his wounds, bathing them with oil and wine. Then he lifted him up on to his own beast, brought him to an inn and looked after him there. Next day he produced two silver pieces and gave them to the innkeeper, and said, "Look after him; and if you spend any more, I will repay you on my way back.' Which of these three was neighbor to the man who fell into the hands of the robbers?" He answered, "The one who showed him kindness." Jesus said, "Go and do as he did." (Luke 10:25-37)

> *5: And there was given unto him a mouth speaking great things and blasphemies; and power was given unto him to continue forty and two months.*
>
> *6: And he opened his mouth in blasphemy against God, to blaspheme his name, and his tabernacle, and them that dwell in heaven.*
>
> *7: And it was given unto him to make war with the saints, and to overcome them: and power was given him over all kindreds, and tongues, and nations.*
>
> *8: And all that dwell upon the earth shall worship him, whose names are not written in the book of life of the Lamb slain from the foundation of the world.*
>
> *9: If any man have an ear, let him hear.*
>
> *10: He that leadeth into captivity shall go into captivity: he that killeth with the sword must be killed with the sword. Here is the patience and the faith of the saints.*

As spoken of earlier, the entrance into the fourth plane, the fourth initiation of the mind, brings a great challenge to the initiate. To be fully conscious of energy, and at the same time to be threatened by the overpowering aspects of the mind, requires careful treading on the spiritual path. Mastery takes time and effort and faith in the Divine. In verses 5-10, the initiate is challenged by the intensified action of the lower psychic aspects of the mind. The lower mind that is attempting to dominate the solar plexus and heart chakra brings forth challenges and lessons of self-importance, spiritual arrogance, intellectual pride, and the notion of entitlement and superiority by virtue of attaining a position of power in the material world. This period of spiritual development, through the challenge of the lower mind, takes 3.5 years of the 7-year initiatory cycle. The struggle can be constant. The seduction of self-importance and its glamour can bind the initiate in golden chains. As Daskalos once described, once you become indispensable to others by virtue of your position, you may start to take yourself too seriously. You might say, "I am the chosen one. God chose me to guide you. Depend on me. I alone can give you what I have. I am special. I am superior, more capable. I am your savior." This egotistic pride puts you in a cage, a prison of your own creation. To be superior eventually leads to the other side of the pendulum in this life or another. To imprison others leads to self-imprisonment; the law of karma makes it so. Most of humanity lives in the illusion of material glamour and worships the beast (lower mind) of false power. To condemn and judge others is to be condemned and judged eventually.

In verse 8, Saint John is saying that those who crave and identify with materiality will suffer bondage and reincarnation, "and all that dwell upon the earth shall worship him"—the beast. But those who are awake to the true self, the higher mind and Spirit-Soul, are individualized and will be liberated from these influences for their names are written in the book of life. When Saint John says, "he who has an ear, let him hear," he is referring to the power of intuition that can give the individual the understanding of these illusions of mind. In verse 10, "killed" refers to condemnation. Whoever condemns will be condemned. "Patience" refers to neutral observation of these illusions of mind, and "faith of the saints" refers to humility, respect, and recognition of the divinity within others. The recognition that we are all children of God, an antidote to the distortion of the social instinct, cultivates the following attitudes: "I belong to God and God's community." "I serve God in humanity and in all life." "To love humanity is to love and serve God."

The Pseudo-Lamb

> 11: *And I beheld another beast coming up out of the earth; and he had two horns like a lamb, and he spake as a dragon.*

The beast with two horns that has resemblance to the Lamb (divine wisdom of the Spirit-Soul) is the pseudo-lamb or the false lamb. The pseudo-lamb symbolizes maya—the illusion that dominates the senses. The pseudo-lamb causes the individual to become identified with and worship the physical body as well as all exoteric forms of beliefs, superstition, carnal love as opposed to the Lamb (divine love). The pseudo-lamb holds illusionary knowledge, ignorance and blindness.

The speech of the pseudo-lamb is motivated by the lower desire nature of the "dragon." The pseudo-lamb promotes negativity or false or superstitious belief, magic for selfishness, sexual misuse and rigid creeds.

> **12:** *And he exerciseth all the power of the first beast before him, and causeth the earth and them which dwell therein to worship the first beast, whose deadly wound was healed.*

Glamour, as self-importance and deception is located in the solar plexus and is subtle and emotional in nature. Whereas maya—sensory—domination is tangible and more etheric in nature, the pseudo-lamb exercises all the power of the "beast" the lower mind's beliefs in deception and self-importance as well as the vital energy of the body bringing sense domination.

> **13:** *And he doeth great wonders, so that he maketh fire come down from heaven on the earth in the sight of men,*

The pseudo-lamb is a false prophet that has the power of magic and the ability to manifest phenomena in the world.

> **14:** *And deceiveth them that dwell on the earth by the means of those miracles which he had power to do in the sight of the beast; saying to them that dwell on the earth, that they should make an image to the beast, which had the wound by a sword, and did live.*

Maya manipulates the unfulfilled wishes of others to bring stronger identification with the body and glorification of the body. One only need think of advertisements and sales pitches that inundate the mind with fantasies of sensory fulfillment or promises of deliverance and false security through temporal forms of outer worship. Be happy, be powerful, be secure, be sexy, and be successful! You can, if you buy this or do that.

> **15:** *And he had power to give life unto the image of the beast, that the image of the beast should both speak, and cause that as many as would not worship the image of the beast should be killed.*

Maya gives etheric energy to the unfulfilled imagination and charges the physical body with the desire to act out the fantasy, challenging anything that would counter it. Among examples of this behavior are the religious sects and cults that hold their believers in fanatical bondage to human authority. The Johnstown tragedy in Guyana is one in which the 900 or so believers under collective hypnosis followed their leader into physical death through cyanide poisoning. The legendary story of the worship of Moloch exemplifies the pseudo-lamb's domain. Moloch was a pagan god of one of the ancient races. He was represented by a gigantic metal monster that took in through its maws, money, gems, wealth, and even young virgins that were sacrificed to it during the ritual. It was a dishonest religious practice done by the priest-craft of that time. Moloch essentially represents the worship of the personality, which is the worship of men. Wisdom can neither be bought, nor sold.

> *16: And he causeth all, both small and great, rich and poor, free and bond, to receive a mark in their right hand, or in their foreheads:*

Illusion drives the individual to use all his/her life force to fulfill its demands (fantasies). One need only think of the almighty credit card and its promises of physical comfort, security, and prosperity—a modern form of the worship of Moloch.

> *17: And that no man might buy or sell, save he that had the mark, or the name of the beast, or the number of his name.*

Once the individual becomes identified with the false values of all forms of illusion, (mental, emotional, sensory) he/she will place great external value on unreal things (maya).

The Self-Preservation Instinct

Psychologically, the pseudo-lamb also relates to the perverted self-preservation instinct, located in the root chakra. The self-preservation instinct exists for physical survival, health, and wellbeing.

Individuals focused on this instinct are concerned primarily with basic survival, health, food, money, home and physical safety, and warmth in personal relationships. They are most practical and responsible in caring for basic needs such as maintaining the home and managing finances. Wounding of this instinct leads to obsessions with the above areas of activity, difficulties with money, and acting out in self-destructive ways. The wounded personality can assume an abuser role in which they assert greed, violence, and control to assure their survival—a kind of dog eat dog attitude. This may manifest as criminality, or a victim role which expresses through poverty, chronic unemployment, hypochondria and hysteria, helplessness, even homelessness, and issues with money management. On the rescuer side of the coin, one could see expressions of excessive philanthropy, sacrificing resources for the safety of others, denying one's basic needs for health, well-being, and comfort for the benefit of others, or being extremely possessive and intrusive to assure the safety of those close to oneself.

The major wounded expressions of this instinct that relate to each of the nine Sephirah and the nine personality types of the Enneagram are as follows:

Realm of the Pseudo-Lamb
Wounded Expressions for the Self-Preservation Instinct for the Nine Sephiroth and Enneagram Personality Types

Sephiroth	Enneagram Point	Vice	Wounded Self-Preservation Instinct	Description
Chokmah	1	Anger	Anxiety	Afraid of making mistakes that could endanger one's survival
Binah	2	Pride	"Me First"	Takes care of others to insure that they will themselves be taken care of
Hesed	3	Deceit	Security	Accumulates wealth and status to feel secure
Tiferet	4	Envy	Dauntlessness	Overdoes risk-taking in order to feel alive
Din	5	Greed	Refuge (Castle)	Seeks space to withdraw for self-protection
Netzach	6	Fear	Warmth	Makes oneself likable and friendly to assure survival and self-preservation
Hod	7	Gluttony	Like-minded Defenders	Attracts those who mirror their own life views in order to feel secure
Yesod	8	Lust	Satisfaction	Externally dominates and controls resources to relieve survial insecurities. Rapacious in drive for satisfaction
Malkut	9	Sloth	Appetite	Substitues non-essential satisfactions for real needs. Over-indulges out of insecurity about not deserving to have needs met

Volume II, Table 3

These illusions act as versions of the pseudo-lamb and kill the Christ Child of spiritual self-preservation in survival matters. Antidotes for the distortion of the self-preservation instinct are the following positive affirmations: "God brings me what I really need for my survival." "I accept God's abundance," "I am given everything I need."

The Feeding of Four Thousand—An Instruction for the Self-Preservation Instinct Given by the Christ

Jesus called his disciples and said to them, "I feel sorry for all these people, they have been with me now for three days and have nothing to eat. I do not want to send them away unfed; they might faint on the way." The disciples replied, "Where in this lonely place can we find bread enough to feed such a crowd?" "How many loaves have you?" Jesus asked. "Seven," they replied, "and there are a few small fishes." So he ordered the people to sit down on the ground; then he took the seven loaves and the fishes, and after giving thanks to God he broke them and gave to the disciples, and the disciples gave to the people. They all ate to their hearts' content; and the scraps left over, which they picked up, were enough to fill seven baskets. Four thousand men shared this meal, to say nothing of the women and children. He then dismissed the crowds, got into a boat, and went to the neighbourhood of Magadan. (Matthew 15:32-39)

Self-Introspection and Healing Practice for All Three Types of Instinctual Wounding (Relational/Sexual, Social, and Self-Preservation)

We all have all three types of instinctual wounding, but in each of us one will appear stronger and be more of a preoccupation in life. To discover your strongest instinct, you can go online and take the free Enneagram Test with Instinctual Variant (www.eclecticenergies.com/enneagram/test.php) to determine your most likely Enneagram personality type—your Enneagram point—as well as your instinctual subtype. Once you have this information, refer to the instinctual subtype tables *(Tables 1, 2, and 3 of this chapter)* and do the following exercise, filling in the blank for each step of the meditation healing practice with your type's characteristic instinctual behavior.

- What is_____for you?
- When have you experienced _____ in your life?
- Where do you experience _____ and with whom do you feel most unresolved about it?
- How do you deal with these feelings? How do they impact you physically, emotionally, and mentally?
- What is the payoff for you to keep this attitude and behavior?

_____

_____

_____

_____

_____

_____

MEDITATION

Healing and Integration of the Instinctual Self

1. Relax your body and close your eyes, focusing on your feet.
2. Visualize a golden healing light flowing up your entire body.
3. Imagine that you are walking into a beautiful garden and standing in the center.
4. Call on your wounded instinctual self for your Enneagram type that you are working on (self-preservational, social, or relational/sexual self) to enter the garden and stand before you.
5. What do you see, feel? What message does your wounded self have for you?
6. Does it present as a victim, an abuser, or a rescuer?
7. Call on Archangel Hanael in the emerald-green light and Rafael in the violet light to enter the garden. For the social instinctual self, see Hanael on your right and Rafael standing on your left side. For the self-preservation instinctual self, call Archangel Sandalfon in a burning pillar of light to your side. For the relational/sexual instinctual self, call Archangel Gabriel in a sky-blue flame to your side.
8. Visualize reaching within your solar plexus (the third-chakra center) for the social instinctual self; for the self-preservational instinctual self, reach into the root-chakra center; for the relational/sexual instinctual self, reach within the sacral chakra (the second-chakra center). Reaching with both your physical hands and etheric energy hands (hands of light), remove all the negative imprints, memories, and qualities of this wounded energy, placing all of it on an elevated platform behind the wounded instinctual self that you are working on. What do you see on the platform?
9. Who in your life contributed to this wounding you witness on the platform? Who is standing there?
10. Speak to them and say "I break all contracts I have made with you to hold this wounded energy. I set myself free of it."
11. Now, taking a sword of light from the archangel or archangels involved in your healing process, tell the wounded instinctual self that it is now free to give back all it is holding to the light.
12. With the sword, make three cuts. First cut the cord of unhealthy energy that the instinctual self before you is holding with you. Then cut the cord of energy between the instinctual self and the accumulated negative energies on the platform. Finally, cut yourself from the source of the wounding (whoever was involved) and let it all go into the holy spiritual fire of the archangels: Hanael and Rafael, for the social instinct; Sandalfon, for the self-preservation instinct; or Gabriel, for the relational/sexual instinct.

13. Ask the archangels to transform the instinctual self before you into a healthier expression of the energy.
14. Embrace the liberated, healed instinctual self and feel you are both lifting together in a golden column of light to a beautiful temple of healing light in your heart.
15. See and feel in your heart that you are being greeted by the Christ. Ask the instinctual self to stand by your side until the healing with the person involved with the wounding is fully completed.
16. Ask the person that you earlier placed into the fiery light of the archangels to enter the temple.
17. As they stand before you, feel the Christ behind you supporting you and filling your spiritual heart with the golden sun energy of divine love, feeling it filling your whole being, cells, tissues, and chakras.
18. With every breath you take, feel yourself becoming the energy and light of the Transfiguration. Reach over and touch with this light whoever contributed to your wounding, seeing it fill them, and share your forgiveness with them. Let them go in peace.
19. Take into yourself the healed instinctual self that accompanied you to the temple of the heart, breathing them into your Being.
20. Feel the Christ taking you by the hands and lifting you, higher and freer, to the healing temple of your seventh-chakra center, right above your head.
21. As you enter the temple, see the Christ standing before you and feel yourself surrounded by the circles of angels, archangels, saints, and masters that reside there, supporting your healing.
22. Hear the Christ say, "My light is your light; my healing hands are your healing hands; my love, your love; my wisdom and oneness, your wisdom and oneness. Enter into my oneness, wisdom, light, and love now." Feel yourself merging with the energy of the Christ. Feel the power of love and light of the instinctual self within you freed for the highest good for you and life.

The Secret Meaning of the Number 666

> *18: Here is wisdom. Let him that hath understanding count the number of the beast: for it is the number of a man; and his number is Six hundred threescore and six.*

Worship of the beast is worship of man and his personality. Numbers are expressed in Greek by the letters of the alphabet. The number of a name is simply the sum of the numerical values of the letters composing it. The Greek word for lower mind is pronounced He Phren (in the actual Greek is composed of 5 letters), the beast in Greek. The first letter is equal to 8, the second letter equal to 500, the third letter equal to 100, fourth letter to 8 and the fifth letter equal to 50, and that totals 666. The number 7 is completion in divine unity. The number 6 is incomplete and strives for something more. When this divine discontent of the initiate (the individual) strives to reach God, it is using its will in the right manner. When it is striving to serve the beast, it is a wrong use of the will. The three elements of discontent within the personality—the thought body, the emotional body, and the physical body can only find peace, fulfillment, and contentment through spiritual completion. But, in a state of discontent, the initiate's thought body, emotional body, and physical body can get caught up in illusion, serving the beast, the red dragon, and the pseudo-lamb (all part of the lower mind, numerically 666).

Chapter 14 of Revelation

Spiritual Instruction to Awaken the Heart

> *1: And I looked, and, lo, a Lamb stood on the mount Sion, and with him an hundred forty and four thousand, having his Father's name written in their foreheads.*

This passage indicates that an alignment of mental ("mount Sion") consciousness and spiritual ("Lamb") consciousness is being made. Mount Sion is one of the hills on which the ancient city of Jerusalem was built. Up until now, the focus of transformation has been upon the external world, the physical dimension, and the inner "psychic" mental and emotional universes. Now the focus is on higher mental/spiritual activation. The "Lamb" is the Spirit-Soul in Keter (crown chakra) who appeared earlier in the awakening of the first seal, and "a hundred forty and four thousand" is the spiritual community of the supernal triad and the magnified spiritual forces of this region. By placing one's attention above the crown chakra for a time in meditation, it is possible to connect both visually and energetically with the realm of the Spirit-Soul. We have already offered a meditation involving the Christ and Saint Mary Magdalene and the surrounding elders, saints, and archangels to raise your attention to the point above the crown chakra so your higher-mind consciousness can connect with your Spirit-Soul and receive a holy transmission of guidance. *(See Volume I, Chapter 6, pp. 124-125)* When you make this connection, you are connecting the Sephirah of Da'at with the supernal triad of Keter, Chokmah, and Binah within yourself.

> *2: And I heard a voice from heaven, as the voice of many waters, and as the voice of a great thunder: and I heard the voice of harpers harping with their harps:*

This vision begins the fifth chorus. The world of Spirit is a world of light and sound vibration and knowledge through direct perception. Knowingness ("a voice from heaven"), or direct cognition, exists beyond time and space. The "many waters" relates to this feeling of sensory knowingness flowing through the initiate, and "the voice of a great thunder" and "the voice of harpers harping with their harps" is the sound current, or Shabda.

> *3: And they sung as it were a new song before the throne, and before the four beasts, and the elders: and no man could learn that song but the hundred and forty and four thousand, which were redeemed from the earth.*

The supernal triad is the spiritual region of the spiritual masters who radiate their unconditional love and higher spiritual instruction Soul to Soul. The direct transmission of spiritual knowledge is sometimes referred to as *darshan*, or receiving the radiant blessings of the Master. The gaze of the Master Soul has the power to liberate the initiate from the fetters of karma and lift the veil of illusion from the initiate who is prepared for self- and God-realization. The direct transmissions given here are not for the profane or for those identified with intellect. In some traditions in the East, by focusing one's meditation practice on the third-eye center and its purification, the veil of ignorance is removed, revealing the presence of the radiant body of the Master that proceeds to take the initiate on a spiritual journey and reveal the secrets of wisdom that the initiate is now worthy to receive.

> *4: These are they which were not defiled with women; for they are virgins. These are they which follow the Lamb whithersoever he goeth. These were redeemed from among men, being the first fruits unto God and to the Lamb.*

The masters of the spiritual hierarchy exist in all dimensions and teach in the wisdom temples. Their consciousness is the pure essence of Spirit (they are "virgins") and is not identified with personal body-desires or emotions ("not defiled with women") Their consciousness is in Atzilut, the realm of the transcendent Christ, the highest expression of the Divine, embodied within the individual Spirit-Soul, God-realized.

> *5: And in their mouth was found no guile: for they are without fault before the throne of God.*

They hold only the highest intention of truth and love, as their Source holds "the throne of God." In fact, they exist in the heart of God, and although individual in expression and function, they speak only the truth.

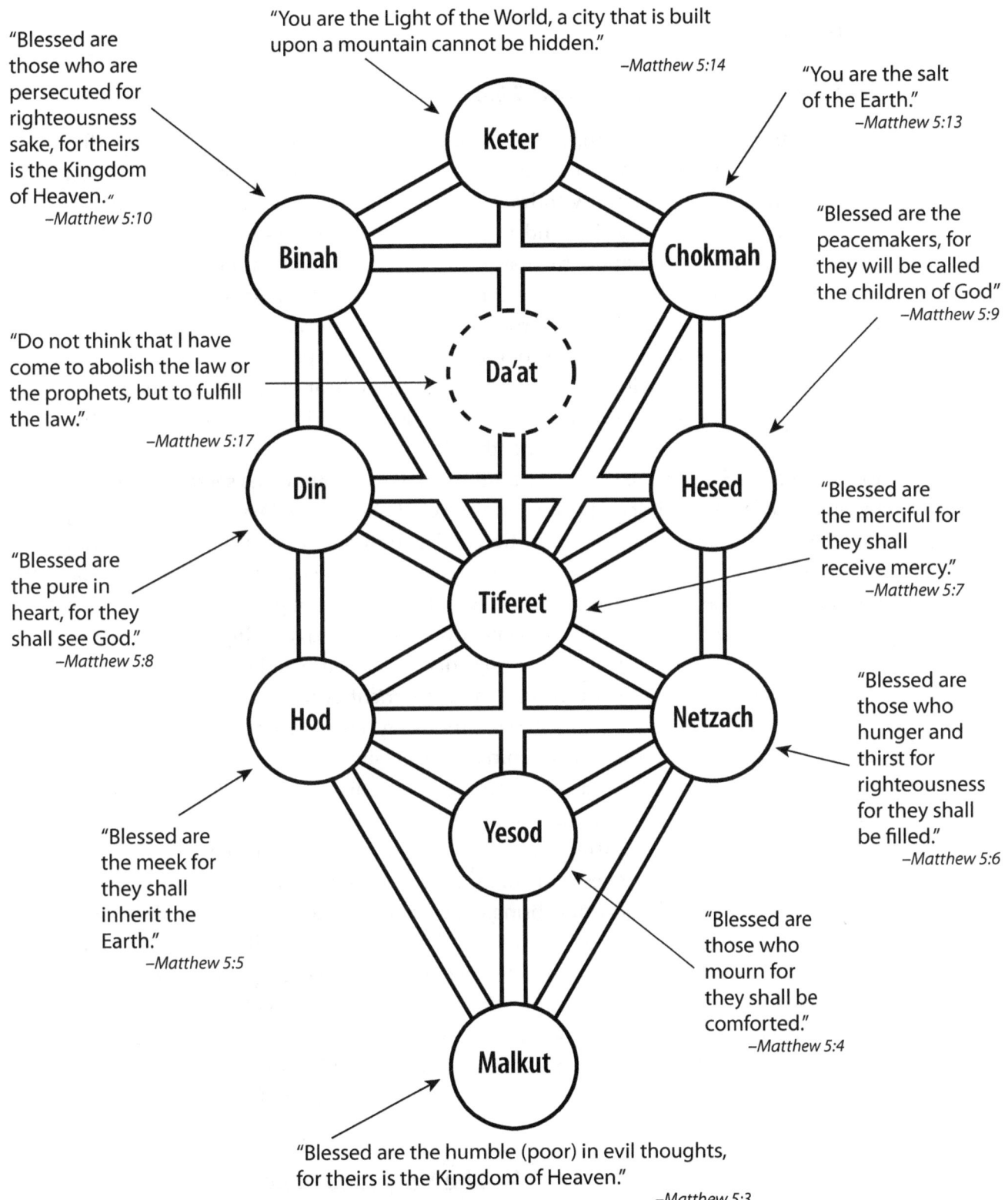

Kabbalah of the Beatitudes and the Harvesting

Volume II, Diagram 3

The Harvesting—Revelation 14:6-20

The distillation and completion of the causal/mental body's healing (the permanent personality) takes place during the harvesting. In fall and winter, when the solar energies of summer withdraw, the vital/mental activities of the year shift toward the harvesting/gleaning and integration of all the lessons gained through experience and transformation, the reaping of all that is good, and the release of all impurities in the heart where the devotional body is purified. This stage of ascension involves the true renunciation of all that was held as impure.

In the Greek mysteries, the gifts of the sun god were ripening grain and turning water into wine—the wine of Dionysius and the wheat sheaf of Demeter—the elements necessary for consecration, as in the offering during the last supper of the bread (the body of Jesus) and the wine (the blood). These elements bring sustenance to the initiate's Soul. In the Hebrew tradition, they were offered as sacramental food by Melchizedek, the priest of the most-high of God, the King of Peace. The harvesting in the Apocalypse suggests the separation of the spiritual life essence from its mortal envelope and the offering up of this essence to God. One can view this process as the passage of the temporary present-day personality through many incarnations of experience, accumulating all that is positive and reflective of higher virtues and ideals, and the illumination of all the things deemed impure and illusionary. All this is registered in the causal/mental body (the permanent personality).

In the story of the lifecycle of Christ, harvesting represents passage through the teachings of the Beatitudes—the culmination of Jesus' ministry and instruction to the multitudes—and the event of the last supper, partaking of the harvest before the crucifixion. The crucifixion represents the final journey through Beriyah and the cleansing of the mind, its mastery and resurrection into the higher consciousness of self-realization (Soul-awareness) in Atzilut, the solar body of the ascended Christ Light. This stage of the journey brings the initiate clearly through Tiferet and completion of the moral triad with Din and Hesed. The crucifixion itself relates more to the pouring of the vials and the later ego death in passage through Da'at to Binah and Chokmah, whereas the purification of the heart centers in the harvest is undertaken as a mastery of the moral triad in Din, Hesed, and Tiferet. The spiritual laws and teachings of Jesus, given as the Sermon on the Mount, are instructions to the initiate for this process of purification—the last supper, the final harvesting and instruction.

The First Harvesting, the Angel—The Holy Idea of Love

Holy love expresses that Absolute Infinite Beingness (God) is the source of unconditional love. Holy love tells us we are beautiful and loving because we are, in essence, Absolute Infinite Beingness.

> 6: *And I saw another angel fly in the midst of heaven, having the everlasting gospel to preach unto them that dwell on the earth, and to every nation, and kindred, and tongue, and people,*

Many of the Ascended Masters continue to convey their divine messages or intuitions to the initiates and to humanity on earth in universal teachings given to everyone with an eye to see and an ear to listen with.

> 7: *Saying with a loud voice, Fear God, and give glory to him; for the hour of his judgment is come: and worship him that made heaven, and earth, and the sea, and the fountains of waters.*

Be aligned with God ("Fear God") and absorb yourself in devotion to "him"— to Absolute Infinite Beingness. His light of spiritual knowledge ("his judgment") is here in the eternal present now. Give devotion, gratitude, and loyalty to the creator of "heaven" (the spiritual world of Atzilut), "earth" (the physical world of Asiyah), "the sea" (Yetsirah, the emotional world), and "the fountains of waters" (the mental world of Beriyah).

The Malkut Type

The first harvesting relates to Malkut in Beriyah, the earth and physical body; the Malkut Type, Point 9, is instructed in the Beatitude "Blessed are the humble [the poor in pride, the poor in evil thoughts], for theirs is the Kingdom of Heaven" (Matthew 5:3). Archangel Sandalfon is a spirit of the earth and connects the supernal light in all matter. Sandalfon carries the secrets of the mysteries of creation and is present in the community, when individuals are together in prayer and meditation, to lift their requests to Heaven. Sandalfon is most actively connected to us when we are in a humble state, free of the desire-thoughts and negative elementals that veil the light from our hearts and cellular awareness. The Sephirah Malkut brings grounding, joy, and abundance into our physical lives. It embodies God's presence within all creation.

Awakening Holy Love in the Heart

Place yourself in the following situation or story, given by Daskalos, visualize Jesus Christ with you, and proceed.

> Two days later, after the morning service, Joshua learnt that thirty of his disciple-healers asked Yiacoub if they might have a private meeting with the God-man. Joshua replied to Yiacoub that he would meet with them, as usual, for the public afternoon lecture in the synagogue. At that meeting, after offering his worship prayer, Joshua said to them, "Beloved ones, all of you, I see confusion in some of you, especially in thirty Israelite disciple-healers among you."

These disciples had asked Zilpah to speak on their behalf, but before he could do so, Joshua turned to him saying, "Dear Ezer, and that is your real name, for the name 'Zilpah,' which you gave to Yiacoub nine months ago, is not yours. I have always known who you are. You are Ezer, the son of an Israelite Rabbi and an informant. You have been reporting to the Sanhedrin on the activities of the Israelites and Essenes in K'far Nahum and Bethsaida.

"In your house in Bethsaida, Ezer, thirty of you Israelite disciple-healers have met with your father and three other Israelite Rabbis. Together you have discussed my teachings at great length and criticized and denounced what you consider distortions of the truth.

"It is your thoughts, Ezer, that drew my attention, for your thoughts shout louder than words. The Israelite Rabbis, without even knowing me, call me a 'cursed Essene' and a 'blasphemous heretic,' and not one of you protested. You, who know me, who have heard so many lectures, you have taken my words and twisted them in your minds." In Aramaic Joshua said,

Blessed are the poor in evil thoughts: for theirs is the Kingdom of the Heavens. (cf. Matthew 5:3)

"My dear Ezer, what do you have to say?"

"Essene Rabbi," said Ezer standing, "you have called yourself the Son of *Alaha* and the Son of Man. This we cannot understand. And you have said that all of us, all human beings, are also sons and offspring of *Alaha*. Who are you? Who are we? How do you differ from us?"

"My dear Ezer," Joshua replied, "all human beings are offspring of *Alaha*—the sons and daughters of *Alaha*. Did I not teach you to call *Alaha* 'Our Father'? You and I as Spirit-Soul-Egos are the same. There is no difference. But as human beings we are different.

"For you, in the world of existence, have wrapped the humanized part of your Spirit-Soul-Self in darkness and in illusion, and have forgotten who you are in reality.

"Humanized as the Son of Man, I am still one with my El Shaddai Self in the One-ness of *Alaha*.

"Ezer, you are now thirty years old. Do you remember who you were before you were born?

"And yet, I know that I Am that I Am. I know my Spirit-Soul-Ego in the One-ness of *Alaha* which was before the material Earth came into existence; before the hills, the mountains, rivers and seas. I know our Father *Alaha*. I know who I am. And that is the difference between us. I know and I feel that you are, and every human being is, and has his life in my El Shaddai Selfhood. I know I am in you as you are in me. And I love you."[8]

MEDITATION

"Blessed are the humble, for theirs is the Kingdom of Heaven."
(Matthew 5:3– Peshitta)

Imagine yourself with the Christ, faced with a group of people who are asleep to their inner light: people who cannot understand you, who feel confused and yet act in harmony on the surface, who hold to and defend traditional fixed beliefs simply to belong, who fear being rejected by you and others. Breathe in their misunderstandings and confusion, the discontent of their inner lives, into your spiritual heart of Christ Light. Breathe out the light into them until your light and their light is of the same brightness. Place a mirror before them, so that they can see their own light. Now say to them, "This is your true nature. You are the embodiment of love."

The Second Harvesting, the Angel—The Holy Idea of Truth

Truth is the perception of multidimensionality; everything is seen as an indivisible unity, beyond the illusion of duality and separation of subject and object.

> *8: And there followed another angel, saying, Babylon is fallen, is fallen, that great city, because she made all nations drink of the wine of the wrath of her fornication.*

The lower nature of "Babylon" has been conquered. The word *fornication* has the meaning of idolatry. Idolatry can be taken to mean the identification with external conditions physically, emotionally, and mentally (*i.e.*, the material worship that enslaves the Soul). Babylon is mentioned elsewhere as the woman in scarlet—personifying the physical carnal expression of the feminine (emotions and body) when disconnected from Spirit. Here is the message that, when you mourn, you cry and release regret.

The Yesod Type

Archangel Gabriel (meaning strength of God) draws Spirit into our feelings and physical body and is associated with motherhood and child-rearing, offering affection, sensitivity, gentle strength, and nurturing to the child of innocence. Gabriel brings strength and support in the most challenging of circumstances. The Sephirah of Yesod, center of the Yesod Type and home of Archangel Gabriel, represents emotional stability, receptivity, innocence, imagination, and security. When Jesus healed, he often touched, embraced, and caressed those in need. His healing touch was the source of many miracles. Since he was in unity with the pure energies of Beriyah in divine will, he had command of all the archangels for the purpose of administering healings.

Awakening Divine Truth in the Heart

Place yourself in the following situation from Matthew 5:4, given by Daskalos, visualize Jesus Christ with you, and proceed.

> An eighteen-year-old Samaritan waiter at the inn asked Joshua and Yiohannan how he might serve them. His eyes were swollen with tears. "Assaf," said Joshua, "I know why you suffer. Come with me." And he led him to a small private room. "My dear Assaf," said Joshua, "your father Hushim is a leper compelled by the authorities for eight years now to live in the caves a mile from here. Your father's nephew, also a leper, lives with him in the same cave and in these caves of Ebal there are ten other lepers. You and two other young men are permitted to go once a week to leave food and clothing for them at a safe distance but you must leave before they approach. From that distance it has been possible for you to talk with them. But now for a month your father has been too ill to come out of the cave. Assaf, my dear, let us go to your father, who you shall kiss now for he is healed."
>
> Coming out of the room with Assaf, Joshua beckoned Yiohannan to follow. As they walked, Joshua spoke to Assaf. "You live with your mother, Elisheba, your grandmother and twin sisters, Lala and Martha, in a small house with a hallway and two little rooms. This house is unsafe and it leaks in the winter rains. Your mother and grandmother work very hard in the vegetable gardens, but there is little time to spare, and you weep because you know your cousin, Eli, waits for you at the caves, and you have nothing to bring them."
>
> "Rabbi," said Assaf bewildered. "How is it you know my name? And the names of my family? And how did you come to hear my father's and cousin's plight?"
>
> "Assaf," said Joshua, "I know all these things because you are in my mind and in my heart. You cannot understand what I am saying, but from this day your family will be poor no more. Your father and cousin will be healthy and strong. You will build in the yard of your house a fine forge for your father, and the neighbourhood will ring again with the sound of his hammer on the anvil."
>
> At the caves Assaf waited at the usual distance while Joshua and Yiohannan went forward. The other lepers were gathered by the wells drawing water. Joshua, entering the cave, found Hushim on a pallet with Eli standing near. Joshua knelt by Hushim's side and took the leper's hand in his saying, "Hushim dear, open your eyes. You are well. Come, get up. Assaf is waiting for you." Hushim, entirely healed, stood with Eli's help. Then Joshua caressed Eli's face and hands saying, "Dear Eli, take off the bandages from your hands and legs. You have no need of them. You are quite well." And so he was. Eli too was completely healed.
>
> The ten other lepers, seeing Hushim and Eli miraculously cured, begged Joshua to heal them too, and they too were healed.
>
> As Joshua healed the lepers he prayed to *Alaha*, his Heavenly Father. And when they were all healed, he stretched out his arms to them, blessing them. And then in Greek and Aramaic he thanked *Alaha* for his great Mercy.
>
> He said "Blessed are they who mourn: for they shall be comforted." And he continued: "Our Father who art in Heaven, your will is done on Earth as it is done in the Heavens."[9]

MEDITATION

"Blessed are they who mourn, for they shall be comforted."
(Matthew 5:4–Peshitta)

Close your eyes and breathe deeply. Allow yourself to imagine that you are walking with Joshua, Yiohannan, and Assaf to visit the leper colony. This is a very emotional time for you because somewhere in the leper colony, perhaps hidden in a cave, is your wounded self—the wounded self that you feel is most disfigured, hidden away from society and from others, perhaps out of social shame or simply because it is a part of yourself that you feel is weak and unacceptable.

Let Joshua take you by the hand and find that child that needs healing, that is afraid of love or be loved. See Joshua taking your hand and guiding you as you go into the cave with a candle in your hand. Somewhere in this darkness is your rejected, unacceptable self, a part of your past, perhaps from your childhood in your current life or perhaps from another life. Allow yourself to feel your tears as you approach this wounded self. *Blessed are those who mourn for they shall receive comfort.*

Feel Archangel Gabriel in a beautiful blue robe of light at the side of Joshua, and feel him reaching over and touching this disfigured part of you, the part of you that feels weak, that feels in some way like a leper. Feel the hands of Gabriel caressing its face, washing its feet, touching its heart, washing away its karma and old energy. Feel it becoming healthy and strong again. And hear Joshua saying, "You are healed, my child; you are ill no more." See the radiance in this child's eyes, in this part of yourself, and feel Joshua taking this child's hand as it begins to run to you to be embraced. Feel your love; feel Gabriel bonded to you. And feel your heart open to this healed part of yourself. And say, "I love you just as you are." And take the child away from the leper colony into a place of peace, beauty, joy, and healing. And feel Gabriel filling the child with his nurturing energy of love. Be born again, alive and free, the child entering your heart.

Feel the manifested Christ, the Healer, in front of you as he says to you, "My beloved, I Am within you and you are within me. You too have the power to heal, to connect with the bodies of others and all life." Feel the strength and the light and the love. Now take a deep breath and exhale. Gently feel yourself returning from your journey, coming back to your physical body. Let yourself stretch, rub your hands, rub your face gently, and return.

The Third Harvesting, the Angel—The Holy Ideas of Strength and Holy Work

Strength is the awareness that the nature of our soul is divine and, by its very nature, brings strength and security. Holy work is the awareness that all manifestations are the result of God's divine plan.

> *9: And the third angel followed them, saying with a loud voice, If any man worship the beast and his image, and receive his mark in his forehead, or in his hand,*

This verse refers to becoming seduced by lower mental fantasies ("If any man worship the beast and his image, and receive his mark in his forehead") or becoming emotionally engaged, wishing to enact these fantasies ("or in his hand").

> *10: The same shall drink of the wine of the wrath of God, which is poured out without mixture into the cup of his indignation; and he shall be tormented with fire and brimstone in the presence of the holy angels, and in the presence of the Lamb:*

> *11: And the smoke of their torment ascendeth up for ever and ever: and they have no rest day nor night, who worship the beast and his image, and whosoever receiveth the mark of his name.*

These verses refer to the potential fall from grace. In the fourth plane initiation, the fall from grace can be severe. According to Meher Baba,[10] if these desires, at this maximum point, overpower the Soul and the powers are misused, the result is that all of the consciousness gained by the Soul is violently disintegrated; the Soul falls from grace and returns to rudimentary consciousness again.

> *11: And the smoke of their torment ascendeth up for ever and ever: and they have no rest day nor night, who worship the beast and his image, and whosoever receiveth the mark of his name.*

The suffering and torment of identifying with the lower mind of fantasy, glamour, and lower desires can bring no peace and will only get worse and worse. If the initiate is successful in overcoming these temptations, he or she will pass on to the next initiation in spiritual consciousness.

> *12: Here is the patience of the saints: here are they that keep the commandments of God, and the faith of Jesus.*

Three "commandments," or principles of instruction and of wisdom, are given here: (1) Follow "patience," observe your personality, and introspect deeply into the thoughts, emotions, and motives of your personality at all times. (2) Follow your inner guidance; learn to trust the voice of the Master within you. (3) Live by the example of the Christ and the Ascended Masters and follow their commandments and the spiritual laws they taught—teachings best embodied by the Beatitudes—for ethical living and non-violence. By following these principles, you will harvest the essential messages and attributes of spiritual life, which will complete the purification of your heart center and awaken you to divine love.

> *13: And I heard a voice from heaven saying unto me, Write,*
> *Blessed are the dead which die in the Lord from henceforth:*
> *Yea, saith the Spirit, that they may rest from their labours;*
> *and their works do follow them.*

You will be blessed through surrendering all your egotistical desires and remaining true to the Soul's values, serving from this Spirit of love and truth.

The third harvesting relates to Hod and Netzach in Beriyah, the third chakra, the lower mind. The Hod Type is instructed through the Beatitude "Blessed are the meek: for they shall inherit the earth" (Matthew 5:5). The Netzach Type is instructed through the Beatitude "Blessed are those that hunger and thirst for justice, for they shall be well satisfied" (Matthew 5:6).

The Hod Type

Archangel Rafael is the illuminator of cosmic ignorance, showing the real truth behind the veil of glamour, illusionary fantasies, and the play of Maya. Rafael brings peace and caring when conflict arises. Jesus often communicated truth in his teachings and demonstrations of mercy, bringing clarity and wisdom. A few examples of this, from the book of John, are when Jesus says to the woman taken in adultery, "go, and sin no more," or to the men who ask about stoning her for her sin, "He that is without sin among you, let him first cast a stone at her." Through his oneness with Archangel Rafael, he offered instruction for purification of the Hod Type. "Blessed are the meek: for they shall inherit the earth." Hod represents logic, clarity of thought, clear perception, and problem-solving. The instruction is to refrain from being boisterous, argumentative, intellectually arrogant, and rigid and fanatical in one's thinking—to instead be receptive and understand in a higher way.

Awakening the Sanctity of Work in the Heart

Place yourself in the following situation or story, given by Daskalos, visualize Jesus Christ with you, and proceed.

> Then the Pharisees went out and plotted how they might entangle him in his talk. And they sent him their disciples..., saying...

"Malpana, we know that you are true, and teach the way of *Alaha* in Truth, nor do you care about anyone for you do not regard the person of men.

"Tell us therefore, what do you think?

"Is it lawful to pay taxes to Caesar, or not?" But Joshua perceived their wickedness, and said, "Why do you test me, you hypocrites? Show me the tax money." So they brought unto him a dinarius.

And he said to them, "Whose image and inscription is this?"

They said unto him, "Caesar's." And he said to them, "Render therefore to Caesar the things that are Caesar's, and to *Alaha* the things that are *Alaha*'s." When they had heard these words, they marveled, and left him, and went their way. The same day, the Sadducees, who say there is no resurrection, came to him and asked him, saying "Malpana, Moses said that if a man dies, having no children, his brother shall marry his wife, and raise up offspring for his brother. Now there were with us seven brothers: The first died, after he married, and having no offspring, left his wife to his brother. Likewise the second also died, the third died, up to the seventh.

And last of all the woman died also.

Therefore, in the resurrection, whose wife of the seven will she be? For they all had her." Joshua answered and said to them, "You are mistaken, not knowing the Scriptures nor the power of *Alaha*. For in the resurrection they neither marry, nor are given in marriage, but are like angels of *Alaha* in Heaven.

"But concerning the resurrection of the dead, have you not read what was spoken to you by *Alaha,* saying, 'I am the *Alaha* of Ibrahim, and the *Alaha* of Is-Shakh, and the *Alaha* of Yiacoub.' *Alaha* is not the *Alaha* of the dead, but of the living." (Matthew 22:15-32)

The newcomers left the synagogue hall, muttering angrily, complaining that this, that this Essene Rabbi was saying indirectly that they should surrender to the Roman conquerors and serve the conquerors.

When they were gone, Joshua said, "In less than a hundred years these war-loving people will believe they are strong enough to drive the Romans from Palestine, and they will declare war. But they will be defeated. There will be great bloodshed and Yerushalayim will be devastated by the Romans. The Romans will destroy the temples and no stone will remain on stone in the place where the great temple of Solomon now stands." In Aramaic Joshua said, "Blessed are the meek: for they shall inherit the earth." (Matthew 5:5)[11]

MEDITATION

"Blessed are the meek: for they shall inherit the earth."
(Matthew 5:5–Peshitta)

Close your eyes again. Breathe deeply and relax your body. Feel yourself with Joshua in the temple in Jerusalem. The 7-year-old child that you once were and you, the adult, are also there. I want you to imagine that, in the audience, there are people who respect and love you, and there are also those who are projecting their criticism, their shadow energy of life. They are your Pharisees, your Sadducees. Perhaps you met them when you were socially introduced to the world, when going to school. Perhaps they were teachers. Perhaps they were someone in your family. Allow yourself to see who they are in your life between 7 and 14 years of age. Who are they? How did they respond to you? What did they say to you that hurt you and injured your self-value and your self-concept?

Let Joshua support you as a child as he stands on one side of you. Let Archangel Rafael stand on the other side. Allow them to help you speak the truth to those who would otherwise attempt to injure you and trap you and wound you through their words. Now remember a major situation you experienced, and take the position of truth with whatever is happening, holding the light of mental clarity and wisdom. Feel this light healing and filling the child. Feel the power of truth as it heals and transforms each event and situation. Let this light shine brightly through the child, and feel Joshua and Archangel Rafael handing this child back to you. Step into the world with confidence and truth in your heart. Know that you exist because of God's love for you and that we are all children of *Alaha*. We are not different from each other in our Soul essence. We all exist because of divine love. Now, very gently, take the child into your heart and allow yourself to return from your journey. Begin to stretch.

The Netzach Type

Archangel Hanael is the guardian of enlightenment on earth; *Hanael* means "grace of God." Hanael is the creative expression that inspires the feelings of devotion to ideals and ascension. When the heart is in the right place about matters of love, you act out of knowing what is right and correct. You know the divine ideal and you attempt to live it, placing it before you as a source of authority in life: "Blessed are they which do hunger and thirst after righteousness: for they shall be filled" (Matthew 5:6). Netzach (victory) holds the qualities of inspiration, creativity, spiritual passion, and higher ideals.

Awakening Strength and Faith in the Heart

Place yourself in the following situation or story, given by Daskalos, visualize Jesus Christ with you, and proceed.

In the visitors' sitting room, Rayis Rabbi Samuel said to the others, "In K'far Nahum four fifths of the population are well-to-do Essenes. Though the Israelites are small, and mostly poor, minority, they are sometimes very provocative. But as they are dependent on the Essenes for their livelihood, they do not dare to actually do harm to any Essene, and the Sanhedrin [which was a Jewish sort of politburo] is, so far, powerless in K'far Nahum. The Sea of K'far Nahum [meaning the province K'far Nahum] owns land north of the Sea of Galilee on which small houses might be built for Essenes who are in need of sanctuary. I am sure many Essenes in K'far Nahum would contribute generously to such a project. I will open a special fund with eight thousand Roman silver denarii from the Sea and four thousand of my own money. We can build small houses and make them ready very quickly."

The Rayis Rabbi Ephrahim responded to this beneficent offer saying, "Reverend Rayis Rabbi Samuel, dearest friend and brother, when you were here in Yerushalayim as a Rabbi Teacher and later as a Rayis Rabbi, you were always so generous, spending your salary on the poor. And not on Essenes only, but Israelites too! We Essenes of Yerushalayim are, as you all know, only a small minority. The Sanhedrin and Herod have their spies everywhere, for they secretly consider us to be heretics. The Sea of Yerushalayim is not rich, but Rayis Rabbi Samuel, I pledge you two thousand silver denarii from the treasury of the Sea and one thousand of my own. It is all I have here in my wooden safe. I would give you more, but I spent some to entertain my brothers and guests here for this meeting. I will send more as soon as I have it. Whenever Joshua comes to Yerushalayim, I will send back with him whatever I can." Joshua looked with great love upon the two white-bearded Rayis Rabbis saying, "Blessed are those that hunger and thirst for righteousness: for they shall be well satisfied." (Matthew 5:6–Peshitta)

"Have no fear," said Joshua, "for the fund you have established today will never lack what is needed to serve its purposes."[12]

―◄o►―

MEDITATION

"Blessed are those who hunger and thirst for righteousness, for they shall be well satisfied." (Matthew 5:6–Peshitta)

Allow yourself to go back in your life to the time of your teenage years, from 14 to 21. As you review this time in memory, who were the people that judged you and rejected you? And who were those that believed in you? Perhaps there is at least one person during those years who believed in you and supported you, even championed you—a real friend to you in your time of need. Perhaps it was a parent, a grandparent, someone who really served you out of their goodness of heart because they could see the best in you. Feel the Christ on one side of you and Archangel Hanael on the other. Now bring the supportive person to you and thank them for their gift of love. Perhaps it was this gift, this encouragement, that allowed you to move on with your life.

Allow yourself to give thanks as you feel yourself being filled with the light and love of Hanael. Let yourself turn to those that judged you or hurt you during your teenage years. Perhaps they misunderstood you, or perhaps you represented something that they could not accept in themselves. Who were those people? Allow the Christ to show them a mirror of themselves. And have the Christ touch you on the body wherever you're holding the wounding from this energy. And through the loving hands of Archangel Hanael, feel yourself filled with healing light, and let these people go. If you like, you can take Hanael's sword of light and realize, before you cut the cord, that these people could only see in a limited way. They couldn't feel or understand through their hearts. Now, take a sword of light in your hands and, at the count of three, let's cut that cord. One, two, three, CUT!

Breathe deeply. Feel the healing light of Hanael and the love of the Christ filling those organs, those cells, those parts of your body that were wounded. As you breathe, feel yourself surrounded by the three archangels. Feel Gabriel behind you in a beautiful white linen cloth, in flames of light. Feel Rafael on your left, a beautiful white solar light with violet wings, and Archangel Hanael on your right, a beautiful androgynous emerald-green embodied Being, a beautiful bright white heart with wings of light, pouring divine grace and mercy on you. Feel Rafael sending his healing energy to you and Gabriel her nurturing energy. And feel from your belly center the Transfigured Christ rising gently into your heart.

With the help of the Transfigured Christ, begin to feel within yourself the Christ Light that exists in your cells and tissues. Acknowledge this light and say, "Wake up." Let the manifested Christ within you awaken all your cells and organs to his light. And feel the great light of the Pleiades connecting through him to you as he touches all the little cells, the organelles, the centrioles, bringing cosmic resonance to you, filling your physical body with light, renewing and regenerating all your cells through his light of love and through these three orders of the archangels with you, healing and evolving any damage that has been done from age 14 to 21 years of age in this incarnation.

As you breathe, feel the light of Archangel Michael and the Christ filling your heart. In your heart center, the Sephirah of Tiferet, Archangel Michael governs the light of the sun that descends from your crown chakra. Let this light flood your physical body and bring you peace. Feel the light of the great star of Alcyone flowing into the light of the physical sun above the crown chakra. Feel this light flowing down into your heart where the great figure of Archangel Michael stands. And very gently, when you are ready, become aware of your body, your breathing, and sense the room. Rubbing your hands, massage your face.

The Fourth Harvesting, the Angel—The Holy Idea of Origin

The holy idea of origin (Source) tells us that we arise out of, and are made of, Beingness. We are whole and complete and lack nothing.

> *14: And I looked, and behold a white cloud, and upon the cloud one sat like unto the Son of man, having on his head a golden crown, and in his hand a sharp sickle.*

The Spirit-Soul of Christ Consciousness, the "Son of man," is the initiate awakening to a higher position of observation and neutrality that brings divine guidance at this stage of his or her journey. The "golden crown" is the light of the crown chakra (Keter). The "sharp sickle" is the ability to discern and discriminate. The practice of detached observation and the receiving of the Soul's guidance empower the initiate's heart to follow the example of Jesus Christ and surrender to inner guidance and instruction. The ego-ridden personality and the lower mind are not allowed to hook and entrap the heart, which at this stage clearly belongs to the guiding hand of the crown center of divine purpose and inspiration. The fourth harvesting involves the surrender of the heart to higher guidance and direction.

The Tiferet Type

The fourth harvesting relates to Tiferet in Beriyah, the fourth chakra, the heart. The Tiferet Type is instructed through the Beatitude, "Blessed are the merciful: for they shall obtain mercy" (Matthew 5:7).

Archangel Michael spiritualizes matter and lifts it to higher ground. Michael embodies the qualities of freedom, independence, self-responsibility, and individuation. Michael supports and strengthens the truth and opens us to higher guidance and spiritual connection. Mercy is that quality of the Christ energy that comes to us when we are asking in prayer for God to intervene or to give us guidance in some area of our life. Tiferet is our great center of Christ love and compassion, and it is into this center that we reach to connect deeply with our Source and receive support and guidance. When we sincerely open our hearts and minds to receive it, the divine mercy of the Christ is then given to us.

Awakening an Awareness of the Divine Origins of the Soul in the Heart

Place yourself in the following situation or story, given by Daskalos, visualize Jesus Christ with you, and proceed.

> Before the sun rose in K'far Nahum, Joshua came to the temple where the novice Is-shaak, standing by the incense burner, was reciting the Psalms of David in Greek.
>
> In the Holy of Holies, before the altar, Joshua offered to *Alaha* his prayer of adoration.
>
> The Rayis Rabbi Samuel found him there, and together they offered to *Alaha* the morning service of worship. After they had breakfast, Joshua went as usual to a quay, two hundred yards from the Essene See, and boarded the fishing boat of Shabbatai. He stood alone there watching the other fishing boats on the See of Galilee.
>
> There was a noisy commotion on shore. Two strong men were holding down and beating a young man as they pulled away his shirt, baring his right shoulder.

A fat man with a leather whip in his hand stood by watching this scene.

The unfortunate young man was Kedar, son of a Bedouin, and slave of the man holding the whip. Kedar's offence was a thwarted to run away from his owner, Madai, a wealthy owner of vineyards and livestock north of Bethsaida. Madai had only one eye, having lost the other eight years before in an accident.

Joshua came down from the boat and went to where Kedar was struggling painfully to free himself. He ordered that the beating be stopped. Madai approached the young Rabbi indignantly. "Rabbi," he said, "this man is my slave. I bought him more than four years ago for fifty silver dalanda in the slave market in Tyre. Look, on the skin of his white shoulder blade is my mark. I branded him with a red hot iron as I do all my livestock. Until recently Kedar has been a good investment, working hard in the vineyards and cow shed. But the last few months he grew lazy, feigning illness and forcing me to use this whip on him. And then three weeks ago he ran off right in the middle of the harvest. Some friend saw him here in K'far Nahum working like a free man on the fishing boats, and here I found him. Kedar is mine, my slave." "Madai," said the God-man, "Are not four years of work enough for Kedar to earn his freedom?" Instead of answering, Madai pointed to the brand on Kedar's shoulder. "This is my mark," he said, "and proves this is my slave."

Then Joshua touched Madai on his chest over his heart, and placing his thumb on the empty eye socket, he said, "Madai, my dear, with two eyes I believe your vision will be better." And thus was Madai healed.

Now caressing the bare shoulder of Kedar, Joshua said, "Madai, where is your mark?" Madai rubbing both his eyes with his fingers stared at the smooth, unblemished skin. "Essene Rabbi," he said, "the things that I heard about you in Bethsaida I did not believe. Now I have seen with my own eyes. Forgive me, Rabbi, I am an Israelite," he continued, "and my father is a Rabbi. Do we believe in different *Alahas*?"

"My dear Madai," said Joshua, "*Alaha* is ONE and what people believe does not change the nature of the ONE *Alaha*. You believe as Moses taught, and we Essenes believe in the *Alaha* of Love and Mercy, the loving Father of us all.

Blessed are the merciful: for they shall obtain mercy." (Matthew 5:7)

Bewildered Madai looked at Kedar. "I understand, Rabbi, that Kedar is not my slave, but what then is he to me?" "Madai," said Joshua, "Kedar is your brother. All human beings are children of *Alaha*. You must love one another as brothers."

"Rabbi," said Madai, "This is the time of the grape harvest. Tell my brother, Kedar, to come back to work for me, not as a slave, but as a free man, and I will pay him well."

"Mara [Sire] Madai," said Kedar, "your vineyards are the best in Bethsaida, and I should know, for I uprooted the old vines that no longer bore fruit and planted new stock. And I love every one of them. Yes, I will work for you as a free man. Did you think that your curses and whip brought you a better harvest? I will work gladly in the vineyard I love."

Joshua took the whip from Madai saying, "My dear Madai, you have no more need of this. And the others, the two you have at home, throw them away too. Kedar will work with you as a free man and a loving brother. *Alaha* will bless you both." And so Joshua left them, to heal the others who gathered along the shore.[13]

MEDITATION

"Blessed are the merciful, for they shall have mercy."
(Matthew 5:7–Peshitta)

Close your eyes and breathe deeply. Put your attention on your feet. Feel the healing white light flowing into your legs, moving into your thighs, your hips and pelvic area. Feel the light flowing into your abdomen, your chest and heart. Feel the healing light flowing over your shoulders, down your arms, to your hands and fingers. Feel the light flowing into your neck, your head and face. And as you breathe, imagine yourself walking along a forest path to a beautiful garden. Imagine that this garden is a vineyard where a part of you works and struggles; that part of you that tries to get ahead in life or attempts to change something in your life; the part of you that feels like a slave, unable to be free, to receive something more from life. You continue to toil in blood, sweat, and tears, to do your job, to put forth effort, to survive.

In the vineyard, Joshua Emmanuel the Christ greets you. And as he takes your hand, let yourself remember some times in your life when you showed someone in your life mercy. Perhaps it was an act of generosity. Perhaps you gave someone something they needed that no one else could really help them out with, but you recognized the need and could fill it. Perhaps you sacrificed a little bit of your time to serve someone or some cause because you felt there was a real need and you felt the suffering. Try to remember at least one event in your life where you acted out of mercy and selfless service to another. It could have been at work, at home, in the family, or with a child. Or it could have been with an animal. Perhaps you took a stray animal in and fed it and nurtured it and brought it back to health. Feel the energy that fills your heart with this memory.

As you look at your struggling self, or this problem in your life where you never seem to move ahead, feel the frustration and powerlessness of the situation. It is time to ask in prayer for the mercy of God for this part of yourself, this problem—not because you showed someone else mercy in your life, but simply because the same mercy is now available for you, if you are ready to receive it. So now, within yourself, as you hold the hands of the Christ, ask in prayer, with sincerity and an open heart, for mercy and divine intervention to help you in this area of your life. Feel the divine mercy lifting this struggling part of you into freedom and light, lifting this burden from you—this burden you carry on your shoulders and in your body, mind, and heart—bringing you the experience of freedom.

And as you look at the struggling self being lifted, breathe light and love and freedom into it from the indwelling Christ in your heart. And feel the support of Archangel Michael in this process shining his bright light of truth, protection, and strength on this situation. And feel yourself filling with the light of Archangel Michael and the indwelling Christ. Breathe deeply. And gently begin to return to your physical body awareness, stretching, rubbing your hands, and massaging your face.

The Fifth Harvesting, the Angel—The Holy Ideas of Omniscience or Transparency and Holy Law

The holy idea of omniscience is the ability to view the inner connectedness of all the parts of the universe as manifestations of the whole. The holy idea of divine law is the realization that the universe, in all its dimensions and parts, is one unified entity in movement and change.

> *15: And another angel came out of the temple, crying with a loud voice to him that sat on the cloud, Thrust in thy sickle, and reap: for the time is come for thee to reap; for the harvest of the earth is ripe.*

The "temple" is the higher mind. The initiate is prompted to inquire deeply into the nature of karmic suffering to uncover the beliefs that still remain that are not aligned with obedience to spiritual laws of life, for the breaking of these spiritual laws causes suffering. The fifth chakra is the place where Din (and Archangel Kamael, keeper of karma) and Hesed (and Archangel Tzadkiel, keeper of grace and blessing) sit, and it is from this center that true spiritual self-responsibility for all one's thoughts, feelings, actions, and deeds emerges. The personality ("the earth") is "ripe"—ready and prepared—and the "sickle"—the power of discernment and discrimination—can now "harvest" the personality, removing the self-created suffering and karmic impact of the ego's struggle and lack of cooperation with the spiritual principles, or laws, of life.

> *16: And he that sat on the cloud thrust in his sickle on the earth; and the earth was reaped.*

Through a non-attached attitude of mind and heart, the initiate extracts the core beliefs of ego separation that have led to suffering and disconnection from Source.

The fifth harvesting relates to Din and Hesed in Beriyah in the fifth (throat) chakra. The Din Type is instructed through the Beatitude, "Blessed are the pure in heart: for they shall see God" (Matthew 5:8).

The Din Type

Archangel Kamael is the divine protector, karmic revealer, and burner. Kamael removes all destructive energy impeding the flow of divine grace. Saint Paul, for example, said, "For I through the law am dead to the law, that I might live unto God" (Galatians 2:19). This suggests that, in the case of Archangel Kamael, the negative elementals get burned away to reveal the Soul of light and the Christ Self within. Kamael is therefore the archangel of divine justice. The Sephirah of Din has to do with that which is limited or bound by form. It carries the spiritual lessons about power, leadership, integrity, honesty, and conscious action.

Awakening the Awareness of Omniscience in the Heart

Place yourself in the following situation or story, given by Daskalos, visualize Jesus Christ with you, and proceed.

> In the first week of Tammuz (July) Joshua returned to the Essene temple in Yerushalayim. Early that morning Stephanos and Yiassounai had everything ready in the temple. The Rayis Rabbi Ephrahim, the other Rayis Rabbis, and the Rabbis were worshipping in the temple when Joshua entered. All stood up to welcome him. He went to the pulpit and, filling the temple with his aura and love, stretched out his arms to the Heavens, saying in Greek:
>
> "*Kodoish, Kodoish, Kodoish Adonai Alaha, Adonai Tsebaoth, Adonai Elohim.* Holy, Holy, Holy is the Lord God, Lord Sabaoth, Lord of the Archangelic Hosts."
>
> Then Joshua reached out his hands to the audience, blessing them and attuning himself to his Divine El Shaddai [Logos] Selfhood, spoke:
>
> "My beloved ones, all of your offspring are mine, Spirit-Soul-Egos, immortal Gods, Ego-Selves, in my infinite Selfhood.
>
> "I am the Lord, your God in you. I'm your Ego-Being-Self. I am the Lord, your God in every other human being. I am the Ego-Being-Self of all human beings. I am the Creator of everything, and I am in everything existing.
>
> "Beloved ones, be still, be calm, and listen to me. I am the everlasting Life, the life in every living being and in every living thing in my Omnipresence. Listen to me. I will speak to you in your mind also, by intuition.
>
> "Listen to me and understand. I, together with the Holy Archangels, have given you a material body, and we are sustaining it continuously for you to live in. I have given you bodies to be my Bat-Salmaynu-Kidmuthenu [image and likeness].
>
> "You are my image and likeness.
>
> "I have given you the Divine Light Body, the Merkabah, in its violet light, to give you the Hokhmah [Wisdom] in my worlds of other dimensions. I have given you a Kuch-ha-guf [the body of sensations and emotions]. Do not allow the Siddim [Evil Ones] to contaminate it with illusions and darkness. I have given you in your material body, the Tzool-mah [etheric double]. Find it, and use it well. Cooperate in it with the archangels in your body in their creative work. Feel your etheric double and fill it with my Neshamah, with Mind-Light-Vitality.

"Be still. Be calm and listen to me. I have given you in your material body a human heart. I am in the pulse of your heart. Hear me in the pulse of your heart. In the pulse of your heart is my love for you. Clean your heart. Make it a crystal clear mirror to reflect my love—your love—to every human being, my offspring. Find me and listen to me. I am Life in your heart. I have given you two eyes well protected in their sockets. You can see the material light and in this light you can see everything material in the material world. Feel me and my Omnipresence. I have given you in your chest two lungs to breathe my air and my Life-giving Vitality. Breathe deeply and feel the air you are breathing in your lungs. You can feel me there and you can hear me in your breath. I am in your breath.

"Beloved offspring, all of you, I am the Life in your bodies. I am the Life everywhere. I am the everlasting Life. I am the Omnipresent, Omniscient, and Omnipotent infinite Selfhood. All of you are my Self-conscious Ego, Spirit-Soul-Beings, immortal Gods.

"Be still. Be calm. Listen to me. I have given you the Mind to use, that you may understand who you are. I am the *Adonai Alaha* [the Lord God]. I am God, your Divine Father. I am the *Adonai Elohim* [the Lord of Hosts].

"I am the lord of the orders of the angels and the archangels.

"The Omnipresent, Omniscient, and Omnipotent *Alaha Elohim*. I am *Alaha El Shadda* [God the Logos] and *Alaha Elohim Shekhinah* [God the Holy Spirit]. See me in the Life-Love-Light in you. I am the light emanating from the material sun. I am in the inextinguishable Mind-Light in the everlasting Wisdom. Feel me and see me in the Strength and Power and Nature. See me and hear me in the storm. Hear me in the wind and see me and hear me in the thunder and lightning. Hear me and see me in the raging sea.

"See me as the beauty of the trees in bloom; see me as the symmetry in all forms; see me in the blossoming flowers; and feel me in their sweet fragrance and see me in their lovely hues. I am the everlasting Life in your immortal Spirit-Soul-Ego-Self in my infinite Selfhood. The Maout [death] is not a reality, but an illusion. The reality is everlasting Life. Your ever-changing bodies are not you. Your Self-conscious Ego-Being is an immortal Spirit-Soul-Being. I am not the *Alaha* of the dead. I am the *Alaha* of everlasting, immortal, Self-conscious Gods, beloved offspring of mine."

Joshua concluded by giving to all present in the temple his El Shaddai Love. The courtyard was already overflowing with the sufferers and their families. Some were men and women moaning in pain. Some were children crying piteously. There were more than two hundred, all waiting expectantly for Joshua....

Caressing their heads and hands most lovingly and taking the children in his arms, he healed them all, saying, "Your sins are forgiven."[14]

MEDITATION

"Blessed are the pure in heart: for they shall see God." (Matthew 5:8)

Close your eyes. Breathe deeply. Relax your body. Imagine that you're among the people that have come to see the Christ in the temple. You are there as he gives his sermon and witness the beauty, the love and grace of his voice, his form, his eyes, his light, and his love. The people are lined up to receive his blessings and healings. imagine that you are next in line. Standing to the left of the Christ is Archangel Kamael in a blazing fire, holding the sword of light of divine justice. To his right stands Archangel Tzadkiel in his beautiful rainbow light body, shining the blessings and grace of God. As you come to Joshua, within your heart say a prayer:

Our Father, who art in heaven,
hallowed be thy name.
Thy kingdom come.
Thy will be done
on earth as it is in heaven.
Give us this day our daily bread,
and forgive us our trespasses
as we forgive those who trespass against us.
And lead us not into temptation,
but deliver us from evil.
For thine is the kingdom,
and the power, and the glory,
forever and ever.
Amen.

And as you look up at Joshua, feel the burning fire of Kamael surrounding you with divine protection and burning away and purifying whatever you hold in your heart that no longer serves you. Burning away whatever karma you no longer need. And feel Kamael forming a protective circle of flames of light around you, and feel the Christ with you. And now allow the Christ to lay his hands upon your body as the blessings of Tzadkiel and the rainbow light flow into you. And feel yourself expanding, being uplifted in this light of healing. And breathe deeply as we complete with the Daskalos prayer:

Absolute Infinite Beingness; God.
Everlasting Life, Love and Mercy.
Manifesting Yourself in Yourself,
as the Total Wisdom and the Almightiness.

Enlighten our minds to understand you as the Truth,
Clean our hearts to reflect Your Love towards You
and towards all other human beings.
Amen.

Take a deep breath, exhale; deep breath, exhale; once again. Slowly return to your physical body awareness. Rub your hands, massage your face, eyes, arms, and return.

The Hesed Type

Archangel Tzadkiel offers divine blessings and lovingkindness according to the degree of our openness and capacity to receive. Tzadkiel brings the abundance of love and the sacred unity of light. Hesed is the carrier of these qualities in God's great mercy, devotion, charity, and the overcoming of rebellion, self-righteousness, and unfaithfulness. This is the Sephirah that embodies the Christ as the forgiver of sins (karma) and imparting God's blessings. "Blessed are the peacemakers: for they shall be called the children of God" (Matthew 5:9).

Awakening the Awareness of the Divine Plan in the Heart

Place yourself in the following situation or story, given by Daskalos, visualize Jesus Christ with you, and proceed.

Joshua healed hundreds daily, giving to all his love and restoring them to health. Among them were the rich and the poor: Israelites, Essenes, Greeks, Bedouins, Romans and others. In his Divine El Shaddai Selfhood all human beings are.

There was no time of the day, or the night, or of the week that he would not heal. He cleansed lepers, gave the blind sight and made the lame to walk. At times he recalled departing Souls to return to their "dead" material bodies.

All over Palestine, as well as in neighboring countries, people heard of the wonders he performed.

But to the Israelite Rayis Rabbis, the Rabbis and the Sanhedrin the reports of these miracles brought grave misgivings for three reasons.

Firstly, the man was an Essene, and the Sanhedrin considered the Essenes to be heretics. Secondly, there was a large number of Israelites among the followers of Joshua. And finally, the Sanhedrin, which had organized a violent underground movement of Zealots to expel the Romans from Palestine, saw Joshua's ministry of Peace and Love as a serious threat. For didn't he reject the Mosaic law of "an eye for an eye and a tooth for a tooth," teaching instead, "to the one who slaps you on your right cheek, turn the other to him also"? The Sanhedrin sent spies to Judea to follow Joshua and to inform on him.

In Yerushalayim Joshua reorganized the group of healer-disciples, which included many Israelites. Three hundred young Israelites and Essenes came to

Joshua's teachings on healing. Yiacoub was designated to train them to use Self-consciously the Mind etheric Vitality and their body's etheric double. Instruction was given four days every month, with daily exercises teaching the proper use of Mind Supersubstance and etheric Vitality in healing and health.

Although many Israelites became good healers, fearing excommunication with the Sanhedrin, they distanced themselves from the Essene communities as they continued to heal in Joshua's name. One of the group of seventy healer-disciples, Yiohannan the Canaanite, came to Joshua saying, "Rabbi, many Israelites are healing using your name. Shall we stop them?"

Joshua said to him, "Yiohannan, to those who are healing, we must give our blessings and our help. Those who are not against us, are ours. Love them and help them in their works of mercy."

Then Yiohannan answered and said, "Master, we saw someone casting out demons in your name…"

The Bible quote reads essentially the same.

"…and we forbade him because he does not follow with us." And Joshua said to him "Do not forbid him, for he who is not against us is for us." (Luke 9:49-50)[15]

As Daskalos has pointed out, due to the degree of political instability in those days, everyone wanted Jesus on his/her side, so to speak. Many of the Israelites wanted him to proclaim himself king of the Jews in order to force an uprising and get rid of the Romans. He lived at a time when there was a lot of political intrigue going on, and so of course it was easy for him to be put in a position of being either the savior or the bad guy. But Jesus didn't want an earthly crown. Being king of the Jews obviously wasn't his mission.

MEDITATION

"Blessed are the peacemakers, for they shall be called sons of God." (Matthew 5:9–Peshitta)

Close your eyes. Breathe deeply. Relax your body. Imagine yourself among the 300 disciple healers of Joshua the Christ learning to use your mind's etheric vitality and your Etheric Double to build your healing energy to serve God as a peacemaker. As you observe Joshua healing others, you observe that no one is excluded from his love. He treats all equally and with the same love and recognition that they are all a part of him. Feel this great spirit of love within him. And imagine sitting next to him, watching him healing others. Israelites come to him, Bedouins, Greeks, Romans, and Samarians—many, many different peoples of different languages, different religions and ways of life. But they all come to him with humility. See his smiling face, his joy, his happiness, how he gives his grace freely.

Sometimes it's simply an embrace that releases someone from a stuck emotion. At other times, it's a handicapped or mentally ill individual that is released from their emotional prison. Or it's simply someone who comes to him seeking a better life, more harmony, more peace, and more freedom. Many people are coming. Watch Joshua the Christ as he treats each one with equality and respect. His blessings are free. And now feel yourself ready to receive his blessings. But before he gives you his blessings, he asks you this question: "My dear one, my beloved child, think to yourself, who or what do you exclude from love? Who is it that you are unable to allow grace to flow to from your love? Who can you not forgive? And why can you not forgive them? For they are in you, in me, as you are in me."

Now allow yourself to think of someone that you have excluded from love and blessings. Think about this person or situation and what emotions you have carried in relation to them. And see this person coming to receive the blessings of healing from Joshua the Christ. Observe him greeting them with the same love, the same respect, that he would greet anyone with, including you. What do you feel, as he blesses them and touches them and heals them? What flows through your heart and mind? Do you feel forgiveness now? Perhaps you're cold, filled with indignation, anger, or pride. Or that person may simply remind you of some shadow part of yourself that is unacceptable to you. Perhaps it is your own inconsideration or neglect.

Now stand before the Christ. What do you see in his eyes and in his heart? Look at the person he has healed, the one you have disregarded, standing by his side now. Can you see the shining light of the Christ's heart within this person now? Can you now surrender what holds you back from forgiveness and love? Let the Christ take in his hands this elemental of judgment of others, criticism, pride, or whatever it is. Perhaps you think "I have been victimized" or "This is such an injustice, how could I ever forgive them? They must pay for their wrong doing." Whatever it is, hand it to him. And now take Michael's sword of light in your hands and cut the connection that has bound you to this energy that holds you back from love and forgiveness. One, two, three, CUT!

Breathe deeply. Feel the Christ placing his hand on that part of your body, that chakra or chakras where you held this old energy. And let the Christ and the presence of Archangel Tzadkiel next to him, in a beautiful rainbow body of light with white wings, fill you with the blessings of God. Breathe in these energies. Hear the Christ say to you, "My beloved, if you follow me, you must also follow my way of love and forgiveness. For everyone is within me and the Selfhood of *Alaha*. Receive this truth, and love as I love. Heal as I heal. Share truth and wisdom as I teach truth and wisdom. Express this joy as I express this joy." And feel Archangel Tzadkiel filling you with more joy and more light until all the cells of your body begin to feel the lightness, the light of joy and peace, the beautiful rainbow light of Tzadkiel, the blessings, the expansion, the growth of this energy, the abundance of good intention and honesty.

Now feel the Christ filling all your chakras with the light of love, the golden light of the Soul, starting with your first chakra, second chakra, third, and so on. As he touches your crown chakra, the Christ says, "My beloved, your Christ Light can now awaken. That's the course of evolution. It's the awakening of the cosmic consciousness in you." Feel this great light and truth growing inside you as he speaks. Feel the deep peace and tranquility. As you breathe, give thanks to the Christ for his love and for this experience, and let the light go out from your heart as you breathe it out into the world—to your family, your workplace, your community—breathing out the love and light. As you inhale, let the old energies be transformed in the light of the peacemaker, the indwelling Christ ascending into the light of the Cosmic Christ, the resurrected Christ within you. "Blessed are the peacemakers, for they will be called the children of God." Take a deep breath. Let yourself begin to stretch a little bit. And rub your hands. And return.

The Sixth Harvesting, the Angel—the Holy Ideas of Will, Freedom, and Perfection

Holy will teaches us that deep within us is the desire to understand ourselves, to know who we really are. This leads to holy freedom—being able to surrender to the flow of what is happening in one's life rather than exerting one's personal will and demands into it. Holy perfection is the recognition that everything is correct and perfect just as it is, because there is the higher hand of perfection in operation within all events and happenings.

> *17: And another angel came out of the temple which is in heaven, he also having a sharp sickle.*

> *18: And another angel came out from the altar, which had power over fire; and cried with a loud cry to him that had the sharp sickle, saying, Thrust in thy sharp sickle, and gather the clusters of the vine of the earth; for her grapes are fully ripe.*

The sixth chakra in the supernal domain of Binah and Chokmah, the "altar" in Beriyah, brings the pure light of the Spirit-Soul and its direct cognitions through the mind (the "temple") and illuminates all held attitudes and beliefs of the mind that impact the heart. The challenge now is to illuminate all beliefs that are contrary to the wisdom of the heart and hold it back from the experiential knowledge of the Soul that enters its domain. The heart is considered by some to be like the fifth part of the brain due to its high concentration of nerve channels interconnecting with its muscle. The heart receives experience directly, which is then assessed by the brain/mind, the higher cortical centers. If the brain/mind holds negative, self-limiting, or outmoded beliefs, it can hold back the heart's evolution to divine love and Christ Consciousness by creating doubt about the heart's higher intuition, spiritual objectivity, and compassionate striving for understanding.

In Revelation 14, verses 17 and 18, the brain/mind has been prepared to receive a greater influx of spiritual light that makes transformation and illumination of all false beliefs possible. The "grapes" represent beliefs, and the "clusters" are groups of beliefs, whether true and synergistic with the heart's development or false and dissonant with the heart's consciousness. The sixth harvesting relates to Binah and Chokmah in Beriyah in the sixth chakra. The Binah Type is instructed through the Beatitude, "Blessed are those who are persecuted for righteousness sake: for theirs is the kingdom of heaven" (Matthew 5:10). The Chokmah Type is instructed through the Beatitude beginning with "Ye are the salt of the earth…" (Matthew 5:13).

The Binah Type

Archangel Tzafkiel carries the great book of life, which holds the Divine Plan of God for humanity. Included is the awareness available to every Soul of its unique divine mission and past life history. Tzafkiel can also bring a deep awareness and inspiration that leads to an awareness of a spiritual community's mission. Tzafkiel can help you answer the question, "Why I am here and what is my spiritual mission?" Tzafkiel also shows us our karmic burdens and what we must learn from them and how to move through it all, graciously, with humility. Tzafkiel also gives us knowledge of how to navigate the various dimensions and our multidimensional nature so we can ascend as gently and harmoniously as possible. Since Tzafkiel is governed by Saturn and sits in the Sephirah of Binah (the Divine Mother), she gives us the knowledge of what is of value in our process of spiritual growth and what is not worth keeping or remaining attached to. She helps us understand the cycles in our lives, what to keep of the harvesting of the seeds and which seeds to plant and why. In the Beatitude, Matthew 5:10—"Blessed are they which are persecuted for righteousness' sake: for theirs is the kingdom of heaven"—she awakens us to the wisdom of divine growth, to the purpose of our karmic debts, and how to endure them in the reassurance that higher consciousness, "the kingdom of heaven," is our goal and reward.

Awakening Freedom and Divine Will in the Heart

Place yourself in the following situation and story, given by Daskalos, visualize Jesus Christ with you, and proceed.

> Blessed are those who are persecuted for righteousness' sake: for theirs is the Kingdom of Heaven. Blessed are you, when they revile and persecute you, and say

all kinds of evil against you falsely, for my sake. Rejoice, and be exceedingly glad: for great is your reward in Heaven: for so they persecuted the prophets that were before you. (Matthew 5:10-12)

Before he departed from Yerushahayim, Joshua explained to his disciples in precise detail what must befall him in less then a month on the Feast of the Passover.

"The time is near when the Son of Man will be arrested on a moonless night by servants and executioners of the Sanhedrin. To satisfy the Israelite Rayia Rabbi Kaiaphas, the judges of the Sanhedrin will convict the Son of Man of violating the Mosaic Law and of blasphemy and will sentence him to death. The Judges will deliver him to the executioners, who will mock him, and abuse him until he is bruised and bloodied. Then the Sanhedrin will deliver him to the Roman Governor, who will authorize the sentence of death.

"My body will be crucified, nailed to a wooden cross. When my body has been killed, two good-hearted Israelites who heard me teaching, friends of the Roman governor, will ask him for my body to place it in a tomb. The governor will grant their request and with two of my disciples, my mother, my aunt Miriam Shalome, Maria Magdalena, and some other good women, they will lay my body in the cave they've prepared for it.

"When three days have passed, I will heal all the wounds and bruises and resurrect my body, leaving only the nail holes in my hands and feet and the deep wound under my ribs where the spear pierced my liver, as proof to whoever may yet doubt, that I have risen from the grave. And thus will I prove to you, my dears, and to all human beings, that the gross material body is not the Self.

"What's really important about life? Is it the body? Or is it the essence, the Soul?

"The body is a gift of *Alaha* that by using it you may express yourselves, but it is not you. When the gross material body dies, and sooner or later it will, your Ego-Self is not annihilated.

"How could it be? Your Ego-Self is your Spirit-Soul-Self, an immortal offspring of *Alaha*. It is for this I have been humanized, becoming a Son of Man. It is for this hour I have come to the world."

Tzafkiel is holding the knowledge of Jesus's divine mission, his destiny. Here he speaks it clearly.

"It is not out of weakness that I will allow them to arrest me, to torture and wound my material body, and to kill it. No, this is my triumph, my victory. This is the proof of what I've taught you of the Son of Man. I tell you this now to prepare you, that you will remain calm when it comes to pass."

Some of the disciple-healers could not grasp what the God-man was saying and they wept openly. Yiohannan the Canaanite, the brother of Simon, stood up and without asking leave to speak said, his voice breaking, "Beloved Malpana, must you go to Yerushalayim to become arrested, tortured, and crucified?"

"My beloved Yiohannan," the God-man said gently, "I know that you and many other here, have not understood me. I will not die upon the cross. It is only my material body that will die, and I will resurrect it. Again I say to you, in this way I will prove to you and to all human beings that you are not your material bodies, but Spirit-Soul-Egos, immortal Beings, the offspring of *Alaha*. As the Son of Man, a human being like you, I have overcome the world….

"The crucifixion and the death of my body is my triumph as the Son of Man. And you, Samuel, will see me here in this room in my resurrected body. I will come to you before my mother, Shabbatai and his family and my companion-disciples return to K'far Nahum. I will show you the signs of the wounds that the nails inflicted.

"A new religious Order will be created in my name and in *Alaha*'s mighty name. Petros will lead it. And you, my beloved Samuel, as a Rayis Rabbi of this new Order will baptize Essenes, Israelites, Greeks, Bedouins, and even Romans in the name of the Father *Alaha,* in the name of the Son, in my name, and in the name of the Holy Spirit. Come my dear, you must not grieve to hear such good news….

"My ministry as the Son of Man is ending. Your ministry in the new Order of Worship begins now."[16]

This is an example of Archangel Tzafkiel's work within the Christ as a part of his energy, in total cooperation with Joshua the Christ who could share openly and calmly these things with his disciples.

◄○►

MEDITATION

"Blessed are those who are persecuted for the sake of justice, for theirs is the kingdom of heaven." (Matthew 5:10–Peshitta)

Close your eyes and breathe deeply. Relax your body. Put your attention on your feet, and feel a beautiful healing white light flowing into your legs. Feel the light flowing up your legs, into your thighs, your hips, your pelvic area. Feel the healing light as it flows into your abdomen, your chest, and your heart. Feel the light flowing over your shoulders and down your arms to your hands and fingers. Feel the healing light flowing into your neck, your head, and into your face. And feel yourself walking along a forest path to the gate of a beautiful garden. Feel yourself entering this garden. This time it's a different garden that begins to appear before you as you walk through it. This is the garden of Gethsemane, in Jerusalem. And it's the night before the Christ is arrested by the Sanhedrin, by the guards. He has clearly instructed his disciples and has spoken of what is to come.

Be with him there in the garden. Be with him in his sorrow. And allow yourself to think of a time in your life when you felt as if you would be crucified. Let the Christ guide you as he takes you through the process of crucifixion. He knows that this is his mission, his destiny, as he walks through the process, fully present to all that is. Now see the Christ being put on the cross and ask yourself: When did you feel crucified in your own life experience? Were you aware of what was happening to you spiritually? Could this have been the way that God was giving you love, by helping you burn off your karma? Recognize what it was that you were burning off, and reflect on it now that it is behind you. Perhaps it was a situation from another life or another time. Whatever it was, you got through it.

See the Christ now in his resurrection. You too burned off the karma and you too healed. He was carrying the karma for the world and for humanity. Your mission is only to carry your own, helped by Spirit to endure it. And you too are resurrected. Reflect on this big event, this situation that you are recalling in your life, and how you came to a higher octave or level of understanding, healing, or acceptance of it. How did you become resurrected? And as you look at that past experience and your suffering, your crucifixion, and your resurrection, recognize that God never left your side. Everything worked out for you. You exist because of God's love for you, and through this experience you became a better human being and a better spiritual being as part of your journey of transformation to the light.

Let the Christ come to you now and see where the wounding of this biggest crucifixion of your current lifetime is. And let the Christ touch those old wounds, those old memories you still have, and let him heal you. Perhaps the Christ will place his hands over the chakra that was most involved. Feel your energy renewed. Feel yourself resurrected from this experience. "Blessed are those who are persecuted for righteousness sake, for theirs is the Kingdom of Heaven." Breathe the healing light into your body. And very gently begin to step away from this place, back toward your physical body awareness, giving thanks that you have been protected through this journey and resurrection. Become aware of your breathing, your body, and begin to stretch yourself. Rub your hands, massage your face, and return.

The Chokmah Type

Archangel Ratziel brings us the divine wisdom and never-ending blessings of God's divine light and mercy. As the great light generator, he is the force, or carrier, of radiant supernal consciousness in Beriyah for the Divine Father. When Jesus referred to the people as "the salt of the earth," he was referring to the real strength ("salt") of the personality ("earth") coming from divine wisdom and blessings that form the very foundation of our lives. Salt is not only necessary for life, but it is a great cleanser and absorber of negative energy. Divine wisdom, the light of Chokmah, is a great cleanser and transformer of our personalities and keeps our heart center purified. We are sanctified, consecrated, by Chokmah's perfect light and wisdom: "Ye are the salt of the earth: but if the salt have lost his savour, wherewith shall it be salted? it is thenceforth good for nothing, but to be cast out, and to be trodden under foot of men" (Matthew 5:13).

Awakening Divine Perfection in the Heart

Place yourself in the following situation or story, given by Daskalos, visualize Jesus Christ with you, speaking to you, and proceed.

"Beloved ones, all of you, my offspring, be still and listen. I speak to you not only in words, but also directly, in your minds.

"I have created all the universes of existence. This is my Will-pleasure.

"I have created my Mind Supersubstance as my Mind Vitality, movement, force, power and energy.

"All that you need to live I have created in abundance.

"I have given you my Light, as much as you as human beings can endure. I have created the elements: fire, water, etheric Vitality, air and matter. With all these elements I have created your bodies.

"Breathe. Fill your lungs with air and hear me and feel me in the air you breathe.

"Breathe Self-consciously. Hear me and feel me in my Mind Vitality. Feel me as the warmth of your red blood. I have given you a material heart. Feel me and hear me in your heart. Hear me in the beats of your heart. I AM the pulse of life.

"Feel the etheric double of your material body, which I have created. Feel it, study it and use it Self-consciously. Through it you can use my Mind Vitality in creating thought-forms, the elementals that compose your present-day personality. Beware that you make good use of my Mind Vitality by creating human-in-nature angels. Do not create human-in-nature demons. Do not allow such demons to enter you and take possession of your mind and heart.

"By using Self-consciously the Mind Vitality in your etheric double, which is the storehouse of Mind Vitality, you will discover that anger, anxiety, enmity, jealousy, hatred, all other human weakness, and especially unbridled lust, exhaust this Mind Vitality, which the Holy Archangels use to create and sustain the material body. When you waste Mind Vitality—your daily bread—the gift of *Alaha*, you allow illnesses to enter your material body.

"Beloved ones, all of you, my children, let your material body, which is my gift to you, be my body, my temple. Let the human-in-nature angels which compose your personality be the congregation in my temple. I will bless them. Make your material heart, my gift to you, my Holy of Holies. On its altar light the lamp with the inextinguishable Light, the Light of Love for all mankind. Let the Light of your Love lead all to the way of righteousness."[17]

MEDITATION

"You are indeed the salt of the earth." (Matthew 5:13–Peshitta)

As you ponder these words, imagine gathering with the people who are part of your daily life, your family, fellow workers, etc. And as you stand with them, make a great circle around the Christ standing in the center. Breathe his light into your heart, and as you breathe out the light, let it fill all the members of the circle. See their brightness and acknowledge that each of them carries this great light and wisdom from Chokmah in their Soul's essence. Feel the perfection and sacredness of each of them and your own perfection and sacredness. Taste and savor the strength. And say together, "We are the salt of the earth."

The Seventh Harvesting—The Winepress

The winepress of God is the spiritual force of Keter, the primordial singularity and source of all. Keter holds the divine plan and divine will of Spirit that guides evolution and higher purpose in our lives. Here is the dissolution of the division of mind and heart as separate entities.

> *19: And the angel thrust in his sickle into the earth, and gathered the vine of the earth, and cast it into the great winepress of the wrath of God.*

The message here is this: To reap the wine is to harvest the essence of the causal/mental bodies—thoughts and feelings.

> *20: And the winepress was trodden without the city, and blood came out of the winepress, even unto the horse bridles, by the space of a thousand and six hundred furlongs.*

The Spirit-Soul (solar body) is emerging from the lower limited bodies—"outside the wall of the city"—through the action of the "winepress," the spiritual force (Keter), through which the transformation is activated. The "wrath" of God is the energy or will of God (or Keter). Wine is "blood," the conveyor of life, the vitality sustained by the spiritual light of our Being. The solar body (body of the sun, or *soma heliakon*) is referenced as being of a great space (1,600 furlongs, or 200 miles) and the spiritual vitality or light fills all the chakra centers ("horse bridles"). The seventh chakra is the domain of Keter in Beriyah, the primordial singularity and source of divine will and purpose. The rising to Keter here embodies the dissolution of the division of mind and heart as separate entities and their ultimate distillation in the winepress of Spiritual love. The words "I Am" embody this expression of unity of heart and mind and the oneness of divine truth. The solar body, or the Spirit-Soul, in its auric splendor emerges beyond the confines of duality, or limited form. It is infinitely large in contrast with the size of the cocoons it was incubated in (the physical, emotional, and mental bodies).

The seventh harvesting relates to Keter in Beriyah in the seventh chakra. The great archangels Metatron (of heaven) and Sandalfon (of earth) merge in the unity of what is referred to as the great Archangel Hua. *Hu* in Hebrew means "he"; *Hua* means "she." Here we can think of Hua as a divine androgyny—the "he" and "she" in unity. These two great archangels, combined into the one archangel Hua, together form the great archangel of the Christ and the Holy Angel of the Apocalypse.[18] Archangel Metatron's form and energy can be likened to the entire universe and its supernal light; Sandalfon's can be likened to the light in the earth. The highest instruction in the Beatitudes are the words of the Christ: "Ye are the light of the world…" (Matthew 5:14). This is also expressed beautifully in the Gospel of John: "The life was in him, and the life is the light of men." (John 1:4 – *The Peshitta*, pp. 1052) So within the Christ is the light, and this light of Christ is within everyone. Archangel Metatron's light within Christ is for the evolution of humanity.

Awakening the Divine Light of the Heart

Place yourself in the following situation or story, given by Daskalos, visualize Jesus Christ with you, and proceed.

> …Aaron [who] cried, "Joshua, I ask you in the name of the Living God to tell me the truth. Who are you?
>
> "Are you the king of the Jews, are you this, are you that? Let me put you in a little category in mind, so that I can then relate to you from there."
>
> So he came to Nazareth, where he had been brought up. And as his custom was, he went into the synagogue on the Sabbath day, and stood up to read. And he was handed a scroll by the prophet Isaiah. And when he had unrolled the scroll he found the place where it was written: "The Spirit of the Lord is upon me, because he has anointed me to preach the Gospel to the poor; he has sent me to heal the broken-hearted, to preach the deliverance to the captives and recovery of sight to the blind, to set at liberty those who are oppressed, to preach the acceptable year of the LORD." (Luke 4:16-19)
>
> Rabbi Aaron ordered that a man who was possessed by demons, and was blind and mute, be presented to Joshua. The man was brought and Joshua healed him.
>
> Again Rabbi Aaron angrily demanded, "Who are you? All of us are convinced, you are a demon."
>
> And Joshua said simply, "*Ehyeh Asher Ehyeh. Ehyeh Beni Alaha, Melekh Shamayyim,*" which means, "I Am that I Am. I am the Son of God, King of the Heavens."[19]

This truth, "I Am that I Am," is Keter; this is the God of Absolute Infinite Beingness.

MEDITATION

"You are indeed the light of the world. A city that is built upon a mountain cannot be hidden." (Matthew 5:14–Peshitta)

Close your eyes, breathe deeply, and place your attention on your feet. Draw the white healing light all the way up your body and fill your whole being with white light. Feel yourself entering a ray of golden white light coming down from heaven, from above, through the top of your crown chakra. And now lift up all of your chakras to the crown, where you will find a great temple of light. Inside this temple, the Christ is teaching, surrounded by the 24 elders, archangels, and masters of the ages. Stand before him and hear his words: "You are the light of the world. Beloved, step into my heart, my love, my body, my blood, my healing hands and light." Step into his presence and feel his heart as your heart, his love as your love, his body and blood as your etheric energy and fire of vitality. Let his light awaken your whole being. Look out onto the world and repeat his words, "You are the light of the world." Slowly return from your journey.

➤*(See Volume II, Chart 1, p. 69)*

Beriyah – Higher Mental Body – 4th Initiation – Approaching Crucifixion – The Last Supper
(Air) – Passage from Tiferet to Din–Hesed (Moral Triad)

7 Harvesters	Correspondences	Virtues of Healing	Beatitudes and Sephiroth	Reaping begins for the Instincts Transformed	Holy Ideas and Virtues Stabilized
1. Aeonian Tidings to those dwelling on Earth	1. Creative Biologic Self-preservation, Instinctual Realm (Subconscious)	"I have infinite worth as a child of God."	**Malkut** "Blessed are the poor in evil thoughts, for theirs is the Kingdom of Heaven."	From sense indulgence (the calf) – Earth (Taurus) to physical mastery, discipline, service to God.	Love Right Action Enneagram Type Nine
2. Fall of Babylon announced to those who drank her wine	2. Psychic, Interpersonal Sexual/Relational Realm (Subconscious)	"I trust every other child of God."	**Yesod** "Blessed are those who mourn, for they shall be comforted."	From passional desire (man) Water (Aquarius) to purified love, higher wisdom	Truth Innocence Enneagram Type Eight
3. Denunciation of those who worship the Beast's image	3. Phrenic Social Instinctual Realm (Subconscious)	"I can do all things through Christ which strengthens me."	**Netzach** "Blessed are those who hunger and thirst for righteousness for they shall be filled."	Same as above	Trust Courage Enneagram Type Six
			Hod "Blessed are the meek for they shall inherit the Earth."		Holy Work Sobriety Enneagram Type Seven
4. Solar Divinity appears, having a sickle	4. Noetic (Consciousness)	"As Love Incarnate, I care for my neighbor and all creation as my self."	**Tiferet** "Blessed are the merciful for they shall receive mercy."	From destructiveness (the lion) – Fire (Leo) to refining, purifying	Origin (Source) Equanimity (Balance) Enneagram Type Four
5. The "over-ripe" harvest is gathered	5. Sympathetic (Consciousness)	"I express my truth freely and fearlessly."	**Hesed** "Blessed are the peacemakers for they shall be called children of God."	Same as above	Compassion Veracity (Honesty) Enneagram Type Three
			Din "Blessed are the pure in heart for they shall see God."		Omniscience Non-attachment Enneagram Type Five
6. The vine is reaped	6. Cerebrospinal (Self-consciousness)	"I perceive the perfection of spirit within all beings."	**Chokmah** "You are the salt of the earth."	From lower vision (Scorpio) to Eagle (Aquilla), Air, spiritual vision, aspiration.	Perfection Serenity Enneagram Type One
			Binah "Blessed are those who are persecuted for righteousness sake."		Freedom Humility Enneagram Type Two
7. The winepress	7. Auric (Self-super-consciousness)	"I am a co-creator with God."	**Keter** "You are the Light of the world."	Same as above including Christ Self or Higher Self	

Volume II, Chart 1

The Movement from Crucifixion to Resurrection—The Dawning of Atzilut

The movement from Beriyah to Atzilut in the ascension process—described in Revelation chapters 15 through 18—is an event of great significance in the incarnation process of the Spirit-Soul, in its spiritual development and return home to self-realization and eventually to God-realization. This is the movement from the Christ story from the crucifixion to the resurrection. The psychological aspect of this process is called ego death (or surrender), and the regeneration brings resurrection (or spiritual rebirth). This is the third great pivot point of transformation. It represents the shift from personal identity to transpersonal identity. This is the surrender of the identification with the personality, the little ego—the "me," "my," "I" way of thinking—and the emergence of the unlimited "I Am" in union with its source in Spirit, tuned to all life with compassion. Initially the process involves dropping deeply into the great psychological void between Da'at (higher mind)—where "the crucifixion" takes place—into the supernal light of Binah-Chokmah—a realm of non-duality, "the resurrection."

The emotional movement of this process is dropping deeply into the void of unexperienced despair. Despair is the state of hopeless futility of the limited identity of the individual ego with its identity in physical, emotional, and mental

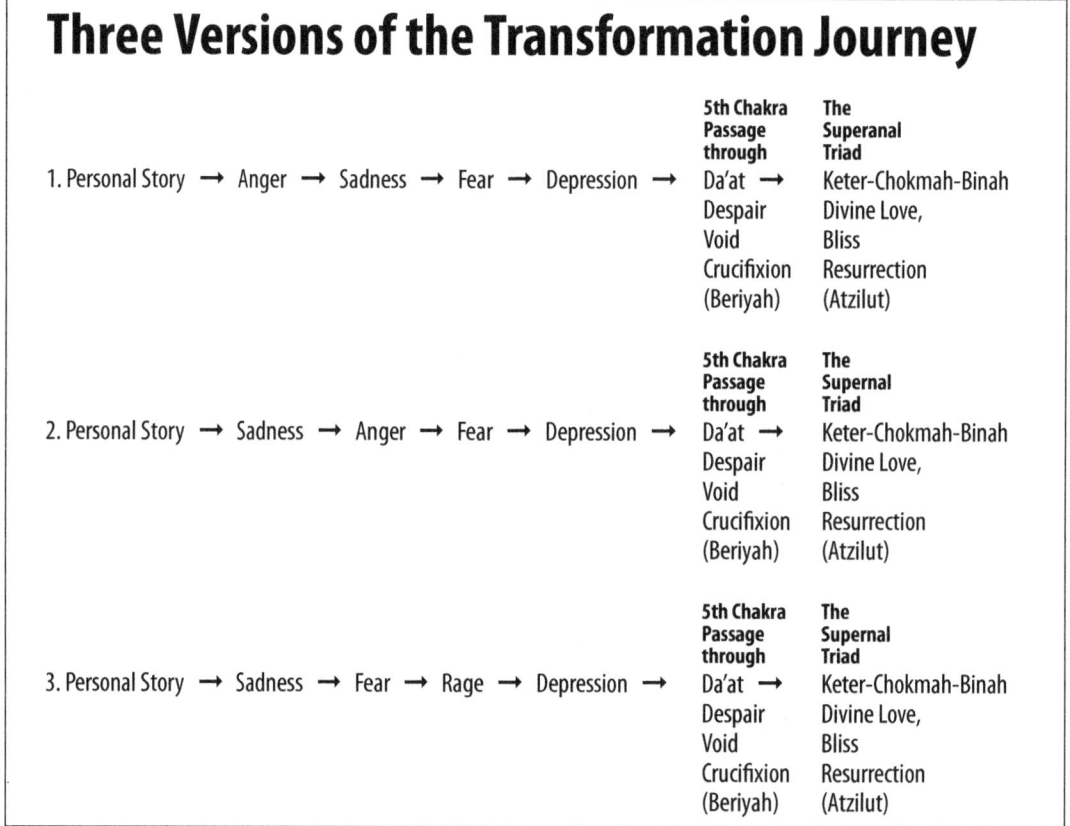

Volume II, Diagram 4

veils of illusion. These veils are like walls, physical and psychic barriers to the ever-present light of divine consciousness. One could say that self-realization is the permanent absence of a belief in a limited "I." When the individual in Beriyah is willing to end all identification with the limited identity of a limited "I" separated from its inner source of authenticity, the personal story gives way to different layers of emotions that eventually lead to despair.

When the identification of the authentic self (Soul) shifts from a particular body (physical, emotional, or mental) to the totality of Being that originally gave rise to duality and separateness in Da'at (the tree of good and evil), the Soul realizes itself as pure, unlimited consciousness in the supernal triad of Keter-Binah-Chokmah. This is the healed, unified Tree of Life. This shift into self-realization is Atzilut (resurrection), the movement from crucifixion (with its accompanying fear and despair) through a "black hole" into the resurrection (bliss, divine love). Three major versions of this story take place, but the fundamental element is despair upon the event horizon of the "black hole" that leads to ego-transcendence. This movement through despair is a personal apocalypse. For example, in the biblical Christ story of the Garden of Gethsemane, we have Jesus's passage into despair and grief.

One can begin to understand the great collective expressions that exist in our world at this current time in history as we plunge into the fifth chakra in our collective movement. The rise of violence and anger, the increase in suicides, the pervasive sadness and despair, the increasing fear of the unknown, more social isolation, the increase of mental illness and mental breakdowns, outbreaks of violence, and the horror of apocalyptic-like events such as natural disasters that appear to make no sense to the logical mind and no explanation brings comfort or relief—these are all examples of our collective passage. The world is in the throes of an ego death and rebirth. The world we have known has reached the event horizon of the "black hole" and is now moving into it.

Ascension Through Adult Spiritual Development

To better understand the psychological implications and qualities of the emergence of this divine consciousness, Elisabeth Liebert's four ascending stages of adult spiritual development are instructive.[20] Stages 1 through 3 represent a purification and breakdown of negative elementals and negative habits and perceptions of separateness and the reintegration of the personality into its higher virtues of expression, the living out of holy ideas and virtues. Stage 4 is the integrated stage, which expresses the Soul's essence of harmony and the cosmic dance of intimacy, thought, feeling, and action in the world with an intimate connection to God-Source and the Divine Plan. This stage is essentially divinity

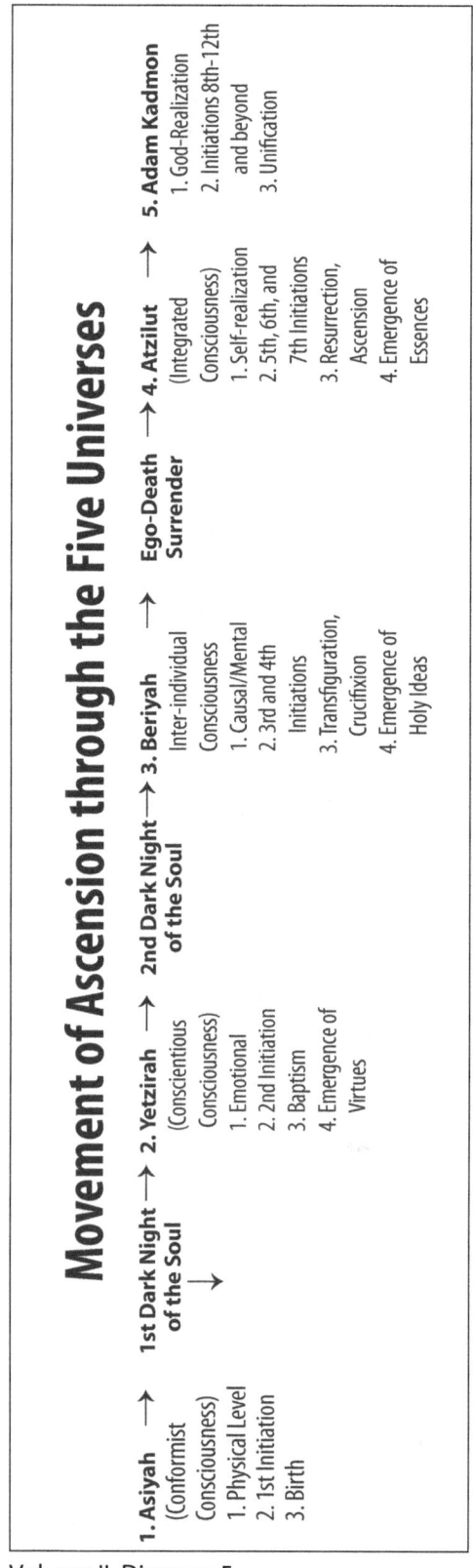

Volume II, Diagram 5

in action, the unification of heaven and earth in consciousness. Movement toward stage 4 involves a deconstruction aimed at the complete transcendence of the personality —a sense of universality and holiness in intent, service, and enlightened consciousness. This is expressed through impersonal or non-attached love in the nine higher aspects of the Soul's essence.

In Saint John's Revelation, the completion of stage 3 would represent the "harvest." The approach from stage 3 to stage 4 would correspond to the "pouring of the vials and the destruction of Babylon." This is more closely linked to what is termed "ego-death." By ego-death we do not mean the annihilation of the ego, but a shift to unlimited, transpersonal ego awareness—awareness not attached to the limited identity of the physical, emotional, and mental bodies. Yet one goes on living in the bodies and allowing the bodies to be the vehicle for higher expression. Daskalos made this clear to me when he said, "Be one within your duality."

The final stage 4 would correspond to the universe of Atzilut, the total integration of divine potentiality and qualities of the Soul. This is described in Revelation as Saint John's experience of the great mandala of wholeness, the New Jerusalem. ➤ *(See Volume II, Diagram 5)*

These first four stages reflect seven initiations. The nine qualities of essence that express the fullness of the Spirit-Soul's light (Christ Self) are given in the following Tree of Life of Atzilut. In this expression of total consciousness, we can no longer speak of particular qualities of essence unique to one Sephirah or personality type but not accessible to another Sephirah or personality type. All Sephirah expressions of Atzilut are available to the self-realized Soul and constitute its divine qualities. The holy scriptures of the world offer many examples of these qualities in the life experiences of Avatars and Spiritual Masters.

➤ *(See Volume II, Diagram 6, p. 74)*

The practice of deep self-inquiry, the Advaita practice recommended by Sri Ramana Maharshi, is the most effective technique for those who are prepared to more fully disengage from the confining enslavement of identity with the physical body, emotions, accompanying instincts, and thoughts. In the Kabbalah, the secret Sephirah "Da'at," in which mind appears and disappears, is the target of self-inquiry. Mind is ever-changing, like the ocean waves in the sea. Waves are temporary forms of water that appear and disappear regularly. Waves of water are in truth only water itself. The same applies to our ever-changing thoughts, emotions, and bodily sensations. They come and go, like the waves of the ocean, sometimes bringing us pain, at other times pleasure, depending on their content and our dualistic, polarized perceptions of them as friend or foe. Yet all these phenomena are part of the ever-changing nature of Da'at (illusionary reality) or, as described before, "relative truth" versus the absolute truth.

When we ask the question "Who am I?" we are digging deeply within ourselves to discover the source of our polarized, conflicted experience of life. When we inquire into the source of our thoughts, we discover they come from mind. And when we inquire into the source of mind, we discover the "I-thought" construct (concept). When we plunge further, we look for the source of the "I-thought." We may ask, "From where does this "I-thought" arise?" We can discover on diligent self-inquiry that this "I-thought" does not really exist. It is only a construct, like the "waves of the ocean" that we take as consensus reality. Behind or beyond this construct is the experience of who we really are, the changeless substratum of consciousness, the "Self," the supernal triad below the waves, the ocean itself, the ocean of bliss and the Soul's qualities of essence. We recognize that the thought and mind itself, the emotions and sensations, are but the ever-changing illusions that support the Soul's ascension journey back home.

Who Am I?

Source without beginning or end

Never changing

Awakened heart! Warmth, joy, laughter

I am that I am

Grace shining its smiling face

on Itself, for Itself, and within Itself

Language of silence speaks

To be still is to know everything!

Nick Demetry
Lucknow, India, 1993

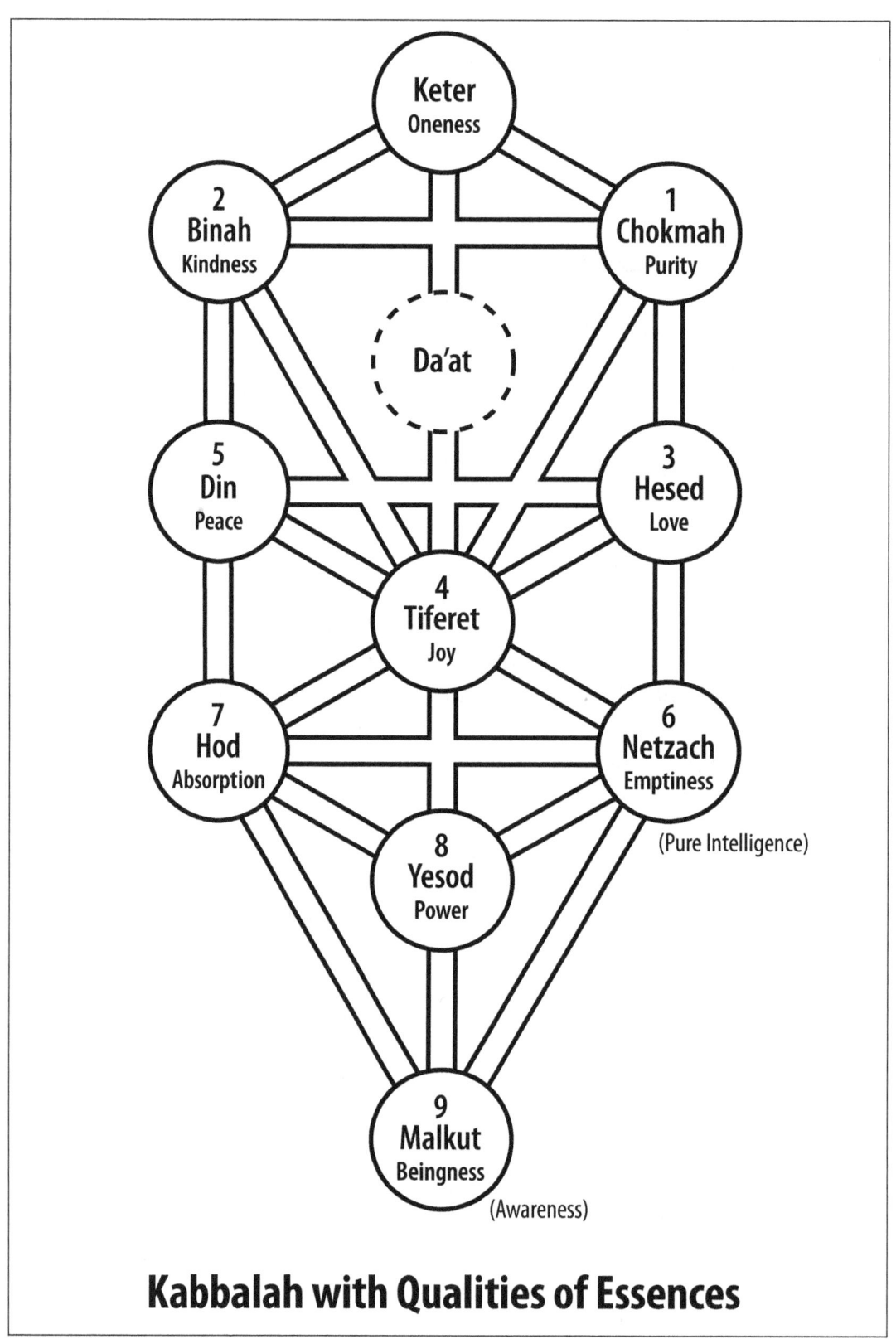

Kabbalah with Qualities of Essences

Chapter 15 of Revelation

Seven Divinities in the Kabbalah

In Saint John's Revelation, Chapters 15 and 16 describe the emergence of seven divinities. The seven divinities may be taken to refer to the Ascended Masters, or Chohans. They may also be interpreted to be the seven orders of the archangels at the level of the Spirit-Soul. Indigenous people throughout the world have referred to the seven androgynous beings of the Pleiades in the constellation of Taurus. In ancient times, the seven divinities or time spirits (planetary spirits) were associated with the seven visible planetary bodies: (1) Moon, (2) Sun, (3) Venus, (4) Mars, (5) Mercury, (6) Jupiter, and (7) Saturn. In Kabbalah, the nine Sephiroth are connected to both seen and what, at that time, were unseen influences. Therefore we need to add the fact of the discovery of Uranus in 1781, Neptune in 1846, and Pluto in 1930. Malkut therefore represents Earth; Yesod, the Moon; Netzach, Venus; Hod, Mercury; Tiferet, Sun; Din, Mars; Hesed, Jupiter; Da'at, Neptune; Binah, Saturn; Chokmah, Uranus; and Keter, Pluto.

Therefore, the energetic influences on the very chakras can involve more than one influence—for example, in the solar plexus, Rafael and Hanael; or the throat chakra, Kamael and Tzadkiel; or the brow chakra, Tzafkiel and Ratziel. Since the right pillar of the Tree of Life contains more male characteristics energetically and the left column more yin or female characteristics energetically, the combined effects of these dual orders are like the androgynous union of both. Symbolically, this was also seen in earlier times in the notion of the Hermaphrodite having both male and female anatomical parts. We also see this in ancient Greece in the combined representation of Hermes (Mercury) and Aphrodite (Venus), who later became known under the Hebraic names of Rafael and Hanael. These are the two energetic influences on the solar plexus chakra, *i.e.*, Rafael in Hod and Hanael in Netzach. We can see this same polarity unified as Kamael (Mars), representing contraction, and Tzadkiel (Jupiter), representing expansion. When polarities become unified, they express a higher non-dual reality that reflects more the qualities of the Spirit-Soul itself. Therefore, the "divinities" are beyond duality, but work within it through the polarities, bringing eventual unification.

> *1: And I saw another sign in heaven, great and marvellous, seven angels having the seven last plagues; for in them is filled up the wrath of God.*

The "seven angels" here refers to the archangels that preside over the Soul's journey through the higher mind of Da'at (crucifixion) into the supernal triad of

Chokmah, Binah, and Keter, as well as the orders governing the other Sephiroth. The four orders of archangels that first appeared governing the four elements—Michael in Tiferet, Rafael in Hod, Gabriel in Yesod, and Uriel in Netzach in the physical body—appear again in Da'at. The other orders include Tzafkiel in Binah, Ratziel in Chokmah, Metatron in Keter, and the orders of Kamael in Din, Tzadkiel in Hesed, and Sandalfon in Malkut. The emergence of mind in Da'at is also the emergence of the mental, causal, astral, and physical bodies. These four bodies are constructed by the divine intelligence of the Holy Spirit, the archangels, as four perfect etheric doubles of each corresponding body.

As each step of ascension takes place, mastery of each body consciousness is actually a process of unification with the perfection already within each etheric double. Our task as humans is to transform the amorphous substance of each body dominated by egotism and the personality and give it a shape and likeness of its perfectly constructed etheric double. At this stage, the work of the archangels in Da'at and the other Sephiroth is to transform any remaining untransformed mental, physical, and astral components, bringing unification with the etheric doubles of each body. The main focus of this work for the initiate is the surrender of the generative instincts of desire that are held in the etheric sheath of the mental body and that bind all the lower bodies in negative expression—namely the beast, the dragon, and the pseudo-lamb. The seven last plagues are the final seven trials, or tests, and the "wrath" of God is the transforming energy to clear unresolved karmas. At this stage, the regenerative instincts of desire form the major area of transformation because the etheric sheath of the mind is interlaced subconsciously throughout all the lower bodies, influencing them. One can think, then, of crucifixion as a process of surrendering one's imperfect sense desires, emotional desires, and negative beliefs that hold one in separation from God Source and moving vibrationally to unity with the etheric double of each body.

In Enneagram theory, this process corresponds to the transformation of the shadow-bound personalities of the belly triad of 8/9/1, the passional realm of the pseudo-lamb (sensory imprisonment and physical addiction); the heart triad of 2/3/4, the passional realm of the dragon (emotional imprisonment, emotional drama, and desire); and the head triad of 5/6/7, the passional realm of the beast (mental imprisonment to false understanding and fixed beliefs). The transformation of each triad of elementals heralds victory over that respective negative force. The deep cleansing is crucifixion, or "ego-death," and the unification with each etheric double corresponds to resurrection. Each initiation therefore brings a kind of crucifixion-and-resurrection process. The pain of crucifixion is simply the pain of suffering engendered by attachment to outer desires. However, the fourth initiation brings the biggest task at hand—surrendering the dominance of mind itself to allow the Christ love of heart and Soul to receive its connection to God Source.

> 2: *And I saw as it were a sea of glass mingled with fire: and them that had gotten the victory over the beast, and over his image, and over his mark, and over the number of his name, stand on the sea of glass, having the harps of God.*

The "sea of glass" represents the higher mind and stilled emotions that are necessary for "the victory over the beast"—releasing the whole of distorted illusionary thinking—"and over his image"—fantasy desire—"and over his mark"—identification with sensory desire. Addiction and separation consciousness carry the meaning of "the number of his name." Those who "stand on the sea of glass, having the harps of God" are those self-realized Souls whose consciousness reflects "the sea of glass"—harmony and self-mastery.

> 3: *And they sing the song of Moses the servant of God, and the song of the Lamb, saying, Great and marvellous are thy works, Lord God Almighty; just and true are thy ways, thou King of saints.*

Moses here represents the spiritual leader whose song of Soul, the "song of the Lamb," was sung as he delivered his people out of Egypt. In the Bible, the Egyptians typify Babylon, the dominating sensory nature separated from Spirit. The verse ends in a chorus of praise and victory.

> 4: *Who shall not fear thee, O Lord, and glorify thy name? for thou only art holy: for all nations shall come and worship before thee; for thy judgments are made manifest.*

Eventually everyone will make the spiritual journey. Once Daskalos said that there are two ways the Soul travels back home to God, either through the "whips of destiny" (subconsciously, *i.e.*, "for thy judgments are made manifest") or "consciously" through introspection, prayer, meditation, and purification.

> 5: *And after that I looked, and, behold, the temple of the tabernacle of the testimony in heaven was opened:*

The higher supernal energy of the Spirit activates the higher mental body in Da'at to activate the fourth initiation of deeper sublimation of impure energies through the crucifixion.

> 6: *And the seven angels came out of the temple, having the seven plagues, clothed in pure and white linen, and having their breasts girded with golden girdles.*

The seven archangels are "clothed in pure and white linen," which represents purity, and as "having their breasts girded with golden girdles"—the girdle of Aphrodite, which is the symbol of innocence, righteousness, and purity.

Metatron, the archangel of Christ, holds the divine mystery and purpose of creation of the one God; Tzafkiel and Ratziel (the female and male complements of holy union), holy form and holy light. The four archangels Michael, Rafael, Gabriel, and Uriel are responsible for the regenerative work of the four elements in the physical body and are the creative manifesting agents of the Holy Spirit in matter. The archangels provide each Soul the etheric and holy templates (the etheric doubles) of each body's divine design. Kamael and Tzadkiel govern the divine balance between working off one's karmic debt and receiving healing blessings and forgiveness. Sandalfon governs the regenerative force of light within the physical body.

The purity of the archangels in white reflects the perfect divine design of each body. As Paracelsus says, "all things when they come from the hand of God are white; he colors them afterwards according to his pleasure."[21] The etheric double of each body is in fact colored in an aura of light—the physical, green; the astral, pink; the causal (lower mental), orange; the higher mental, blue; and the etheric sheath of the mind, violet.

Auric Colors and Mantra Sounds

Kabbalah	Universe	Body	Color	Sounds
Asiyah	I	Physical	green (etheric double)	adonai
Yetzirah	II	Astral	rose pink (etheric double)	el shaddai
Beriyah	III	Causal	orange golden (etheric double)	alaha elohim tzavaot
		Mental	blue (etheric double)	yeshua messiah
		Etheric	violet (etheric double)	alaha elohim alaha
Atzilut	IV	Soul	golden	Ehyeh Asher Ehyeh
Adam Kadmon	V	Spirit	white	Hu or Hua

Volume II, Diagram 7

Each initiatory step of ascension occurs through the activation of the Holy Spirit and Christ Light of the corresponding etheric double of the body in which the new initiation is taking place. The process is the cleansing and purification of the corresponding imperfect body of elementals the personality holds at that level that, when transformed, reflects the perfect etheric double and color of that corresponding body and, by the law of co-vibration, brings union and mastery of that level of initiation in the ascension process.

> 7: *And one of the four beasts gave unto the seven angels seven golden vials full of the wrath of God, who liveth for ever and ever.*

The beast that "gave unto the seven angels seven golden vials" is the emotional body representing the water bearer, the sign of Aquarius. The vials are shallow cups that represent drink/offerings to the gods, and they contain the etheric life-giving energy (spiritual will force) of a new vibration and a new age—the Aquarian energy. The "wrath of God," again, refers to the transforming principle of the purification, wisdom, and illumination of the eternal God.

> *8: And the temple was filled with smoke from the glory of God, and from his power; and no man was able to enter into the temple, till the seven plagues of the seven angels were fulfilled.*

The temple of the Spirit-Soul is filled with illumination ("smoke from the glory of God, and from his power"), but the initiate is not yet ready for entering this consciousness until the purification of the "seven plagues of the seven angels" takes place. For awareness of divine love to enter the vehicle of the physical body in the physical world, purification and transformation of the deepest levels of illusion and separation from God must take place. Hence, the purification of the lowest is mirrored in the highest as well. The actual level of purification is the etheric veil of the mind, which contains the deepest subconscious roots of separation, the misdirected instincts as reflected in all the lower bodies. This purification process is happening collectively as a result of the astrological configuration of Uranus squaring Pluto from 2012-2017.

Seven major transformational pulses are occurring as each square brings reactivation at a new chakra level, revealing what is really needing to be changed in humanity and in the world. This state of purging and cleansing the old consciousness to bring in the new Aquarian paradigm marks the process of the pouring of the vials and the deep physical, emotional, and mental purification taking place now.

Chapter 16 of Revelation

Outpouring of the Vials—The Cleansing of the Etheric Veil of the Mind

Daskalos used the psychospiritual term "negative elementals" to describe desire-thought-action complexes that draw the personality away from the Spirit and enslave the Soul in addictive thought, desire, and behavior. The corresponding players in Saint John's Revelation, as mentioned before, are (1) the beast (desire-mind thoughts), (2) the dragon (passion or vice, addictive emotions), and (3) the false seer of sensuality in materialism, the pseudo-lamb (negative, self-destructive, or addictive behaviors justified by the mind's negative imagination and false belief).

What the mind holds in its imagination at the lower levels of desire, the pseudo-lamb in the realm of bodily activity manifests in the world. The temporary satisfaction of outer desire fulfilled reinforces and solidifies the mind's imprisonment in imaginary cravings and dissatisfaction that only grow. Over time, the negative elementals become so entrenched that the individual remains possessed by the addictive desire and continually justifies its negative behaviors (the behaviors of the pseudo-lamb) as being right and correct. As discussed in the last chapter, the creature or animal that activates the "seven angels" is man, which corresponds to the element of water and therefore to the emotional nature and psychic regions. When a human being indulges in egotistic, passional desire, the behavior becomes destructive. As higher emotion, or feeling, it becomes purified love and wisdom.

> 1: *And I heard a great voice out of the temple saying to the seven angels, Go your ways, and pour out the vials of the wrath of God upon the earth.*

The Spirit-Soul, or force of spiritual will, initiates the process of cleansing by sending out the seven light streams of transformation and purification to the egotistic personality.

> 2: *And the first went, and poured out his vial upon the earth; and there fell a noisome and grievous sore upon the men which had the mark of the beast, and upon them which worshipped his image.*

The first vial is poured "upon the earth" (Malkut, or the root chakra center) by Archangel Sandalfon. This is the realm of perverted self-preservation instinct. It is the arena of the pseudo-lamb or sensory domination by the desire-mind ("the beast") and its physical responses and addictive negative behaviors of indulgence and destructive actions. The "grievous sore upon the men" indicates a purging or throwing off of poisonous desire from the lower bodies of the impure etheric matter. The "men which had the mark of the beast" refers to those individuals identified with the lower desire-thoughts that catalyze these destructive, deceptive behaviors and indulgent fantasies.

> *3: And the second angel poured out his vial upon the sea; and it became as the blood of a dead man: and every living soul died in the sea.*

The second vial is poured "upon the sea" (the second chakra center of Yesod) by Archangel Gabriel. This is the realm of the perverted sexual/relational instinct of lower passional emotions of desire. The "blood of a dead man" refers to the realm of the dragon's self-desire and perverted instinct that only brings emptiness and deadness emotionally, as it never obtains fulfillment because it is only outer-directed, seeking to fulfill what can only be fulfilled through divine love. In general, "blood" refers to divine love but can only come to a man or women living in connection to the inner light and higher desire aspiring to love and wisdom, the hallmarks of the Aquarian Spirit.

> *4: And the third angel poured out his vial upon the rivers and fountains of waters; and they became blood.*

The third angel (representing the combination of Rafael in Hod and Hanael/Uriel in Netzach) "poured out his vial upon the rivers and fountains of waters." This represents the purifying energy taken into the solar plexus center, the seat of the beast and the perverted social instincts that lead to bigotry, intolerance, and the rigid fixed beliefs of exoteric religious worship. That "they became blood" reflects the purification process that transforms the solar energies into the spiritual will and desire to achieve higher love.

> *5: And I heard the angel of the waters say, Thou art righteous, O Lord, which art, and wast, and shalt be, because thou hast judged thus.*

> *6: For they have shed the blood of saints and prophets, and thou hast given them blood to drink; for they are worthy.*

The perverted social instincts of the solar plexus, which engender the lower thoughts and feelings of persecution and hatred, lead to the shedding of "the blood of saints and prophets"—the contamination and degradation of the will to higher love ("saints") and higher wisdom ("prophets") in the initiate's solar plexus consciousness. Yet God gives the divine love ("blood") that brings true feelings of worthiness and self-value, feelings that can never be obtained through the lust for domination and outer expressions of false power and rulership in the world.

> *7: And I heard another out of the altar say, Even so, Lord God Almighty, true and righteous are thy judgments.*

Nevertheless, the eternal power of spiritual will, given to the initiate by God, will prevail and bring true self-value.

> *8: And the fourth angel poured out his vial upon the sun; and power was given unto him to scorch men with fire.*

The fourth vial is poured "upon the sun" (on the center of Tiferet, the fourth chakra) by Archangel Michael. The fourth chakra is also considered the seat of the beast, as it represents the intellectual forces of the mind that veil the heart in debate, conflict, and rationalizations to defend its egotistic position of pride and dogma. The light of Michael reveals the truth of the mind's illusionary and empty thinking.

> *9: And men were scorched with great heat, and blasphemed the name of God, which hath power over these plagues: and they repented not to give him glory.*

The light of truth illuminates the egotistic pride and false self-importance of this center in the initiate, revealing its separation from the light. As Daskalos once put it, pride is "a devil disguised as an angel of light." It rebels and fights to hold its false identity until the light of truth prevails and purifies it.

> *10: And the fifth angel poured out his vial upon the seat of the beast; and his kingdom was full of darkness; and they gnawed their tongues for pain,*

The fifth vial is poured "upon the seat of the beast" (the centers of Din and Hesed, the fifth chakra) by Archangel Kamael (in Din) and Tzadkiel (in Hesed). The self-created darkness of all our subconscious shadow emotions and thoughts are karmas that we project out onto others. With the pouring of the fifth vial, they are now brought to the surface of our consciousness to be examined and re-owned by Archangel Kamael. Once we own these impure elements as our own creations (sins), we are lifted in forgiveness by the Christ Light (love) in Tiferet by Archangel Michael, and we receive the blessings and healings of God through Tzadkiel (Hesed). These three Sephiroth—Din, Tiferet, and Hesed—represent the moral triad of the Kabbalah. If we remain identified with the shadow we have created (in Din), we stay locked into our guilt and fear of a punitive God who will never forgive us. Once we release "the seat of the beast" as projected shadow, the kingdom full of darkness, and the self-inflicting pain ("they gnawed their tongues for pain"), we can begin returning to the light of forgiveness. Until then, we continue to fear God and perceive ourselves as victims, remaining rebellious and mistrusting of God.

> ***11:** And blasphemed the God of heaven because of their pains and their sores, and repented not of their deeds.*

> ***12:** And the sixth angel poured out his vial upon the great river Euphrates; and the water thereof was dried up, that the way of the kings of the east might be prepared.*

The sixth vial is poured on the sixth chakra, or centers of Binah and Chokmah, by Tzafkiel in Binah and Ratziel in Chokmah. The sixth chakra is, as mentioned before, deeply connected to the whole action of the cerebral spinal axis and the Kundalini life force flowing through the spinal column—"the great river Euphrates." The Euphrates appears in Genesis 2:14 as one of the four rivers flowing out of the Garden of Eden. Rivers hold a sacred symbolism in many cultures, examples being the Ganges, the Nile, and the river Jordan. In Saint John's Revelation, the river Euphrates is the river flowing through the New Jerusalem, and it symbolizes the divine power of the spiritual current of ascending conscious awareness (values and higher energy). The phrase "the water thereof was dried up" suggests that the lower energy and thought-emotion complexes of personal ego have given way to the new flow of transpersonal energy; "that the way of the kings of the east might be prepared" refers to the cleansing that will allow the transpersonal light of the Spirit-Soul to flow unimpeded into consciousness, ascending upwards instead of following its former motion downward into the lower chakras to feed the negative elementals held in force by the beast, the dragon, and the pseudo-lamb.

> ***13:** And I saw three unclean spirits like frogs come out of the mouth of the dragon, and out of the mouth of the beast, and out of the mouth of the false prophet.*

The "unclean spirits" are what Daskalos called negative elementals. These negative elementals are collected in the three lower bodies. In the physical body, they motivate impure and destructive actions (the pseudo-lamb) and lie in the cellular substance of the physical body. In the emotional realm (the astral body), they exist as passions (vices) of desire, and in the mental realm, or mental body, they are illusionary beliefs and negative beliefs and attitudes. At this level of cleansing, the deepest and most "evil" of the perverted instincts are discarded ("come out of the mouth"). The "frogs" symbolize the physical/emotional elementals in a human, as frogs inhabit the watery, murky depths of the earth (the water element). In psychological terms, these three "unclean spirits" are the perverted, misused instincts of self-preservation of all personality types—the perverted, unhealthy, misused instinct of sexual/relational energies and the perverted, unhealthy, misused instinct of the social energies—primarily the instincts of the three lower chakras in each body (physical, astral, and mental). As each of these bodies is discarded by the Soul in its ascension journey to higher dimensions after death, these discarded elementals remain in the collective realm of these three planes until, eventually, they are reabsorbed into the great abyss Saint John refers to in this chapter as Armageddon.

In the initiate, the purging of these impure and perverted elementals that dominate the instincts takes place in the fourth initiation in Beriyah to totally purify the three bodies, purging them of these unhealthy energies. Armageddon (in Da'at) psychologically would then refer to the battleground of the self-observing Soul in its efforts to observe and release the hold these forces have on it at a deep subconscious level. The three instincts, when dominated by ego survival strategies, lead to the blockage and entrapment of the spiritual flow of consciousness and deplete the initiate of the etheric life force necessary for the higher task of self-realization. All three instincts in the nine Enneagram personality or Sephiroth types become dominated by the ego's survival fears. The sixth chakra opens the channel of direct cognition and clear self-observation (or neutrality) so the initiate can see what was not seen before.

The psychospiritual dynamic of the "three unclean spirits" works in the following way. Each mental fixation (realm of the beast) held by the personality is run by a particular passion (realm of the dragon). Happiness is sought through acting out the passion (realm of the pseudo-lamb) in an attempt to fulfill one of the three lower (animal) drives: (1) self-preservation, for survival of the individual unit, (2) sexual, for reproduction of the individual unit, and (3) social, to establish hierarchy and the role of the individual unit in the herd. As long as the individual's consciousness identifies itself as the body, then these three animalistic drives mediate all of life. These drives run the mental fixation below the level of astral passion (vice). They fuel the fixation's passion and, until these drives are addressed, the passions of fixation will continue to run and dominate the individual. These three drives are sublimated into the ego's desire for happiness and acted out through the passions of fixation. The result is increasing levels of selfishness leading to greater indulgence, which brings greater suffering and more limiting consciousness. As long as life is lived for survival, sex, and social status, it is a life lived for "me." ➤ *(See Volume II, Diagram 8, pp. 86-87)*

Complete fulfillment, peace, and love can only be found in the selfless life. Then true fulfillment (as opposed to selfish motives for survival), true intimacy and love (as opposed to selfish motives for sexual gratification and relational dominance), and true bliss and peace (as opposed to selfish obsessive thoughts of mental fixation striving for social status) can bring transcendence and the selfless life of spiritual consciousness.

Diagram of "The Three Frogs" As They Manifest in The Nine Sephiroth or Enneagram Types

Chokmah Type I
Separation Consciousness
(Lost Connection to the Holy Idea of Perfection)

Instincts	Passion	Mental Fixation: Resentment
self-preservation →	anger →	anxiety — making a mistake endangering survival
sexual, relational →	anger →	jealousy — the judging of one's partner's intentions in intimate situations
social →	anger →	inadaptability in social settings

Binah Type II
Separation Consciousness
(Lost Connection to the Holy Idea of Will)

Instincts	Passion	Mental Fixation: Flattery
self-preservation →	pride →	"me first" — because they give so much, they have the right to preserve their own well-being
sexual, relational →	pride →	seductive aggressiveness in intimate situations
social →	pride →	ambitious to get attention and position of association with important other people

Hesed Type III
Separation Consciousness
(Lost Connection to the Holy Idea of Hope)

Instincts	Passion	Mental fixation: Vanity
self-preservation →	deceit →	material security as a sign of self-worth
sexual, relational →	deceit →	ideal image of male/female
social →	deceit →	prestige/status in social groups

Tiferet Type IV
Separation Consciousness
(Lost Connection to the Holy Idea of Origin)

Instincts	Passion	Mental fixation: Melancholy
self-preservation →	envy →	reckless — taking risks provides them with the emotional intensity, the need to preserve an authentic sense of themselves
sexual, relational →	envy →	competition — to compete with the rival for a desirable mate to feel self-value
social →	envy →	shame for not meeting the group's expectations

Volume II, Diagram 8

(Continued from previous page)

Din Type V Separation Consciousness (Lost Connection to the Holy Idea of Omniscience)	**Instincts** self-preservation → sexual, relational → social →	**Passion** avarice → avarice → avarice →	**Mental fixation: Stinginess** castles to preserve themselves they establish castles for personal safety and intrusion confidences to bond privately to another in an intimate situation totem they create their own niche by offering their group specialized expertise
Netzach Type VI Separation Consciousness (Lost Connection to the Holy Idea of Faith)	**Instincts** self-preservation → sexual, relational → social →	**Passion** doubt → doubt → doubt →	**Mental fixation: cowardice** warmth fear using warmth to disarm the harmful intent of others strength and beauty fear to counter their fear of intimate situations duty fear to adhere to duty to its social rules
Hod type VII Separation Consciousness (Lost Connection to the Holy Idea of the Divine Plan)	**Instincts** self-preservation → sexual, relational → Social →	**Passion** gluttony → gluttony → gluttony →	**Mental fixation: Planning** like-minded defenders surround themselves with the security of like-minded individuals to ensure a sense of personal security suggestible suggesting sharing a realm of fascinating options with the partner sacrifice willing to endure temporary limitations to achieve a brighter future in social situations
Yesod type VIII Separation Consciousness (The Lost Holy Idea of Universal truth)	**Instincts** self-preservation → sexual, relational → social →	**Passion** lust → lust → lust →	**Mental fixation: Vengeance** satisfactory survival to control personal environment for personal well-being possession to control the partner before they become vulnerable to love friendship with people who will stand up to them
Malkut type IX Separation Consciousness (The Lost Holy Idea of Unconditional Love)	**Instincts** self-preservation → sexual, relational → social →	**Passion** sloth → sloth → sloth →	**Mental fixation: Indulgence** appetite for non-essential interest to replace real wants in the area of personal well-being union to be absorbed on all levels with a mate participation for a sense of fellowship

> **14: For they are the spirits of devils, working miracles, which go forth unto the kings of the earth and of the whole world, to gather them to the battle of that great day of God Almighty.**

The vices ("spirits of devils") are deceitful and give meaning (by "working miracles") to what is not true and important—the mental fixations, "the kings of the earth"—creating a battleground for the self-aware observing Soul seeking separation from them.

> **15: Behold, I come as a thief. Blessed is he that watcheth, and keepeth his garments, lest he walk naked, and they see his shame.**

The "thief," the Spirit-Soul, brings true happiness and transcendence by awakening divine love, peace, and bliss through diligent self-examination of the personality and its underlying passions (vices) and perverted instincts.

> **16: And he gathered them together into a place called in the Hebrew tongue Armageddon.**

The word *Armageddon* literally means "mountain of Megiddo." The plain of Megiddo was one of the great battlegrounds that involved the people of Israel (Kings 9:27). Armageddon, taken as a mountain, would mean a higher vantage point (the sixth chakra) from which the conflicting instincts, passions (vices), and fixation of the personality can be viewed and transformed through deep introspection.

> **17: And the seventh angel poured out his vial into the air; and there came a great voice out of the temple of heaven, from the throne, saying, It is done.**

The temple in heaven is the Spirit-Soul in the triad of Binah, Chokmah, and Keter. The "air" represents the divine messages coming from the Spirit-Soul; the "throne" is the heart of God. The saying "It is done" represents the impulse of the great Archangel Metatron, activating the full flow of the Kundalini energy current from the lower Sephiroth centers of Malkut, Yesod, Hod and Netzach, through the heart center of Tiferet, onward to Da'at, then Binah, Chokmah, and Keter. The words "It is done" are similar to the culminating point of the crucifixion of the Christ when he said "It is finished." The transformation in the lower three centers of the instinctual urges of each of the lower bodies is now complete.

> **18: And there were voices, and thunders, and lightnings; and there was a great earthquake, such as was not since men were upon the earth, so mighty an earthquake, and so great.**

The great shift in consciousness is a movement from personal ego-consciousness to transpersonal consciousness. This shift reorganizes consciousness in an entirely new way. The throat chakra is represented by "voices," the crown chakra by "thunders," and the heart chakra by "lightnings," so "there were voices, and thunders, and lightnings" can be seen as the awakening and alignment of these higher chakras with the lower three chakra centers. The transformation here is much greater, much more complete than before, as indicated by "so mighty an earthquake, and so great."

> *19: And the great city was divided into three parts, and the cities of the nations fell: and great Babylon came in remembrance before God, to give unto her the cup of the wine of the fierceness of his wrath.*

The "great city was divided into three parts, and the cities of the nations fell." The "great city" is the enslaved ego of all nine mental fixations holding consciousness in the past and recreating itself in the future, unaware of the eternal presence of the divine union of the nine holy ideas. That "cities of the nations fell" indicates a surrender, transformation, and release of the nine passions (vices) that hold the mental fixations in place.

"Great Babylon" represents the three materializing instincts in the egotistic personality now transformed by the spiritual will "wrath," and the illumination of the shadow ego (egotism), by the awakening of Soul-awareness. That "great Babylon came in remembrance before God" represents the awakening of the initiate's lower consciousness into the light of the eternal presence of God.

> *20: And every island fled away, and the mountains were not found.*

The egotism that creates isolation and separateness ("every island") and pride ("the mountains") is now gone.

> *21: And there fell upon men a great hail out of heaven, every stone about the weight of a talent: and men blasphemed God because of the plague of the hail; for the plague thereof was exceeding great.*

When Spirit comes on its own terms in concentrated form ("and there fell upon men a great hail out of heaven"), human egotism (the "men") reacts in discontent, frustration, and unrest, because it can no longer fulfill its selfish desires and keep everything in life under its control. The new spiritual light of unity and its flow through the chakras and the initiate's physical consciousness is much too strong to be resisted by the petty human egotism.

MEDITATION JOURNEY

(FREE MP3 RECORDING AVAILABLE AT WWW.ETHERIKOS.COM)

Close your eyes and breathe deeply. Place your attention on your feet. Feel the healing white light flowing into your legs, into your thighs, your hips and pelvic area. Feel the healing light moving into your abdomen, your chest, and your heart. Feel the healing light flowing over your shoulders, down your arms to your hand and fingers. The healing light flows into your neck, your head, and your face.

And with your healing hands of light, feel yourself building a large circular disk in white light on the ground before you. And on the disk build a beautiful temple in white light. And step into the temple and stand in its center. Feel Jesus the Christ and Saint Mary Magdalene coming to you. The Christ stands on your right and Saint Mary Magdalene on your left. Feel their great love for you. And feel Archangel Rafael behind you. Feel Rafael touching your heart at your back, opening your spiritual sun and the vibrating light within you, the Christ Self. And feel this love and light filling you.

Feel the Christ and Saint Mary Magdalene reaching into your physical hands and taking the hands of your astral body. Inhale a rose pink-colored energy, feeling yourself immersed in it. Feel your astral body in this rose-pink light, vibrating with its own light. And feel a column of light coming down from heaven to lift you up to the healing temple of your astral body. Feel the Christ and Saint Mary Magdalene lifting you now. Lighter, freer, higher and lighter, freer and higher, lighter and freer, lifting up to the healing temple of your astral body, a temple of great light and joy, uplifting emotions, and celebration.

Stand in the center of this temple. And feel the Christ and Saint Mary Magdalene placing their hands into your astral body as they take the hands of your mental body and begin to lift you out of your astral body, into your mental body. Inhale a vibrant sky blue-colored energy, feeling immersed in it. The mental body is in a blue light. Feel yourself being lifted into a column of blue light. Higher, freer, lighter, higher and freer, freer and lighter, lighter and freer, lifting you to the temple of your mental body, another great temple of light, a very expansive energy and awareness. Now feel the differences between this mental temple and the astral temple. And as you stand in the center of the temple of your mental body, feel that your light is growing brighter and brighter in a beautiful clear blue aura.

Now feel the Christ and Saint Mary Magdalene reaching into your mental body and taking the hands of your Soul into a beautiful golden light. And feel yourself being lifted into this beautiful column of light. Higher, freer, lighter, higher, freer, higher, lighter and freer, freer and lighter, higher and freer to the beautiful healing temple of your Soul. Feel yourself in the healing temple of your Soul, radiating your golden light in the temple.

Here in the temple of your Soul is the great Divine Mother. Her body looks like the sun. Her head has a crown with twelve stars, and under her feet is the moon. And in her belly she holds the Christ Child yet to be born. And she says to you "my beloved child, it is time for your solar body to be born, for you to enter the temple within yourself, to let the seven great archangels pour their vials of golden light on all of your chakra centers within your three bodies, to eradicate the pseudo-lamb, the dragon, and the beast." And the Divine Mother says, "My eyes of wisdom are yours; my heart of love is your heart of love; my healing hands, your healing hands, my beloved. Step into my body, my heart, my eyes, my hands, my love, and my light." And feel yourself doing so.

As you feel the Divine Mother's holy love and wisdom, her radiant body of solar light, her healing hands, her love, feel yourself unifying with the Christ Child in her belly, your solar body of golden light ready to be born, your Christ Self, with the symbol of a circle upon your forehead. As you merge into the body of the Christ Child, feel all seven of your chakra centers becoming golden suns—the first center, the second center, the third center, the fourth center, the fifth center, the sixth center, and the seventh center. See and feel this golden emanation of light from all your centers.

Now feel and hear yourself being told that it is time to be birthed. And see the great archangels Metatron and Sandalfon there to birth you in the temple. Gently, as you feel yourself in the golden light of your Soul, your solar body is being born. Sing the seven names of God in sequence: *Adonai, El-Shaddai, Alaha Elohim Tzavaot, Yeshua Messiah, Alaha Elohim Givor, Alaha Elohim Alaha, Ehyeh Asher Ehyeh*.

Feel all the great archangels surrounding you as they accompany you into the column of light as you descend back to the healing temple of your mental body, standing in the temple in the radiant golden light of your Soul. There in the temple awaiting you, is your radiant blue mental body to be purified by the archangels and released from its attachment to the beast.

Feel Archangel Sandalfon pouring the first vial/cup of golden light on the root chakra of your mental body. Give back your laziness to the beast. At the count of three, cut your thoughts and beliefs about laziness. One, two, three, CUT! Feel the root center growing bright as a beautiful golden star appears in it, a six-pointed star of light.

Now feel Archangel Gabriel pouring the second vial/cup of golden light into the second chakra of your mental body. Give back the thought impressions of lust and domination to the beast. At the count of three, let us cut that connection. One, two, three, CUT! See Gabriel placing the six-pointed golden star of light into your second chakra.

Now feel the two great archangels, Rafael on your left, Hanael on your right pouring their third vial/cup(s) of golden light, transforming the two centers of your solar plexus. From the right side of your solar plexus, give back your fear to the beast. And from the left side of your solar plexus, give back your gluttony to the beast. Now take your swords of light, both Rafael's sword and Hanael's sword, and at the count of three cut both of these connections. One, two, three, CUT! Breathe deeply. Feel and see Raphael placing the six-pointed golden star into the left side of your solar plexus, and Hanael on the right side doing the same. Take a deep breath.

And now feel Archangel Michael pouring the fourth vial/cup of golden light into the heart center of your mental body. And give back to the beast your thoughts of jealousy and envy. Take the sword of light and, at the count of three, let us cut this energy. One, two, three, CUT! Breathe deeply. Feel Archangel Michael placing the six-pointed golden star of light into the heart chakra of your mental body.

Now feel the two great archangels, Tzadkiel and Kamael, Tzadkiel standing to the right and Kamael standing to the left of the throat center of your mental body. Let them both pour the fifth vial/cup(s) of the golden light of purification onto your throat chakra as you give back to the beast, on your right, the energy and thoughts of deceit and dishonesty and, on your left, the energy and thoughts of greed. At the count of three, let Kamael and Tzadkiel cut these cords. One, two, three, CUT! Breathe deeply. Feel Kamael and Tzadkiel place golden six-pointed stars on both sides of your throat chakra as you feel the spiritual energy current rising to your sixth chakra center.

Now focus on the sixth chakra of your mental body. And here feel, on the left, Archangel Tzafkiel and, on the right, Archangel Ratziel. Let Ratziel and Tzafkiel pour the sixth vial/cup(s) of golden light and purifying energy on your sixth chakra. And give back to the beast the pride you hold on the left of the chakra and the thoughts of anger you hold on the right. See Ratziel and Tzafkiel raising their swords of light and, at the count of three, cutting these connections to the beast. One, two, three, CUT! Breathe deeply. Feel them placing their golden stars in the sixth chakra, left and right. Breathe deeply, feeling the light of the spiritual energy, the golden light, flowing up the central column of your spine, and moving to the crown chakra of your mental body.

And now feel Archangel Metatron pouring the seventh vial/cup of the golden light on the crown chakra of your mental body. Feel yourself giving back to the beast those false beliefs of separation from God that your mental body holds. And, at the count of three, feel Archangel Metatron cutting this cord, as you give back all this energy to the beast. One, two, three, CUT! And now breathe deeply. Feel Metatron placing the golden six-pointed star in your crown chakra. Let yourself, as Soul, enter your mental body with the stars of light shining brightly within it. Embrace your mental body with your Soul and say, "My beloved mental body, you are my servant. I Am the Soul. I Am a spark of God, and I exist because of God's love for me. I Am." And let your Soul's light fill the stars of your mental body. These are the threads of connection your Soul has with your mental body. Your mental body is glowing blue with the golden stars within, the stars of divine intelligence.

Breathe deeply. Feel your brothers and sisters of the light, the archangels, as you begin to leave the temple of the mental plane, coming down the column of light to your astral temple of light. Feel yourself standing in the astral temple of light. The holy archangels surround you. You are now the Soul connected to the mind, and it is time now to heal and connect to the astral body. As the beast went into the light of oneness and disappeared from the mental body, so here, if you look at your astral body in its rose-pink light in front of you, before it is the dragon. It is now time to give back to the dragon the negative elementals experienced as feelings and emotions within you.

Let Archangel Sandalfon pour on the root chakra of your astral body the first vial/cup of golden, purifying light. And give back to the dragon your emotional attachment to laziness and apathy. Take Sandalfon's sword of light and cut this connection to the dragon. One, two, three, CUT! Breathe deeply. Feel Sandalfon placing into your root chakra a beautiful candle flame of light, your astral body connection, in the root chakra to your Soul.

And now feel Gabriel pouring into the second chakra of your astral body the second vial/cup of golden healing light. And feel yourself taking this emotional attachment to the energy of lust and possessiveness giving it back to the dragon, and at the count of three cutting this cord with the sword of Gabriel's light. One, two, three, CUT! Breathe deeply. Feel Gabriel placing the candle flame in the second chakra center of your astral body. Take a deep breath.

Feel Raphael on your left and Hanael on your right, pouring the third vial/cup(s) of the golden healing light of purification into the solar plexus of your astral body. And give back to the dragon your astral fear—your emotional attachments to fear, to overconsumption and gluttony, to fanaticism and intolerance and prejudice. And see and feel Rafael and Hanael with their swords of light, as you give these energies back to the dragon, along with the violence of perceived differences and ethnic hatreds. And one, two, three, CUT! Breathe deeply. Feel Rafael and Hanael placing, to the left and right of your solar plexus, the golden-orange flames of light into your astral body.

Feel Archangel Michael pouring his fourth vial/cup of the golden liquid light of purification into the heart center of your astral body. And give back to the dragon all emotional attachment to jealousy and envy. And, at the count of three, you can let Archangel Michael cut this cord of energy, breaking the connection to any tyranny and cruelty that your heart may carry from its woundings, any residues of suffering and unhappy sacrifice or feelings of masochism toward yourself, any self-hatred or low self-value. Give this back to the dragon now—whatever keeps your heart from the light of divine love. At the count of three, let us cut it. One, two, three, CUT! Breathe deeply. Feel Archangel Michael placing in the heart chakra of your astral body the golden-orange flames of light.

And now feel Archangel Kamael at the left side and Archangel Tzadkiel on the right side of your throat chakra in your astral body. Feel them pour the fifth vial/cup(s) of golden healing light and purification into both sides of the throat chakra in your astral body. Give back greed on the left side, dishonesty on the right, to the dragon. Give back poverty and isolation, self-centeredness and narcissism, verbal manipulation and control; give it back to the dragon. And see the two great archangels lifting their swords of light. At the count of three, let us cut this cord in your astral body. One, two, three, CUT! Breathe deeply. Now, see and feel Kamael and Tzadkiel place two flames of golden-orange light in your throat chakra.

Now as the energy rises to your sixth chakra center, feel Archangel Tzafkiel on the left and Ratziel on the right filling your sixth chakra with the sixth vial/cup(s) of golden healing light, the light of purification. And give back to the dragon emotions that you are attached to, your pride on the left and your anger on the right. At the count of three, let us cut these energies on both sides. One, two, three, CUT! Breathe deeply. Now allow these two great archangels to place their two great golden-orange flames in the brow chakra of your astral body, and give the old energy back to the dragon.

And now feel the energy rising to the seventh chakra of your astral body. Archangel Metatron pours the seventh vial/cup of purifying golden healing light into this seventh chakra. Give back to the dragon all your feelings of separation from God's light and love. At the count of three, let us cut this connection. One, two, three, CUT! Breathe deeply. And feel Metatron placing into your astral body's crown chakra a beautiful golden-orange flame of light.

Now feel and see your beautiful rose-pink astral body with the flames of golden-orange light in each of its centers. And feel your Soul in its beautiful, unified, golden healing light connecting to each of the flames. These flames of light in your astral body chakras are threads through which the intelligence of your Soul flows to your astral body. And from your Soul's light, as you did with the stars and your mental body, just think and feel these flames to bring your astral body into perfect resonance with your Soul. For your Soul is truly like the Son of Man in the vision of Saint John. Embrace your astral body and say to it, "My beloved, I Am the Soul. I Am a spark of God. I exist because of God's love for me. I Am." Connect your astral and mental bodies to the light of your Soul; bring them into your Soul's light.

Now with the great archangels, feel yourself leaving the astral temple and coming down the column of light to the physical etheric temple where you started your journey. And here, standing before you, is your physical body with its five senses, addicted to the pseudo-lamb that stands behind it. As you stand as Soul, let Sandalfon pour the first vial/cup of the golden healing light of purification into the root chakra of your physical body as you give back to the pseudo-lamb whatever behaviors or sensory indulgences that lead to apathy and laziness. And at the count of three, cut this connection. One, two, three, CUT! Breathe deeply. Feel Archangel Sandalfon placing into the root chakra of your physical body a beautiful white-domed temple of light. And breathe in deeply.

Now feel Gabriel pouring into the second chakra of the physical body the second vial/cup of golden purifying light as you give back to the pseudo-lamb the sensory expression of your cravings and any lustful feelings that draw your energy away from love and lower your chi energy. And at the count of three, let Gabriel cut this connection. One, two, three, CUT! Breathe deeply. Feel Gabriel placing a beautiful white-domed temple of light into the second chakra center of your physical body.

And as you breathe, now feel Raphael on the left of your solar plexus and Hanael on the right pouring the third vial/cup(s) of the golden healing light of purification into your solar plexus center as you give back to the pseudo-lamb all the physical expressions of fear and gluttony that you carry. And let us cut these connections. One, two, three, CUT! Breathe deeply. Feel the two great archangels placing beautiful white-domed temples of light into the right and left sides of your solar plexus.

Feel now Archangel Michael pouring the fourth vial/cup of golden healing light into the heart chakra of your physical body, removing any physical expressions of envy or jealousy, betrayal and hurt; any suffering or pain expressed through your physical body. And give it all back to the pseudo-lamb. At the count of three, let us cut this connection. One, two, three, CUT! Breathe deeply. Feel Archangel Michael placing into the heart center of your physical body a beautiful white-domed temple, filling your heart center with healing energy, for all these temples are connected with the energy of your Soul's light.

And now feel at your shoulder level, at the throat chakra, Kamael on the left and Tzadkiel on the right, as they pour the fifth vial/cup(s) of purifying golden light into both sides of your throat chakra. And give back to the pseudo-lamb all greed on the left and dishonesty on the right in your expressions in speech. As they raise their great swords of light, and at the count of three, give this energy back to the pseudo-lamb. One, two, three, CUT! Breathe deeply. Feel the two great archangels placing the white-domed temples of light into both sides of your throat chakra, healing your throat chakra. For each of these domed temples in each of your chakras is a gateway through which your Soul energy can flow to heal your physical body so it may remain healthy and strong. In all your organ systems, feel this connection to your Soul's light—the stars, the flames, and the temples—the organizational system of your Soul within the three bodies.

Now feel the archangels Tzafkiel and Ratziel, Tzafkiel on your left and Ratziel on your right, at the level of your sixth chakra. And feel them pouring the sixth vial/cup(s) of the golden healing light of purification into your brow chakra. Give back to the pseudo-lamb any expressions of pride on the left and anger on the right in your physical actions. Give all this back to the pseudo-lamb and, at the count of three, let us cut these cords. Watch now as Tzafkiel and Ratziel cut them with their swords of truth. One, two, three, CUT! Breathe deeply. And feel each of these great archangels placing two beautiful domed temples of white light into your brow chakra, on the right and on the left, over the two lobes of your brain.

And, finally, feel Archangel Metatron pouring the seventh vial/cup of the healing golden light of purification on the crown chakra of your physical body as you release to the pseudo-lamb any feelings of separation from your source in God and your Soul's light. Send these feelings back to the pseudo-lamb, at the count of three. One, two, three, CUT! Breathe deeply. Feel Archangel Metatron now placing in the crown chakra of your physical body the beautiful circular white-domed temple of light. And the pseudo-lamb dissolves into the white light as Archangel Michael carries him up above. Feel yourself now as the Soul in your great solar light, embracing this physical body with its aura of green light and the beautiful white temples shining in all its centers. Say, "My beloved physical body, I Am the Soul. I Am a spark of God. And I exist because of God's love for me. I Am."

Embrace the physical body as you connect it to the astral and mental bodies, as you bring them into the oneness of your Soul, saying, "I Am. I Am. I Am." Give thanks to the great archangels for their work and for the great work of the Christ and Saint Mary Magdalene, and the saints, prophets, and angels, and the twenty-four elders, and the transformed energies of the four animals of John's Revelation, the four bodies—the physical body, the calf; the emotional body, the man; the mental body, the lion; and the spiritual body, the eagle—for they also celebrate their transformation in this meditation today. So be it. Slowly, slowly, leave the temple, dissolving it behind you. And just feel your solar light shining on everything around you. Say to yourself, "I Am the light and the sound of God. Amen." Breathe deeply. Slowly feel yourself coming back to your physical body awareness. Rub your hands. Massage your face, your eyes and ears. And return.

Chapter 17 of Revelation

Transformation of the Whore of Babylon

> 1: *And there came one of the seven angels which had the seven vials, and talked with me, saying unto me, Come hither; I will shew unto thee the judgment of the great whore that sitteth upon many waters:*
>
> 2: *With whom the kings of the earth have committed fornication, and the inhabitants of the earth have been made drunk with the wine of her fornication.*
>
> 3: *So he carried me away in the spirit into the wilderness: and I saw a woman sit upon a scarlet coloured beast, full of names of blasphemy, having seven heads and ten horns.*
>
> 4: *And the woman was arrayed in purple and scarlet colour, and decked with gold and precious stones and pearls, having a golden cup in her hand full of abominations and filthiness of her fornication:*
>
> 5: *And upon her forehead was a name written,* MYSTERY, BABYLON THE GREAT, THE MOTHER OF HARLOTS AND ABOMINATIONS OF THE EARTH.

The meaning of Babylon is multilayered and deserves explanation. Babylon symbolically represents the human body, the materializing instincts, the lower ego function enslaved and caught in desire in the realm of Malkut, separated from the higher light and love principal of Tiferet. Without spiritual light, Malkut is simply passive and entrenched in itself with impure negative passions (vices), elementals that breed by virtue of its separation from Source and its own etheric double. Here, in isolation, it remains dissatisfied, addicted, and contaminated.

Since Malkut, or the earth domain, is the physical expression of the virginal Divine Mother—"the sun-moon woman," or Binah, who lost her divine connection to her daughter in Malkut, in the separation and fracture of humanity into ego-consciousness represented by the fall from Eden—there is a longing of Binah for her daughter in Malkut. Only through the agency of Tiferet, which stands in the heart between human love (Tiferet-Yesod-Malkut) and divine love (Keter-Binah-Chokmah-Tiferet), can there ever be a reconnection and return to the Garden of

Eden, transforming the tree of good and evil (polarity) into the unified tree of knowledge.

We have discussed before that all this symbolism may well reflect the cataclysmic trauma on the earth 12,000 to 14,000 years ago and humanity's loss of unified consciousness. Christ (representing the activation of Tiferet) appeared 2,000 years ago to activate the healing of this fracture in the human psyche. Symbolically, the "Virgin Mary" represents Binah descended from the supernal heavenly state as the archetype of the divine female returned to heal this fracture through her son in Tiferet. Jesus Christ, centered in the heart of divine love in Tiferet, links the sephirah of the Tree of Life by exorcising Mary Magdalene; she then becomes unified with Tiferet and ascends in consciousness to the supernal triad with the Christ.

In the biblical story of Jesus meeting Mary Magdalene, this reconnection happens. It is said that when Jesus was baptized by John the Baptist in the river Jordan (the awakening of Yesod), Mary Magdalene became aware of her desire to search for him, and the spiritual life and light she missed, for she had been raised in a material way without connection to spirituality. This story reflects the notion of Malkut (the earth domain) being separated from the light, as seen in Daskalos' account:

> Maria had arrived in a horse-drawn cart, dressed as elegantly as any noble woman had. When her uncle saw her, he ran towards her shouting vile names and slapping her as he pushed her into the house where she fell in a heap. When Joshua entered, Zakharias was still shouting, and kicking the fallen woman. Joshua ordered him to stop and he helped her to stand. Her face was swollen, bruised badly, and her fine clothes were bloodstained. Joshua led her to a stool and, asking the trembling woman to look into his eyes, he took out of her personality seven human-demons: 1. Adultery; 2. Pride; 3. Stealing; 4. Lying; 5. Cruelty; 6. Hatred and Enmity; 7. Malice and Aggression.[22]

From a psychological perspective, when divine love (transpersonal love) lifts the lower consciousness of ego and cleanses it of illusion, this leads to ego-death and rebirth. This is very similar to Mary Magdalene's own ego-death and rebirth, with Tiferet connecting to Malkut through the astral cleansing of Yesod, connecting her awareness to Tiferet and then to God, which is the unification of Jesus and Mary Magdalene in Yesod. At the time that Jesus was baptized by John the Baptist in the river Jordan, activating Yesod or the water element, Mary was also awakened to this level.

It is interesting to consider that Mary Magdalene may well have been the wife or partner of Jesus[23] and that she spent much time in communion, not only with Jesus Christ, but with his mother, the embodiment of Binah in the divine biblical story. There is the outer story and there is the inner knowledge (or alchemy) that is part of the initiate's journey to Christ Consciousness. In Saint John's Revelation, the "harlot"—the physical body—must be disciplined and purified to allow the full reconnection of the divine love and supernal light in Keter-Tiferet-Yesod-Malkut.

> *1: And there came one of the seven angels which had the seven vials, and talked with me, saying unto me, Come hither; I will shew unto thee the judgment of the great whore that sitteth upon many waters:*
>
> *2: With whom the kings of the earth have committed fornication, and the inhabitants of the earth have been made drunk with the wine of her fornication.*

"The great whore that sitteth on many waters" represents the passional desires that support her. The personality—"the kings of the earth"—is intoxicated and enmeshed in its false desires.

> *3: So he carried me away in the spirit into the wilderness: and I saw a woman sit upon a scarlet coloured beast, full of names of blasphemy, having seven heads and ten horns.*

The "scarlet coloured beast" represents material prosperity accumulated through the ego's wiles and the corrupted lower mind fixated on false beliefs of immortality from accumulated riches and royalty—the ego-pride and arrogance of having a special position.

> *4: And the woman was arrayed in purple and scarlet colour, and decked with gold and precious stones and pearls, having a golden cup in her hand full of abominations and filthiness of her fornication:*
>
> *5: And upon her forehead was a name written, MYSTERY, BABYLON THE GREAT, THE MOTHER OF HARLOTS AND ABOMINATIONS OF THE EARTH.*

The "golden cup in her hand full of abominations" is the contaminated etheric energy, at one time pure and reflecting truth, rendered impure with distortions and confusion. In a similar manner, in Daskalos' account of Mary Magdalene, we see the Christ saying, "Gold in dung is still gold. This gold is like the Soul of your niece, and isn't a Soul more valuable than gold? With water and sand you cleaned the coin. Maria, with tears of repentance, is now washing away her sins. Maria's sins are forgiven."[24] This is the cleansing of Malkut and Yesod so it can raise itself to Tiferet and reconnect with the Divine Mother Binah and God.

> *6: And I saw the woman drunken with the blood of the saints, and with the blood of the martyrs of Jesus: and when I saw her, I wondered with great admiration.*

The ego is so clever that it can even kidnap one's best intentions at spiritual practice and transform even the sincerest intentions into pride: "Look how evolved and how spiritual I am." By acting in a saintly manner, one seeks admiration, self-importance, indispensability, and power over others. Despite outward appearances, these actions are not selfless, but come with a hidden agenda. This is ego specialness. Daskalos called this getting caught in "golden chains."

> *7: And the angel said unto me, Wherefore didst thou marvel? I will tell thee the mystery of the woman, and of the beast that carrieth her, which hath the seven heads and ten horns.*

The "seven heads" refer to the fixations that are controlled and ruled by "the beast"—the lower mind that controls the body and "that carrieth her." The "ten horns" (egotism) are the perverted powers of the ten Sephiroth. The seven fixations dwell in the chakras, and the ego misuses the etheric energy of the seven chakras to reinforce its illusion through strong, bodily felt sensations of an illusionary nature that go contrary to higher perceptions of the truth.

> *8: The beast that thou sawest was, and is not; and shall ascend out of the bottomless pit, and go into perdition: and they that dwell on the earth shall wonder, whose names were not written in the book of life from the foundation of the world, when they behold the beast that was, and is not, and yet is.*

The "beast that was, and is not, and yet is" refers to the illusionary and impermanent nature of negative elementals once they are de-energized or transformed. The mind creates and destroys itself and remains impermanent in nature. The ones "that dwell on the earth..., whose names were not written in the book of life from the foundation of the world," are those Souls not initiated, whose personalities continue to incarnate, learning unconsciously through what Daskalos called "the whips of destiny."

> *9: And here is the mind which hath wisdom. The seven heads are seven mountains, on which the woman sitteth.*

The deeper wisdom reveals itself to the initiate and gives insight into the state or condition of Babylon. The contaminated physical body—the harlot and separated realm of Malkut—contains "seven mountains"—seven chakras. These "mountains" are separated from their Source, and their lofty positions suggest arrogance, ego-inflation, and pride. The ego—"the woman"—sits on them with control, ruling the usage and expression of their energies.

> **10:** *And there are seven kings: five are fallen, and one is, and the other is not yet come; and when he cometh, he must continue a short space.*

"And there are seven kings: five are fallen" likely represents the first five chakras, or ego-aspects of the personality, that have been dominated by ego but have now been subdued, surrendered, and transformed. The initiate is currently in the sixth chakra center, awaiting entry into the seventh (through completion of the Kundalini's flow to the crown chakra) and unity consciousness. According to Grove,[25] the five "fallen" kings may also refer to the seven incarnations during which initiation is completed. Saint John, the initiate, has completed five incarnations, is in the sixth, and one more remains. In Buddhism, this sixth stage is called "sakadagami" ("he who returns once"), because only one more incarnation is necessary.

> **11:** *And the beast that was, and is not, even he is the eighth, and is of the seven, and goeth into perdition.*

On the Hawkins scale (discussed in Volume I, Chapter 4), the eight levels of negative force are (1) shame, (2) guilt, (3) apathy, (4) grief, (5) fear, (6) desire, (7) anger, and (8) pride.[26] The "beast," or lower mind, represents the eighth level. The seven chakras are controlled by the seven "dragons" of passional desire, which correspond with the first seven levels of negative force. Pride ("the beast"), at the eighth level, controls the seven forces below it, keeping them in the shadow of the personality. Pride "goeth into perdition" in the abyss as the elemental self that will desire existence one more time. Upon the seventh incarnation, pride will be put to final rest. After pride, courage (at the ninth level) is the first purely positive state of real power, and it is here that the ego surrenders its hold and acknowledges a higher power is at work in one's life.

> **12:** *And the ten horns which thou sawest are ten kings, which have received no kingdom as yet; but receive power as kings one hour with the beast.*

The "ten kings" are the illusionary desires "which have received no kingdom" because they have no true power from the Source, only ego-forcefulness and ego-control. They represent the ten Sephiroth dominated by false values. As the beast (which "goeth into perdition," verse 11) holds the deepest wounding of the personality in its state of separation from its true power or Source, it represents the hidden inferiority of the ego's hurt pride—the shame of separation—that attempts to compensate by creating a false sense of authority and superiority.

> **13:** *These have one mind, and shall give their power and strength unto the beast.*

Again, the seven negative emotional states of shame, guilt, apathy, grief, fear, desire, and anger are of "one mind" and "shall give their power and strength unto the beast," the eighth negative emotional state, which is pride. Pride is the stronghold of the beast and is the negative force of mind that controls the seven below.

> **14:** *These shall make war with the Lamb, and the Lamb shall overcome them: for he is Lord of lords, and King of kings: and they that are with him are called, and chosen, and faithful.*

The Spirit-Soul that expresses itself through the pure positive powers of Source—(1) courage, (2) neutrality, (3) willingness, (4) acceptance, (5) reason, (6) love, (7) joy, (8) peace, and (9) enlightenment—is the "Lamb," the true "King of kings." "They that are with him" are the physical (Asiyah), emotional (Yetzirah), and mental (Beriyah) bodies and their respective chakra centers, and they "are called, and chosen, and faithful"—they will be aligned with the purpose of the Soul.

> **15:** *And he saith unto me, The waters which thou sawest, where the whore sitteth, are peoples, and multitudes, and nations, and tongues.*

The emotions ("waters") are controlled by the "whore" (the ego) and are supported by the collective energies of the world, the "peoples, and multitudes, and nations, and tongues."

> **16:** *And the ten horns which thou sawest upon the beast, these shall hate the whore, and shall make her desolate and naked, and shall eat her flesh, and burn her with fire.*

The desires of the mind ("the beast") identified with its body, in separation from the Source, causes the ego ("the whore") deep frustration and suffering, bringing the ego to feel self-critical, inferior, different, shameful, and isolated.

> **17:** *For God hath put in their hearts to fulfill his will, and to agree, and give their kingdom unto the beast, until the words of God shall be fulfilled.*

The "beast"—the source of all desire—plays an important role in assisting in the evolution and individuation of the Spirit-Soul in manifestation. Like the prodigal son (Luke 15:11-32), we are all destined to return to our home, individuated and evolved in consciousness as self-realized Beings. One could say that even the "beast" works for God by showing what is illusionary, thereby leading the Soul to what is authentic and real in Spirit.

> *18: And the woman which thou sawest is that great city, which reigneth over the kings of the earth.*

The ego, or "woman," is the "great city," or authority, that dominates the personality fixations, the "kings of the earth." In Chapter 18, the great transformation from personal self to transpersonal self and spiritual awakening is underway.

Understanding Zorba

I dance the pain until it stands
   in acrid drops like olive brine
      upon my face
I dance the crystalline tears
   that long ago turned
      my shoulders into stone
I dance the sorrow
   of love turned to hatred
      and hatred to indifference
I dance the fear of loneliness
   and the anguish
      of abandonment
I dance the anger
   until it rages free
      and runs down my arms
   like rivers
I dance the disappointment
   of expectations unfulfilled
      and dreams too long
   deferred
I dance all my demons
   into dust beneath my feet
      sweeping them away
   in spiraling centrifuge
Only then can I dance
   that which sings
      the heart and blood
In the space
   between the spaces
      that lie between the words
Where words have no meaning
   I dance and joy IS...
       —Donna Overall, ©2015

Chapter 18 of Revelation

The Process of Ego-Death and Spiritual Awakening

> *1: And after these things I saw another angel come down from heaven, having great power; and the earth was lightened with his glory.*

The "angel" represents the Spirit-Soul and "the earth" the personality. The personality is being "lightened with his glory," illuminated by deeper awareness of its Soul's presence. The agents in Beriyah that mediate this transition for the evolving personality are Metatron, the archangel of Keter (representing "heaven"), and Sandalfon, the archangel representing Mother Earth ("the earth"). Together, Metatron and Sandalfon bring light to matter. The union of the two is the great Archangel Hua, suggesting that the ascension process, through union of Keter and Malkut, is approaching in the initiate's consciousness.

> *2: And he cried mightily with a strong voice, saying, Babylon the great is fallen, is fallen, and is become the habitation of devils, and the hold of every foul spirit, and a cage of every unclean and hateful bird.*

"Babylon" is symbolic of the sensory domain and all that is corrupt and tainted with egotism in the human being as a result of the identification of ego with its materializing instincts. Before the fall of Lemuria and Atlantis, all the Sephiroth remained aligned in creation, from Binah on down through the remaining Sephiroth, creating perfect archetypal forms and links in matter (etheric doubles) as expressions of the virginal, spiritual consciousness. With the fall of Lemuria and Atlantis (probably the Garden of Eden of biblical lore), the negative and positive polarities were created and Spirit and matter were separated by ego-consciousness. This gave rise to dissatisfaction and addictive desire ("the habitation of devils"), to the creation of negative elementals imprisoning the Soul ("the hold of every foul spirit"), and to negative mental fixations ("a cage of every unclean and hateful bird").

> *3: For all nations have drunk of the wine of the wrath of her fornication, and the kings of the earth have committed fornication with her, and the merchants of the earth are waxed rich through the abundance of her delicacies.*

Babylon is referred to as a feminine entity here. She represents the "harlot," the contaminated etheric energy field of all three bodies, physical, emotional, mental, and the misuse of these sacred bodies through selfish desire, self-gratification, and narcissistic preoccupations that lead to perversion of the sex function, addictions, and abusive behaviors.

The original intent of Spirit in the supernal triad of Keter, Chokmah, and Binah was to support the evolving Soul through perfect archetypal expressions of divine laws and virtues (the etheric doubles of each of the bodies) to inspire the ascending Spirit-Soul-Ego-Self to individuate and manifest itself in matter in the likeness of the Divine, in the image of God.

"Kings of earth" refer to false inner beliefs of illusion in the personality considered with authority by the lower collective nature. "Merchants" refer to overconsumerism, (elementals of overconsumption and allurement).

> *4: And I heard another voice from heaven, saying, Come out of her, my people, that ye be not partakers of her sins, and that ye receive not of her plagues.*

In other words, don't engage any longer in your personality's egotism, lest you create more karmic bonds (partake "of her sins") and self-created suffering ("her plagues").

> *5: For her sins have reached unto heaven, and God hath remembered her iniquities.*

The light of higher consciousness is illuminating the ego's entrapment in egotistic elementals.

> *6: Reward her even as she rewarded you, and double unto her double according to her works: in the cup which she hath filled fill to her double.*

Surrender your egotism and the great suffering it has cost you through your great determination and skill of self-introspection.

> *7: How much she hath glorified herself, and lived deliciously, so much torment and sorrow give her: for she saith in her heart, I sit a queen, and am no widow, and shall see no sorrow.*

The ego, when defended through arrogance and pride, believes itself to be invulnerable to discomfort, emptiness, sorrow, and suffering.

> *8: Therefore shall her plagues come in one day, death, and mourning, and famine; and she shall be utterly burned with fire: for strong is the Lord God who judgeth her.*

Her karmas ("plagues") come in "one day" but in three distinct stages, "death, and mourning, and famine." This process suggests the act of disengaging or de-energizing negative elementals mentally, emotionally, and physically. Being "utterly burned with fire" represents illuminated thought, which energetically is "strong"—of a higher power than the lower egotism.

> **9:** *And the kings of the earth, who have committed fornication and lived deliciously with her, shall bewail her, and lament for her, when they shall see the smoke of her burning,*

The mental beliefs of the egotistic personality ("the kings of the earth") will no longer be enlivened when they become de-energized through the dissolution of egotism ("when they shall see the smoke of her burning").

> **10:** *Standing afar off for the fear of her torment, saying, Alas, alas, that great city Babylon, that mighty city! for in one hour is thy judgment come.*

When illusionary beliefs and thoughts are brought to light, they are struck with the lightning of illumination and quickly rendered ineffective—"for in one hour is thy judgment come." As the light of self-awareness approaches illusionary beliefs, they tend to withdraw "afar off" and hide in fear of being made conscious and exposed to change. These illusionary beliefs and thoughts literally fear their own death, even though they are of the ego's creation. They also perceive the end of their materialistic origins; they know the ego will come to an end soon. This is reflected psychologically in the ego-death process, a state of mental despair that we compared, in Chapter 14, to the event horizon of a "black hole."

> **11:** *And the merchants of the earth shall weep and mourn over her; for no man buyeth their merchandise any more:*

The "merchants of the earth" are the feeling or emotional desire component of the negative elementals. As the emotional component of your egotism dies, you can no longer satisfy yourself through feeling special or above others intellectually, emotionally, or materially.

> **12:** *The merchandise of gold, and silver, and precious stones, and of pearls, and fine linen, and purple, and silk, and scarlet, and all thine wood, and all manner vessels of ivory, and all manner vessels of most precious wood, and of brass, and iron, and marble,*

> **13:** *And cinnamon, and odours, and ointments, and frankincense, and wine, and oil, and fine flour, and wheat, and beasts, and sheep, and horses, and chariots, and slaves, and souls of men.*

> *14: And the fruits that thy soul lusted after are departed from thee, and all things which were dainty and goodly are departed from thee, and thou shalt find them no more at all.*

Verses 12, 13, and 14 express the process of ego-death as the ego releases its attachments to the things it found desirable and that made it feel special and satisfied.

> *15: The merchants of these things, which were made rich by her, shall stand afar off for the fear of her torment, weeping and wailing,*

These emotional attachments to false feelings of specialness and security will no longer be able to feed off the sacred etheric energy. They will be experienced by the personality as withdrawal, suffering, sorrow, and unfulfillment, *i.e.*, emotional despair.

> *16: And saying, Alas, alas, that great city, that was clothed in fine linen, and purple, and scarlet, and decked with gold, and precious stones, and pearls!*

> *17: For in one hour so great riches is come to nought. And every shipmaster, and all the company in ships, and sailors, and as many as trade by sea, stood afar off,*

> *18: And cried when they saw the smoke of her burning, saying, What city is like unto this great city!*

The first stage of ego-dissolution occurs. Those who "trade by sea" represent the laborers of the sea of life—the sensory realm. The negative elementals attached to sensory or bodily sensations are now being de-energized and witness from "afar off" the illumination of the ego.

> *19: And they cast dust on their heads, and cried, weeping and wailing, saying, Alas, alas, that great city, wherein were made rich all that had ships in the sea by reason of her costliness! for in one hour is she made desolate.*

All those who toiled—the "sailors," the sensory-based elementals—to build and maintain the prideful ego, its false image and its false specialness, will perish with the ego's death because they were created in the egotistic state of separateness.

> *20: Rejoice over her, thou heaven, and ye holy apostles and prophets; for God hath avenged you on her.*

God's holy ideas and pure light source "hath avenged you on her" — illuminated the hold the ego has had and exposed her falseness.

> **21:** *And a mighty angel took up a stone like a great millstone, and cast it into the sea, saying, Thus with violence shall that great city Babylon be thrown down, and shall be found no more at all.*

Divine love puts an end to the ego's domination and false pretense. It is interesting to note that Plato's account of the destruction of Atlantis has a similar tone to it. Ego's domination and subsequent demise are mirrored in the historical accounts of many world powers of the past — Atlantis, Babylon, Rome, etc. Saint John's account can be seen, in part, as representing the deep collective memories of near-extinction of the human species and the post-traumatic stress resulting from a traumatic global catastrophe that almost destroyed the earth approximately 12,000 to 14,000 years ago.

> **22:** *And the voice of harpers, and musicians, and of pipers, and trumpeters, shall be heard no more at all in thee; and no craftsman, of whatsoever craft he be, shall be found any more in thee; and the sound of a millstone shall be heard no more at all in thee;*

The enlightened, self-realized initiate will continue to enjoy life in a state of neutrality, without attachment. Even his or her skills will be learned and practiced without the ego's personal desires, through impersonal love.

> **23:** *And the light of a candle shall shine no more at all in thee; and the voice of the bridegroom and of the bride shall be heard no more at all in thee: for thy merchants were the great men of the earth; for by thy sorceries were all nations deceived.*

In this verse, "the light of the candle" (the intellect), the voices of polarity ("of the bridegroom and of the bride," *i.e.*, the sexual nature), and all aspects of everyday life will no longer be "deceived" and corrupted by ego-strivings (the "merchants," the "great men of the earth"). The personal ego is being put to rest to allow the transpersonal self that lives by grace alone to emerge. The individual may not appear different outwardly and will continue to be engaged in life as before, but the ego is no longer running the show. Spirit is navigating the individual's life existence. Ramana Maharshi was once asked, "How can I tell if a man is enlightened?" He answered that it is difficult to see outwardly, but that person would exemplify at least three qualities — kindness, tolerance toward all living beings, and acceptance.

24: *And in her was found the blood of prophets, and of saints, and of all that were slain upon the earth.*

This phrase may refer to the materializing consciousness, now purified—made virginal again—through the "blood"—the divine love of prophets (sixth chakra) and saints (seventh chakra). This is the holy vision and wisdom of the supernal triad.

The Egoless Life

Embracing the spiritual life brings a radical change in one's value system. The shift is from outer to inner and then to wholeness-consciousness, where both outer and inner are held as sacred expressions of God's love. From this point on, a life lived in love is a blessed life, full of grace and harmony.

MEDITATION JOURNEY

Close your eyes and breathe deeply. Relax your body. Place your attention on your feet, and feel a beautiful healing white light flowing into your feet and legs. Feel the healing light flowing up into your thighs, your hips and pelvic area. The healing light flows into your abdomen, your chest, and your heart, relaxing you. With every breath, the light in your heart grows stronger and brighter. The healing light flows over your shoulders and down your arms to your hands and fingers. The healing light flows into your neck, your head, and face. And as you breathe, looking down at your healing hands of white light, build a large circular disc in white light on the ground before. And on the disc build a beautiful domed temple of white light.

Step into the temple and stand in its center. Call on Archangel Michael in red flames of light on the right side of your body, and breathe in this light of faith and courage and strength. Call on Archangel Rafael and the violet flames of light to the left side of your body, and breathe in the violet flames of wisdom and clarity and focused attention as they gather all your consciousness into one point for your work. Call on Archangel Gabriel and the sky-blue light to your back, along your spine. As you breathe in the sky-blue flames of light into your heart, ask Gabriel to support you with love and compassion and forgiveness on your journey. And call on Archangel Uriel and the silver-white flames of light to the front of your body. Breathe in Uriel's healing light of peace and harmony, letting it fill you.

As you stand in the center of your temple, call on Joshua Immanuel the Christ to stand on your right and Saint Mary Magdalene to stand on your left, and feel them touching your back. Feel a beautiful golden-yellow spiritual sun emerging in your heart center, the light of the Christ filling you. And feel Saint Mary Magdalene sending a beautiful rose-pink light into the center of the spiritual sun like a beautiful rosy flame. Feel this rose light and the golden light of the Christ both filling you. Feel them supporting you in this process. Feel above you, to your left, levitating in the sky to your left above you, the great Archangel Tzafkiel, the Divine Mother of Binah, with her shining face of gold, clothed in the Milky Way galaxy with millions of shiny stars within her body. She is holding the book of your memories in her hand. Connect with her, and breathe deeply, and exhale.

Feel to your right above you, at the same level, levitating to the right side of you, the great Archangel Ratziel, clothed in a beautiful white cloud, as rainbow rays pour out of his body of radiant sunlight behind the clouds. He holds a staff in his left hand, and in his right hand is a crystal-clear sphere. Feel Tzafkiel supporting you with divine love and Ratziel supporting you with divine wisdom. And let Archangel Michael, standing on the periphery, create a circle of fire around you as protection. Feel your love and wisdom and power growing, strengthening, with every breath you take.

And now, entering the temple for transformation and yet standing outside of the fiery sacred circle of Michael's protection, are three men. The first is the king of the earth, dressed with his seven crowns and ten horns of destructive power, representing the desire-mind and distorted thoughts. The merchant next to him represents distorted feelings, and the sailor next to the merchant represents distorted physical behavior. All three are intoxicated with materiality and arrogance and egotism, filled with pride and intolerance, cruelty, bigotry, false beliefs, idolatry, racism, and hatred, and all support separatism and separateness from God.

Now ask yourself, as you go back in your memories of growing up, "Who in my life growing up represented this energy to me? Who seduced me into these energies in some manner or form? Who was it that was involved in selling me these ideas as being real and true to life?" Bring that person into the temple to stand before you. Speak to them. Tell them you are no longer willing to carry these beliefs, these feelings and behaviors, that make you forget your real task in life, your real purpose; that make you forget your Soul and the wisdom that it carries to light your way to truth. Give back this energy now. Perhaps this person or this society was attaching this energy to you through the feeling of loyalty: "You have to be loyal to me. It is only right." Maybe the merchant said, "You have to sell, you have to make money, you have to survive." Or the sailor said, "You have to work until you are exhausted and you drop, and it is all about survival." And maybe the king said, the king of the earth, "Yes do all that, because it is all for me after all. I take it to glorify myself."

Give back these energies to whoever was involved in your life that taught you this way. And tell them they can give this back to the king of the earth, to the merchant and to the sailor, if they choose. Give the energies back now. And at the count of three, taking Archangel Michael's sword of light, cut this connection of loyalty to this way of life. One two, three, CUT! And breathe deeply. Feel the Christ filling you with the golden healing light of wisdom as the king, the merchant, and the sailor are taken by Archangel Michael into a great lake of fire and dissolved in the light, and let whoever was involved go to a place of healing and peace. Breathe deeply.

And as you breathe, coming into the temple of transformation is the Harlot of Babylon riding the scarlet-colored beast. She is dressed in scarlet and purple, and her arms and body are filled with gold and jewels. She holds in her hands a golden cup filled with dirt and mud, and she proclaims herself queen of the world. Seven crowns are on her head, and the ten powers of the distorted Sephiroth of the Tree of Life surround her. All the vices are with her. Look at her, the false pride and passion, the arrogance.

And now, ask this question, "Who in my life represented this energy in some manner, the energy of self-gratification, narcissistic love, sexual abuse, selfishness. Who was it? Who tried to teach me that this is the way of love?" Let this person enter the temple and stand before you. Look at them; speak to them. Tell them, "I can't carry this for you anymore. I can't be loyal to your way of life. I need to be free, to learn love." Give back whatever you have carried for them, the greed, the selfishness, self-absorption, the narcissism, self-gratification, whatever you are holding of that energy, the sexual abuse if it happened to you, being treated as an object of desire. Whatever it might be, give it back, every bit of it now. And tell this person they can also send it back to wherever they received it, from the Harlot. And now, at the count of three, let us cut this cord with Archangel Michael's sword of light. One, two, three, CUT! Breathe deeply.

Feel Mary Magdalene filling you with her rose-colored light of love. She is the bride, and the Christ is the bridegroom. Just let the Harlot of Babylon move into the lake of fire as Archangel Michael moves this energy out. Feel the Christ and Saint Mary Magdalene, as they fill you with their light, as Mary Magdalene takes your feet, sending her fiery light of devotion to God through you, her passion for God as it flows up your body, rose-pink light. And now the Christ takes your head and sends down the golden light of wisdom and love, love for God and love for the bride. And feel these energies meeting in your heart. Feel above you, to your left, Archangel Tzafkiel, and above you, to your right, Archangel Ratziel as they pour their divine love into you. With every breath, feel this energy pouring into your crown chakra and through all your chakras as love and wisdom come together in you. As the bride and bridegroom, wisdom and love, mind and heart merge in you. And feel yourself becoming clothed in a white linen gown. And feel yourself holding in your hands a beautiful white lily flower.

Now the Virgin Mary in a turquoise-blue light comes to your back and gently touches you, touching you with her grace, filling you with her grace and mercy. And let her grace and mercy flow through all of your bodies, all the way to your core. Her grace and mercy is flowing through your physical body, your astral body, your causal body—your body of memories—and your mental body, your instinctual mind, and into your Soul, as you become the pure light of love and wisdom, the purity of the lily, the grace of God.

Now feel yourself surrounded by all the great archangels as they support you with their holy spiritual energy. And into the temple comes a great white horse with a rider wearing a golden crown, and the rider's eyes are focused with a great fire, and the rider holds in his hands a double-edged sword. And feel the great spiritual power in this image as this energy flows into you, for nothing can hold you back from your spiritual destiny, your destiny as bride of the Lamb. You are the Soul seeking union in God. Feel the great energy of the horse and rider touching you. And as you kneel on you knees in prayer, with your head bowed in humility toward the earth, feel the rider touching each of your shoulders with his sword, preparing you for the next step of your journey, your initiation to the light of trueness and faithfulness to your True Self within. Let this energy enter you.

And the Virgin Mary—Sophia—supports you from behind. And say now, "I Am the Soul. I Am a spark of God. I exist because of God's love for me. I Am. I Am." And each time you say "I Am," feel the old energy of the collective memories and traumas of past incarnations falling away. Beginning now, "I Am." First incarnation of the past falls away. "I Am." Second incarnation falls and is transformed. "I Am." Third incarnation falls and is transformed. "I Am." Fourth incarnation falls and is transformed. "I Am." Fifth incarnation of the past falls away and is transformed. "I Am." Sixth incarnation is now, and it is ready to fall to the past, and it falls away now into the lake of fire and is transformed. Breathe deeply. And as you breathe, one more step remains to be taken.

Feel Archangel Michael protecting you as the dragon enters the temple. Now see Archangel Michael chaining the dragon, and raising his sword to cut your second chakra away from the dragon. One, two, three, CUT! Breathe deeply.

As Archangel Michael takes the dragon to the bottomless pit, the deep subconscious of the collective, feel the light of Gabriel, Sandalfon, Raphael, Hanael, Michael, Kamael, Tzadkiel, Tzafkiel, Ratziel, and Metatron filling you with the light of transformation. Feel the peace descending from heaven, for the real meaning of the Apocalypse is the peace and stillness of Spirit. Feel the peace filling all your chakras. In your seventh chakra, it brings illumination and inspiration and divine purpose. In your sixth chakra, it brings divine vision and the light of wisdom. In your fifth chakra, it brings the words of truth and the communication of love. And in the fourth chakra, it brings divine love and compassion and forgiveness. In the third chakra, it brings a spiritually directed will, real courage and strength; and in your second chakra, joy, celebration, connection, emotional attunement to all life, and the happiness of your Soul. And in your first chakra, it brings a sacred connection to the earth and abundance. Hear the words, "Peace be with you in all your centers of awareness. Peace be on the earth. Amen." Breathe deeply.

And feel yourself gently leaving the temple, dissolving it behind you, giving thanks to the Christ and Saint Mary Magdalene and all the great archangels—especially Michael, Tzafkiel, and Ratziel—and to the Divine Mother. And slowly begin to become aware of your physical body, stretch yourself, and rub your hands, Massage your face and ears and shoulders.

Chapter 19 of Revelation

The Dawning of Self-Realization and the Seventh Chorus

> 1: And after these things I heard a great voice of much people in heaven, saying, Alleluia; Salvation, and glory, and honour, and power, unto the Lord our God:
>
> 2: For true and righteous are his judgments: for he hath judged the great whore, which did corrupt the earth with her fornication, and hath avenged the blood of his servants at her hand.

The seventh and final chorus from the world of the supernal triad of Keter, Binah, and Chokmah sings its joy to the Spirit of God. The "great whore" is the egotism that has now been fully revealed and unveiled for its illusions. The "earth" is the human personality, and "fornication" is the living out of external desire through the ego's false attachment to outer forms in its separation from Spirit. The initiate's purified Soul ("his servants") has been freed of its suffering ("the blood") at the hands of its egotism.

> 3: And again they said, Alleluia. And her smoke rose up for ever and ever.

The word *Alleluia* in the Aramaic language that Jesus spoke translated to *Alaha Hu*. According to Daskalos, this mantra or word of praise means "God in manifestation, who is": God of manifestation and God of Beingness as one. The word suggests the union of the Sephiroth of the Tree of Life, anticipating the holy or sacred marriage of the initiate's Soul with Spirit. The purified etheric doubles and corresponding three bodies of the initiate are now ready to reflect this self-realization consciousness, where heaven and earth meet in spiritual unity and wholeness—the arrival into Atzilut and spiritual resurrection while in the physical body existence.

> 4: And the four and twenty elders and the four beasts fell down and worshipped God that sat on the throne, saying, Amen; Alleluia.

As the initiate approaches spiritual self-awakening, the 24 elders from stage 1 at the beginning of Revelation—the revelation, or coming of the light—now reappear at the end of stage 3—the final destruction of personal egotism and the three faces of the ego's instinctual desires. The "four beasts" in this verse represent the fourfold nature of the human being—spiritual, mental, emotional and physical—that has now surrendered to God.

> 5: *And a voice came out of the throne, saying, Praise our God, all ye his servants, and ye that fear him, both small and great.*
>
> 6: *And I heard as it were the voice of a great multitude, and as the voice of many waters, and as the voice of mighty thunderings, saying, Alleluia: for the Lord God omnipotent reigneth.*

A messenger of the supernal triad of Spirit speaks to the initiate, reminding the initiate to cultivate constant mindfulness, or self-awareness, in all aspects of life, "both small and great." Mother Teresa once shared that it is not possible to do great things in life, only small things with great love. We are only passing through this schoolhouse on our way home. By recognizing the power and purpose of creation in God's agenda for humanity, we can bring the best of ourselves to every situation and challenge in life. We are here to learn to love and be loved.

> 7: *Let us be glad and rejoice, and give honour to him: for the marriage of the Lamb is come, and his wife hath made herself ready.*

The "Lamb" represents the Christ Self, or bridegroom, who awaits his union with "his wife"—the Soul (bride), the initiate who is now prepared for the sacred marriage of Spirit and Soul.

> 8: *And to her was granted that she should be arrayed in fine linen, clean and white: for the fine linen is the righteousness of saints.*

The initiate's personality—consisting of the mental, emotional, and physical bodies—has been purified and has become in the likeness of the etheric doubles of each body. This is symbolized by "fine linen, clean and white." The "righteousness of the saints" connotes the holiness, the sacredness, of each of the three purified bodies with their respective etheric doubles. According to Pryse, the word *linen* is "bussus"—a fine cloth of yellow color representing the auric color of a saintly man.[27]

> 9: *And he saith unto me, Write, Blessed are they which are called unto the marriage supper of the Lamb. And he saith unto me, These are the true sayings of God.*
>
> 10: *And I fell at his feet to worship him. And he said unto me, See thou do it not: I am thy fellow servant, and of thy brethren that have the testimony of Jesus: worship God: for the testimony of Jesus is the spirit of prophecy.*

The experience of divine union ("the marriage supper of the Lamb") can only be received in the deep state of meditation when all bodies—the physical senses, emotions, and thoughts—are in abeyance, stilled. In deep silence and inner stillness, the peace and inner voice of God can be heard. In this consciousness of union, God's purpose for human life reveals itself. The temptation of the initiate is to worship this experience and Source, but he or she is advised to remain humble as all things and guidance can only come through the spirit of humility. Daskalos was often asked if he was a guru, an outer figure of authority representing the seeker's true self. He would say "I prefer to be seen as a brother guide." In the same Spirit, the seeker is advised not to worship or praise the messenger, but to recognize "I am thy fellow servant, and of thy brethren that have the testimony of Jesus"—I am one of many who carry the Spirit of the Christ in community with others. Hold your worship for the highest—"worship God" only.

> **11:** *And I saw heaven opened, and behold a white horse; and he that sat upon him was called Faithful and True, and in righteousness he doth judge and make war.*

The "white horse" from Revelation 6:2, the opening of the seals—Yesod in Yetzirah (second chakra)—has reappeared. Sitting upon this pure source of energy is the initiate's Soul, "Faithful and True." The Soul was, is, and will always be eternal, faultless, and faithful; it embodies truth itself. The Soul is indestructible and untainted in its essence as a holy spark of God. Here the initiate's Soul is the warrior of peace, with the power of spiritual discernment ever ready to bring truth to all experiences, whether they are mental, emotional, or physical in nature.

> **12:** *His eyes were as a flame of fire, and on his head were many crowns; and he had a name written, that no man knew, but he himself.*

The initiate has full spiritual vision ("his eyes were as a flame of fire") and has acquired mastery over the various bodies and inner planes ("on his head were many crowns"). Having "a name written, that no man knew, but he himself" refers to the initiate's spiritual name and self-realized state that make him (or her) a citizen of the inner worlds, unseen by the profane. Throughout Saint John's vision, the various archangels make their appearance. The one whose "eyes were as a flame of fire" is Archangel Tzadkiel (the influence of Jupiter, God's blessings and grace). Here the self-realized Soul is at-one-ment with the holy ideas of the archangels.

> **13:** *And he was clothed with a vesture dipped in blood: and his name is called The Word of God.*

The soul of the initiate carries the divine love ("blood") of God and divine will ("The Word of God").

> *14: And the armies which were in heaven followed him upon white horses, clothed in fine linen, white and clean.*

All in the spiritual hierarchy ("the armies which were in heaven") are consciously in contact with the initiate, supporting his or her continual journey to Christ Consciousness and service to the Divine. This hierarchy includes the archangels, saints, and Ascended Masters and the divine ideas and qualities of the Soul's essence.

> *15: And out of his mouth goeth a sharp sword, that with it he should smite the nations: and he shall rule them with a rod of iron: and he treadeth the winepress of the fierceness and wrath of Almighty God.*

In Saint John's vision, "out of his mouth goeth a sharp sword" refers to Archangel Kamael (the Mars influence, power and rulership). The expressions of the Soul's essence in Din (peace) and in Hesed (love) are the dual qualities indicating mastery and service and a spirit of peace and love, whereas in Beriyah the Soul is separated in its awareness from the holy ideas the archangels hold. Here the Soul is in union with these qualities. It is also interesting to consider that, in the Kabbalah, these qualities are located at the level of the fifth chakra, where we are today in our collective consciousness.

The "rod of iron" suggests attainment of spiritual willpower, which is also a quality of the fifth center, and "the winepress of the fierceness and wrath" suggests the never-ending stream of life-force or energy that is accessible now that the Soul has reached the positive power states of love and peace. On the Hawkins scale,[28] level 500 is love and level 600 is peace—both very high levels of energy on the scale of human consciousness.

> *16: And he hath on his vesture and on his thigh a name written, KING OF KINGS, AND LORD OF LORDS.*

The "name written" indicates the self-realization that brings omnipotence, omniscience, and self-mastery, inwardly and outwardly. The Soul has returned home and shares in the consciousness of the Source.

> *17: And I saw an angel standing in the sun; and he cried with a loud voice, saying to all the fowls that fly in the midst of heaven, Come and gather yourselves together unto the supper of the great God;*

The angel "standing in the sun" is Archangel Michael in Tiferet who banished the dragon from the heavens. He calls forth "to all the fowls that fly in the midst of heaven" the powers of reason and thought and introspection to de-energize the negative ego elementals of perverted instinctual desires.

> *18: That ye may eat the flesh of kings, and the flesh of captains, and the flesh of mighty men, and the flesh of horses, and of them that sit on them, and the flesh of all men, both free and bond, both small and great.*

Now you, the initiate, "may eat" (de-energize) the fixed thoughts that have ruled you ("the flesh of kings"), the negative emotional desires that dominate you ("the flesh of captains"), the physical sensations that addict and enslave you through their illusionary power ("the flesh of mighty men"), the instinctual life energies or lust that you have been perverted by ("the flesh of horses"), and the false qualities of ego-pride and strength, false humility, and false authority based on image and outer performance.

> *19: And I saw the beast, and the kings of the earth, and their armies, gathered together to make war against him that sat on the horse, and against his army.*

> *20: And the beast was taken, and with him the false prophet that wrought miracles before him, with which he deceived them that had received the mark of the beast, and them that worshipped his image. These both were cast alive into a lake of fire burning with brimstone.*

The lower desire-mind of fixed beliefs—"the beast," or perverted social instincts—and "the false prophet"—the perverted survival instincts of worshiping material illusions of glamour, idolatry, and maya—are "cast alive into a lake of fire burning with brimstone." The "lake of fire" is the lower astral world from which these negative elementals originate and to which they return by co-vibration when they are no longer held through ego-attachment by the enlightened Soul.

> *21: And the remnant were slain with the sword of him that sat upon the horse, which sword proceeded out of his mouth: and all the fowls were filled with their flesh.*

All the remaining imperfections are illuminated by the rider of the white horse, or self-realized Soul, through the power of direct cognition and intuition. "The sword of him that sat upon the horse" is the self-realized Soul's wisdom and qualities of essence that immediately remove ignorance through awareness of one's true Self.

Chapter 20 of Revelation

The Threefold Domains of Consciousness

Chapter 20 of Saint John's Revelation deals with the relationship and interaction between the threefold domains of consciousness: (1) super-consciousness, the supernal triad, (2) consciousness, the moral triad, and (3) subconsciousness, the action triad.

> *1: And I saw an angel come down from heaven, having the key of the bottomless pit and a great chain in his hand.*

An "angel coming down from heaven" suggests the illuminating truth and intuition of Archangel Michael, the bringer of truth and light, the great defender of heaven. Psychologically, the angel represents the divine intuitions of the super-consciousness of the Soul that holds the power ("the key") to regulate and limit ("chain") the flow of destructive subconscious elementals from the subconsciousness of the personality and its influences from the lower astral plane. The super-conscious (transpersonal) self now has the power to restrict these influences. The "bottomless pit" can be taken as a kind of abyss in the lower astral realm that contains all the collective negative elementals and their seed desires, or passions (vices), for humanity.

> *2: And he laid hold on the dragon, that old serpent, which is the Devil, and Satan, and bound him a thousand years,*

The "dragon" represents the contaminated subconscious instinctual desire-body of the relational/sexual instinct. Let us consider that the "dragon, that old serpent"—the source of worldly desire and separation—is the sum total of negative elementals below 200 on the Hawkins scale[29] (pride, anger, desire, fear, grief, apathy, guilt, and shame) that dominate the subconscious personality and keep it imprisoned at the lower energy levels. As long as there is nothing to counter these lower energies, they run rampant, manifesting physically from the lower astral plane.

The super-conscious spiritual power of an enlightened being—1,000 on the Hawkins scale—would counterbalance, subdue, and neutralize the collective negative energy of millions or billions of lower-vibrating individuals who are living subconsciously, thereby keeping their negative tendencies from manifesting in the physical world. Such an "angel" of super-consciousness could easily bind the negative collective state of humanity—"the Devil, and Satan," the illusions of maya for "a thousand years."

The number 1,000 is 10^3 and represents completeness. One who has reached the super-conscious state (the level of 1,000 energetically) could symbolize the lasting power of the self-realized or God-realized Soul that binds the negative forces in the lower astral world from manifesting physically "for a thousand years." The iconic pictures of Christ banishing the devil to the bottomless pit are similar to his actions at the time of crucifixion and resurrection. In psychological terms, the personal ego can no longer entrap, hijack, and influence the Soul's impulses and intuitions in the three bodies—mental, emotional, and physical.

> *3: And cast him into the bottomless pit, and shut him up, and set a seal upon him, that he should deceive the nations no more, till the thousand years should be fulfilled: and after that he must be loosed a little season.*

After self-realization, the super-consciousness of the Soul uses its conscious mind and its divine ideas to discern and not allow negative subconscious drives to influence or direct the initiate into negative conditions mentally, emotionally and physically. When subconscious elementals arise, they are dealt with through continual self-inquiry and self-introspection, which builds more conscious self-awareness. Therefore, the loosing of the lower energies for "a little season" takes place as a natural consequence of living in the schoolhouse of learning to further progress the initiate. As Daskalos said, we can either grow through the "whips of destiny" (that is, subconsciously) or consciously.

> *4: And I saw thrones, and they sat upon them, and judgment was given unto them: and I saw the souls of them that were beheaded for the witness of Jesus, and for the word of God, and which had not worshipped the beast, neither his image, neither had received his mark upon their foreheads, or in their hands; and they lived and reigned with Christ a thousand years.*

Each body—mental, causal, astral, and physical—is now under the dominion of the super-conscious awareness of the Soul and remains in the state of harmony of the Christ Light until new subconscious material emerges for examination and to be neutralized.

> *5: But the rest of the dead lived not again until the thousand years were finished. This is the first resurrection.*

Subconscious elementals cannot dominate, for the Soul is now guiding.

> 6: *Blessed and holy is he that hath part in the first resurrection: on such the second death hath no power, but they shall be priests of God and of Christ, and shall reign with him a thousand years.*

The "first resurrection" occurs as the self-realization experience while in the physical body. The "second death," the dropping of the physical body, will not impact the Soul's unfolding journey, for the lower astral plane which the Soul will pass through on its journey into the higher dimensions after physical death has already been reviewed and mastered and will not slow down the Soul's journey of ascension. When life-review is done while in the body, the afterlife transition is done in an already enlightened state; "they shall be priests of God and of Christ, and shall reign with him a thousand years" indicates that the Soul will remain attuned to Christ Consciousness and the higher energy levels and planes of afterlife existence. Psychologically, we could say that the experience of self-realization in the supernal triad in Keter, Binah, and Chokmah brings a period of extended grace, *i.e.*, "a thousand years," as being in higher states of realization can be likened to being outside time and space as we know it in the physical world. Daskalos, for example, indicated that the after-death state of time of the Soul feels extended over physical time. Because the astral state is so much more intense and vibrating far faster than physical time is perceived, it is conceivable that, subjectively, 1,000 astral years is roughly equivalent to 100 earthly years.

> 7: *And when the thousand years are expired, Satan shall be loosed out of his prison,*
>
> 8: *And shall go out to deceive the nations which are in the four quarters of the earth, Gog and Magog, to gather them together to battle: the number of whom is as the sand of the sea.*

The people of Magog, like the locusts (Revelation 9:3), represent collective negative elementals that have no "I" consciousness. They are false collective values that create guilt and lower consciousness, and they are numerous ("the number of whom is as the sand of the sea"). All of these influences are in the collective unconscious mind of humanity, what Jung called the collective shadow.[30] These subconscious elementals attack all four bodies—the mental, the causal, the emotional, and the physical—bringing suffering and illusion to the four-fold personality, "the four quarters of the earth."

> 9: *And they went up on the breadth of the earth, and compassed the camp of the saints about, and the beloved city: and fire came down from God out of heaven, and devoured them.*

The subconscious elementals emerge in the personality ("the earth") and disrupt the Soul's super-conscious control of its conscious mind ("the camp of the saints about, and the beloved city"). Immediate attention to the Divine brings down the higher thought energy—the wisdom of divine ideas—from super-consciousness ("and fire came down from God out of heaven"), and the lower-energy elementals are "devoured"—de-energized and neutralized by the higher divine ideas of wisdom.

> **10: And the devil that deceived them was cast into the lake of fire and brimstone, where the beast and the false prophet are, and shall be tormented day and night for ever and ever.**

With regards to "the lake of fire," Lansdowne's idea of a threefold, or triple, light is worth exploring.[31] According to Lansdowne, the light of God has three components: (1) the infinite light of Absolute Infinite Beingness (the super-conscious light), (2) the light of the Soul focused in the mind (the conscious mind), and (3) the light of the personality (the personal self). All three, when blended, create the "lake of fire." The "lake" is the Soul, "fire" is thoughts of God, and "brimstone" is the light of the personality. When the power of this three-fold light transforms the perverted instincts—the beast and the pseudo-lamb—they are forever scrutinized through the power of mindfulness. Both "the beast and the false prophet" have already been banished, and now the "devil that deceived them" is being scrutinized ("tormented") and overcome.

> **11: And I saw a great white throne, and him that sat on it, from whose face the earth and the heaven fled away; and there was found no place for them.**

The "great white throne" is the supernal or super-conscious light of God's heart—the seed of Chokmah, the Divine all-wise Father, and Archangel Ratziel in Beriyah is the personification of this great light. The infinite light absorbs all form and is formless by nature, a pure light generator of infinite grace and blessings that contains no duality.

> **12: And I saw the dead, small and great, stand before God; and the books were opened: and another book was opened, which is the book of life: and the dead were judged out of those things which were written in the books, according to their works.**

The Divine Mother, Binah, holds the secrets of creation, and Archangel Tzafkiel holds "the book of life" of each Soul. The book of life holds all karmic records of the Soul, including its purpose and gifts and its tasks on earth in each incarnation. This book is like a divine standard by which all one's thoughts, feelings, and actions can be "judged"—evaluated by the super-conscious transpersonal self, the infinite "I Am" of self-knowledge. This is a kind of life-review in the afterlife and also a review of all one's ongoing experiences and choices in life while in the physical body.

> *13: And the sea gave up the dead which were in it; and death and hell delivered up the dead which were in them: and they were judged every man according to their works.*

The "sea gave up the dead which were in it" refers to the astral or emotional body giving up all its negative elementals, and "death and hell delivered up the dead which were in them" refers to all the subconscious emotions that are brought forth for the self-conscious Soul to evaluate. The Soul decides on their value under the guidance of the super-conscious Spirit of God.

> *14: And death and hell were cast into the lake of fire. This is the second death.*

All the negative elementals—pride, anger, desire, fear, grief, apathy, guilt, and shame—are "cast into the lake of fire." The negative desires that have been repressed, held in the subconscious, are eliminated. Though this process happens in the after-death state as a life-review process in which all negative and unnecessary astral elementals are cast into the abyss from which they arose, leaving the spiritualized and higher vibrational energies of the Soul to continue upward, this same process takes place in the initiate's self-realization process while in the physical body.

> *15: And whosoever was not found written in the book of life was cast into the lake of fire.*

All lower thoughts, emotions, and behaviors that are found unworthy—that is, of lower vibration and inconsistent with the Soul's self-knowing (truth)—are released. The fifth initiation, self-realization, is now complete. The self-realized Soul can now determine its own destiny. The resurrection is complete.

MEDITATION JOURNEY

Close your eyes. Relax your body. Put your attention on your feet. Feel the healing white light as it flows into your feet and legs, moving into your thighs, your hips and pelvic area, moving up into your abdomen, your chest and your heart. The healing light flows over your shoulders and down your arms, to your hands and fingers, into your neck, your head, and face. Feel the healing light flowing through you. And now feel yourself with your healing hands of light, white healing hands, building a large circular disc on the ground before you.

And on this disk build a beautiful temple of white light. Stand at the entrance of the temple. Feel the Christ coming to greet you and Saint Mary Magdalene. And feel them taking the hands of your physical body, reaching into the hands of your physical body, and taking the hands of your purified astral body, the radiant body of the first resurrection. Feel them taking the hands of your astral body and lifting your astral body out of your physical body. Feel your radiant astral body, your astral body full of light, and feel the saints surrounding you. Feel this radiance of your first resurrection, this great light and energy. Stand at the entrance of the temple.

And now feel the Christ and Saint Mary Magdalene as they reach into your astral body. And they take the hands of your causal body, your memory body, that also contains your mental/intellectual body and your instinctual mind. And feel them lifting you into this causal body, full of radiant light with an aura of orange, blue, and violet expanding outwardly from your heart and filling the space around you. Feel yourself in your combined mental body—causal, orange; higher mental, blue; and instinctual, violet—and let them take you to a white throne that sits in the middle of your temple as you emanate these three colors of orange, blue, and violet. And let yourself sit on the white throne.

As you sit on the white throne in the temple, breathe deeply. Feel the pure light emanating from this combined body of memory, intellect, and instinctive mind—orange, blue, and violet—a body of three colors, three layers. And feel yourself sitting on the throne, at the center of an equilateral cross on the floor of the temple, with Mary Magdalene on your left, Jesus Christ on your right, and above you, levitating on your left, the great Archangel Tzafkiel, representative of the Divine Mother. Tzafkiel is the holder of all the memories in your life and in all your incarnations. And levitating above you, on your right, is Archangel Ratziel, carrying the great wisdom of the Divine Father in the light—a never ending light of divine blessings—showing you the meaning of everything that has happened in your life and what you must take with you, as you rise up into the solar or Soul body, of your life experiences. And the Divine Mother shows you all the memories that are critical for your understanding. She carries all the pictures from your lives. And the Divine Father carries the wisdom and light of blessing that heals the pictures. And he brings to you the understanding of how the beast—the lower desire-mind—and how the dragon—the emotional images—and how the pseudo-lamb—the material instincts—have all served you, served your Soul, as part of the negative force that works for the Lamb to polish you as a Soul and promote you toward self-mastery, and to bring you into the light of your solar body, the Soul, and into the Christ itself. For according to the Law of Unity, all things serve God.

Facing the entrance on the bottom right quadrant of your temple appears a child that contains all the energies of your incarnation as a child. Look at this child. What illusions does this child carry from the beast, the dragon, and the pseudo-lamb? And what does this child need to be released from in its illusions, to bring itself back into the light of Spirit, to embrace the Divine? How has this child served the beast, the dragon, and the pseudo-lamb out of fear in its separation from God? Look at the child with neutrality, with objectivity, with the acceptance and courage that you hold in the heart of your Higher Self, as Saint Mary and the Christ support your heart. And look before you, and say to these three forces, "Look at this child. You have taught the child what it is not, so that it can learn who it really is." Let the Christ Light into your heart and the spiritual sun begins to emerge. And let Archangel Michael stay in the connection with the child, allowing the great solar light to come down through Archangel Michael, and through your heart as you sit on the throne, and into the child as you and the child say to the three forces, the beast, the dragon and the pseudo-lamb, "It is done. I Am the Soul. I Am a spark of God. I exist because of God's love for me, and deep inside all of us there is God."

Now see, within each of these three, the golden light of God beginning to emerge and fill them. Let the beast transform into wisdom. Let the dragon transform into divine love, and let the pseudo-lamb transform into the spiritual will. And let them go. And if you wish, Archangel Michael can raise his sword and cut the old residues, the old contracts you have had with all three—the beast, the dragon, the pseudo-lamb—that have assisted the child in this learning process. One, two, three, CUT! Breathe deeply. Let these transformed energies go to the light. And take the child back, bringing the child into your Christ heart. The essence of this child is love. Allow only the positive, enlightened elements to enter. And as you breathe, take in the love, the wisdom, and the will of courage, the great gifts of the three forces in this transformation, the gifts behind the illusions of the beast, the dragon, and the pseudo-lamb.

Breathe deeply, looking toward the upper-right quadrant before you in the temple. Call in the composite adolescent from all your lifetimes. What illusions is this composite adolescent from all your lifetimes carrying? What is it carrying as illusion? Look behind it at the beast, the dragon, and the pseudo-lamb who were instructed to influence it through this illusion and maintain its separation from God. What has it carried from them? From your throne and your Christ Love speak to these three: "Thank you for being the illusion that supports the reality of the Lamb, the Christ. You have done your job. It is done." And see the great solar light of God from above flowing through Michael and through your Christ Love into the adolescent. See it flow into these three aspects of illusion, transforming the energy of the beast into wisdom, the energy of the dragon into divine love, and the energy of the pseudo-lamb into the spiritually directed will, true power.

Now feel these energies filling the adolescent—wisdom, love, and power. And together with the adolescent say, "I break all contracts with the work of the beast, the dragon, and the pseudo-lamb." Feel behind the beast Archangel Michael's solar light, transforming it from inside out into wisdom; from inside out, transforming the dragon into love; and the pseudo-lamb, from inside out, transforming it into spiritual power. Feel the same energies within the adolescent, the belly center of spiritual power, a golden light, the heart center of divine love in golden light, and the head center of divine wisdom in golden light. And at the count of three let Archangel Michael cut any residue of illusion or contracts that you had with the illusions of the beast, the dragon, and the pseudo-lamb that only separated you from your Christ Light, from the Lamb. At the count of three, let us cut these contracts. One, two, three, CUT! Breathe deeply. Let them go to the light. And receive the adolescent into your Christ heart, as you received the child into the Christ Light.

Breathe in deeply and, as you breathe, turn to the upper-left quadrant of the temple. And there call in the composite adult from all your incarnations. What appears for you in the temple? And what does this adult still hold in the way of illusion of the beast, the dragon, and the pseudo-lamb for your adult life? Feel the spiritual light in your heart, the Christ Light. What does the adult carry? Look behind it at the beast, the dragon, and the pseudo-lamb and feel the great light of God from above pouring down through Archangel Michael into your Christ heart on the throne, into the adult, and to these three illusions. And say to them, "Thank you for serving this adult in my lifetimes. I don't need you any longer to serve this adult. It is done. I Am the Soul. I Am a spark of God. I exist because of God's love for me. I Am. I Am. I Am."

And let this great light of God flow in and, from the core of the beast, transform the beast into the light of wisdom. Let it transform the dragon into the light of divine love, and let the light transform the pseudo-lamb into spiritual power and spiritual will. And feel in the belly center of the adult the great spiritual power, the golden light activating. And in the heart center of the adult, divine love is activating the spiritual sun, and in the head center, the golden light of wisdom is activating the spiritual sun. And with Archangel Michael's support, let us cut any residues of illusion that the adult may hold and any contract that it has held with these three forces of illusion to support its evolution and growth. One, two, three, CUT! Breathe deeply. Let the three forces go to the light. Embrace the adult within your Christ Light on the throne, and feel how the Christ child, the Christ adolescent, and the Christ adult are all a part of you. Feel your inner bodies growing more and more as the light of the causal, mental, and etheric bodies begin to transform into the solar body of Christ Light. Slowly, slowly the blue aura, the violet aura, and the orange aura transform into a golden aura.

At the lower-left quadrant of the temple, call in the composite energies of all your elderly lifetime memories, of the lifetimes in which you experienced yourself in your old age—the composite image, the composite memory—and behind this image, see the illusion of the beast, the dragon, and the pseudo-lamb. What is this elderly adult carrying in its body as an expression of this illusion? Look into the eyes of the elderly adult and speak to the beast, the dragon, and the pseudo-lamb as the great solar light of God flows down through Archangel Michael into your Christ heart, into the elderly adult, and into the beast, the dragon, and the pseudo-lamb. And just say to them, "Thank you for your work. We don't need you any longer. It is done. The work is done. You may leave now." And feel the beast transforming from inside out, through the golden light of God into divine wisdom; the dragon transforming from inside out into divine love; and the pseudo-lamb transforming from inside out into the light of spiritual power and spiritual will. And feel the same energies in the elderly adult, the belly center transforming into spiritual power and spiritual will, the heart center into divine love, and the head center into divine wisdom. And with Archangel Michael's sword of light, cut any residues that may still exist of the illusion of the beast, the dragon, and the pseudo-lamb. One, two, three, CUT!

Now let them go to the light. Feel the elderly adult filled with spiritual power, love, and wisdom coming back to you. And simply say, "I break all laws, vows, and contracts with the illusion of the beast, the illusion of the dragon, and the illusion of the pseudo-lamb, the lower worlds of existence. I embrace the higher teachings of the Soul and the Spirit of God and the inner light, to show me divine power, divine love, and divine wisdom, in every experience of my life, that I may see the unity of God." Embrace all the spiritual laws of life. Breathe deeply. As the elderly adult enters your Christ heart, all four of these phases of your life experience—the illusion of childhood, the illusion of adolescence, the illusion of adult life, and the illusion of the elderly adult phase of life—and all time and space collapse into the eternal presence of your Soul.

Now feel the Christ and Saint Mary Magdalene transforming any residue of your memory, your intellectual mind, and your instinctive mind into the solar body of the Soul. Feel a great column of light coming from the heavens above and the solar energy of God lifting you—higher, freer, lighter, freer, higher, lighter, lighter, freer, freer and higher and freer—all the way to the healing temple of light, of your Soul. Feel yourself in the Soul body, your body of solar light. And say, "I Am the soul. I exist because of God's love for me. I Am a spark of God. I Am. I Am. I Am." For the solar body is fed continuously by the solar forces of God above. And say, "I surrender to the Spirit of God, to the Holy Lamb, that I may undergo the marriage and union with my beloved Spirit. I Am. I Am. I Am." Feel the power, feel the love and the wisdom. Feel the peace. Feel the freedom. And feel the Virgin Mary, the Divine Mother, embracing you like a child, touching you with her grace and blessings, as we finish with the prayer of Daskalos:

> Absolute Infinite Beingness; God.
> Everlasting Life, Love and Mercy.
> Manifesting Yourself in Yourself,
> as the Total Wisdom and the
> Almightiness.
> Enlighten our minds to
> understand you as the Truth,
> Clean our hearts to reflect Your
> Love towards You and
> towards all other human beings.
> Amen.

Slowly, slowly feel yourself coming down the column of light in your solar body. And take on your etheric body, your intellectual mind body, your causal body of memory, taking them into your solar body, filling them with your golden light. Now, enter your astral body and physical body filling them with your golden light. You are one being, one whole. So be it. Let yourself leave the temple, dissolving it behind you, knowing you can return at any time. And slowly begin to stretch yourself a little bit, rub your hands, and massage your face, your eyes, ears, and neck, and return.

Atzilut – Spiritual – Movement from 4th Initiation (Crucifixion) to 5th Initiation (Resurrection)

Passage from Daat into Binah-Chokmah-Keter

Seven Vials	Seven Stars Pleiades	Qualities of Essence	Enneagram Type	Seven Archangels (Divinities)	Seven Spirit-Soul Expressions
1. Libation on the Earth (Root Chakra)	Atlas	Beingness	9	Sandalfon	Abundance, Self-sufficiency, Resourcefulness
2. Libation on the Sea (Second Chakra)	Celaeno	Power (Shakti)	8	Gabriel	Attunement, Humility, Gratitude
3. Libation on the Rivers (Third Chakra)	Taygeta	Emptiness, Pure Intelligence, Absorption	6	Hanael/Uriel	Faith, Courage
			7	Rafael	Commitment to Higher Ideals
4. Libation on the Sun (Fourth Chakra)	Electra	Joy	4	Michael	Love, Compassion
5. Libation on the Throne of the Beast (Fifth Chakra)	Maia	Love	3	Tzadkiel	Grace, Blessings
		Peace	5	Kamael	Creativity, Divine Plan in Expression
6. Libation on the River Euphrates (Sixth Chakra)	Merope	Purity	1	Ratziel	Mental Objectivity
		Kindness	2	Tzafkiel	Intuition, Reason
7. Libation poured on the Air (7th Chakra)	Alcyone	Oneness Self-Realization		Metatron	Wisdom, Inner Knowng, Oneness

Volume II, Chart 2

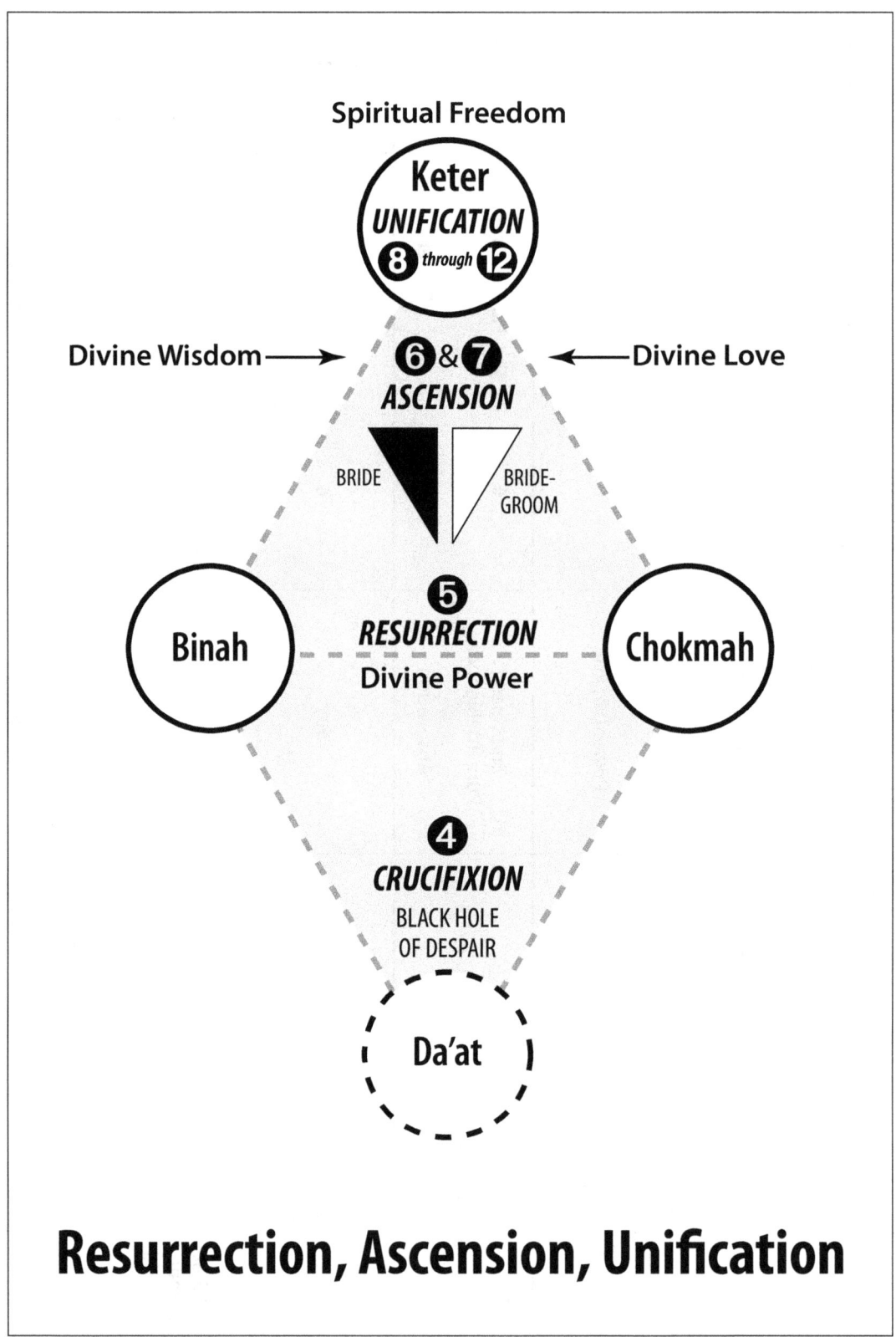

Resurrection, Ascension, Unification

Volume II, Diagram 9

Chapter 21 of Revelation

Resurrection, Ascension, and Unification

Resurrection/self-realization corresponds to the element of Spirit-Space, the transcendence of the fifth chakra (throat center). This transcendence represents the dawn of self-realization (I Am That I AM) and the inflow of supernal light transforming all levels of consciousness—full Soul awareness—and, at the same, the purification and upliftment of all the lower bodies now under the Soul's mastery. The sixth and seventh initiations (ascension/spiritual realization) is the full awakening of the brow and crown chakras (We are many, yet we are one.); it is the preparation for the divine marriage of Soul and Spirit and their union in Chokmah and Binah (holy marriage). The 8-12th initiations (unification/God-realization) are the final conscious unification of the merged bride and bridegroom with God; this is true Christhood or God-realization in chakras eight through twelve. (I AM One in the many.)

> *1: And I saw a new heaven and a new earth: for the first heaven and the first earth were passed away; and there was no more sea.*

With the transcendence of the fifth chakra, the initiate has been resurrected, reborn into a whole new state of consciousness ("a new heaven and a new earth"). The initiate now realizes there is no astral world ("the first heaven and the first earth"), only the sum total of all the collective imaginings of humanity—a function of the relative truth of the mind—that does not actually exist. Verse 1 may also relate to the prophecy of the Aquarian age. In many ways, the Piscean age was astral-dominant, preoccupied with the highs and lows of astral emotional experience. The Piscean Soul made astral emotions its learning lab and identified its experience of God through outer forms of devotional worship. Imagination ruled all. The Aquarian spirit relies more on the higher wisdom of holy ideas. Understanding God as Self and how one creates thought and imagination (consciousness), metaphysical realities are more dominant. As the external world loses its power to internal realities, so too are the preoccupations with outwardly anchored astral emotions weakened, revealing that we are at the center of all that we perceive and create.

> *2: And I John saw the holy city, new Jerusalem, coming down from God out of heaven, prepared as a bride adorned for her husband.*

The initiate, "John," witnesses the "holy city, new Jerusalem." The "holy city" the purified, awakened Soul in dynamic balance and unity consciousness—"a bride adorned for her husband"—the true androgyny of Soul. Here, alchemy of the two polarities is taking place in the supernal triad of Chokmah, Binah, and Keter. The bridal city is the initiate himself in the solar (or Soul) body, resurrected and ascended. This begins the sixth initiation as described in the introductory paragraph of this chapter where the merging of male-female aspects is taking place in the brow chakra between Chokmah and Binah. This process is also related anatomically to the pineal gland in the crown chakra and the pituitary gland located in the region of the sixth chakra, making energetic connection.

> *3: And I heard a great voice out of heaven saying, Behold, the tabernacle of God is with men, and he will dwell with them, and they shall be his people, and God himself shall be with them, and be their God.*

The "great voice out of heaven" is the Soul speaking to the "men"—the personality of thought, feelings, and actions. The purified Soul is saying that "they shall be his people"—in other words, all aspects of the personality are under the Soul's control.

> *4: And God shall wipe away all tears from their eyes; and there shall be no more death, neither sorrow, nor crying, neither shall there be any more pain: for the former things are passed away.*

No longer is the initiate in separation consciousness that caused desire, suffering, limitation, and the three bodies' host of illusions that veiled the Soul's eternal identity. All this has passed.

> *5: And he that sat upon the throne said, Behold, I make all things new. And he said unto me, Write: for these words are true and faithful.*

The lower self, the little "I" that has undergone many incarnations of experience, death, and rebirth in the physical body, has served its purpose in evolution and creation. The initiate is now a new being.

> *6: And he said unto me, It is done. I am Alpha and Omega, the beginning and the end. I will give unto him that is athirst of the fountain of the water of life freely.*

The eternal, omnipotent, ever-present God who made his appearance in Revelation 1:8 returns and proclaims the spiritual journey is complete ("It is done"). The Source guided the initiate through all the trials and tribulations of Asiyah,

Yetzirah, and Beriyah to awaken to "the fountain of the water of life" of Atzilut, the initiate's rebirth as a complete spiritual being. The "water of life" represents all the qualities and essence of the purified Soul unified with God: Beingness, power, emptiness, absorption, joy, love, peace, purity, kindness, and oneness (unity).

> *7: He that overcometh shall inherit all things; and I will be his God, and he shall be my son.*

Ascension is now underway. The initiate has entered his or her divine home in Keter, Chokmah, and Binah, returning like the prodigal son and receiving his wholeness and rightful place in God's kingdom. When Christ said, "I and the Father are one," he was expressing the wisdom of this spiritual reality.

> *8: But the fearful, and unbelieving, and the abominable, and murderers, and whoremongers, and sorcerers, and idolaters, and all liars, shall have their part in the lake which burneth with fire and brimstone: which is the second death.*

Yet while living in the body, one must remain ever mindful of fear, doubt, perversions, hatred, lust, misuse of psychic power, and exoteric worship of the world, for when these energies arise in consciousness, they will be cast into the lower astral abyss through the supernal light of God Consciousness (Keter, Chokmah, Binah).

> *9: And there came unto me one of the seven angels which had the seven vials full of the seven last plagues, and talked with me, saying, Come hither, I will shew thee the bride, the Lamb's wife.*

The "bride" is the purified Soul, while the "Lamb" is the Spirit, the Christ Consciousness of the initiate.

> *10: And he carried me away in the spirit to a great and high mountain, and shewed me that great city, the holy Jerusalem, descending out of heaven from God,*

Here the ascension (the sixth and seventh initiations) is taking place in the brow chakra—"a great and high mountain"—and the initiate is being shown "that great city, the holy Jerusalem"—the unified state of mystical marriage, the union of male-female polarities, which is now coming from Keter (Adam Kadmon) to Atzilut (Chokmah-Binah).

> *11: Having the glory of God: and her light was like unto a stone most precious, even like a jasper stone, clear as crystal;*

The light of John's Soul is illuminated with the radiance of Atzilut, "clear as crystal." The "jasper stone" is believed to have been the opal stone, which is basically white in color, the color of the radiant light of Atzilut.

> **12:** *And had a wall great and high, and had twelve gates, and at the gates twelve angels, and names written thereon, which are the names of the twelve tribes of the children of Israel:*

All aspects of the city are a part of the city and represent the unified perfection of the Soul's divine expression. The wall of the city is considered a powerful aura (of the Soul's light) and offers protection. The number 12 represents spiritual perfection. Therefore, the "twelve gates" embody the perfect spiritual out-flowing of the initiate's service to life; the "twelve angels," the divine perfection of spiritual essence, or gifts of the Soul; and the "twelve tribes," the perfect obedience and devotion likened to the sons of Jacob, the biblical twelve tribes. The "twelve tribes" are also symbolic of the twelve astrological signs.

> **13:** *On the east three gates; on the north three gates; on the south three gates; and on the west three gates.*

The number 12 is symbolic of cosmic order, completeness, and salvation. The number 12 is the product of 3 and 4, the "three gates" of the four directions, or cardinal points, of this verse. As the third and final quaternary, 12 completes the manifestation of the divine order on earth through our conscious co-creation with God, the divine pattern of organization. The four cardinal points are the four planes of consciousness. North is the body; west, the mind; south, the emotional body; and east, the spirit. In looking at the practical meaning of the four directions, we can consider north as wisdom and understanding—the body. West is what challenges us in our growth and what we need to complete and transform—the mind. South is nurturing and sustenance—the emotions—and east is creative guidance and support—the spirit. If we think of the twelve astrology signs, three are earth, or body; three are water, or emotion; three are fire, or mind; and three are air, or spirit.

Each astrological sign has a gate through which it enters the higher light of Spirit and carries special gifts of God to give in service to life. The twelve astrological signs are symbolic of the twelve perfected personalities, yet all are part of the Soul's greater consciousness. The self-realized Soul can express all these gifts freely when called to do so, regardless of its personality traits. In Liebert's four ascending stages of adult spiritual development,[32] the fourth stage of growth (the integrated stage) expresses the Soul's essence of divine gifts in a harmony, unity, and the cosmic dance of intimacy, thought, feeling, and action in the world. This is essentially divinity in action, the unification of heaven and earth in consciousness.

One only needs to look at the lives and expression of the great spiritual masters on our planet to understand that all gifts are available to them to express in service to all when called for. They are not bound by their astrological signs or individual attributes.

> *14: And the wall of the city had twelve foundations, and in them the names of the twelve apostles of the Lamb.*

When the twelve disciples ascended to the supernal triad of Keter, Binah, and Chokmah during Pentecost, they were consciously given unity with the power of the Holy Spirit ("the Lamb") to activate all the gifts needed for their service and ministry to the world. These gifts express through the mental, emotional, and physical bodies of the "apostles"—self-realized initiates—but do not create or accumulate negative personal karmas. Their acts henceforth are karma-less, or without karma; that is, they only serve the evolutionary plan for humanity. The "wall of the city" represents divine protection in which there are "twelve foundations," the divine pattern and plan of organization for working as conscious co-creators with God.

> *15: And he that talked with me had a golden reed to measure the city, and the gates thereof, and the wall thereof.*

The "golden reed to measure the city" may indicate that it is a sacred measuring or evaluation instrument to assess to what degree "the city," the self-realized Soul, meets the standards of divine perfection.

> *16: And the city lieth foursquare, and the length is as large as the breadth: and he measured the city with the reed, twelve thousand furlongs. The length and the breadth and the height of it are equal.*

> *17: And he measured the wall thereof, an hundred and forty and four cubits, according to the measure of a man, that is, of the angel.*

According to Pryse, "the cubical city, when unfolded, becomes a cross, symbolizing the human form."[33] Numerically, it may represent the perfect divine dimensions for the perfected Soul. As numbers relate to physical dimensions, perhaps the harmonious combination of spiritual and physical traits come together in the self-realized Soul in Atzilut, "a new heaven and a new earth" of Revelation 21:1. The height of the city is "twelve thousand furlongs," and the height of the walls "an hundred and forty and four cubits." If we consider these numbers symbolically, we see that twelve thousand is 12×1000—twelve (the divine pattern) times one thousand (completeness or fulfillment) of the Divine Plan or pattern. The number 144 is 12×12.

As discussed in Volume I, Chapter 7, the divine pattern of Spirit (God Source) exists on all levels of creation and links all levels. Each level exists autonomously and yet is linked by the reflection in divine oneness of universal patterns. Since archetypal number laws exist in the human psyche, the twelve astrological signs, and the structure of the physical body (twelve cranial nerves, twelve organ systems, and its cellular genetic code of approximately 144,000 genes), we can read many symbolic meanings into the archetypal figure of the New Jerusalem. In Jungian analytical psychology, it most certainly stands as a mandala of wholeness reflecting many hidden facets, which is the nature of an archetype of the Self. If "man" is the human personality, and "angel" the Soul, then the measure of a perfected personality is synonymous with the self-realized Soul of which the personality is a part, or aspect, of its expression in the world.

> *18: And the building of the wall of it was of jasper: and the city was pure gold, like unto clear glass.*

Here "jasper," as before, is likely the opal stone that is white yet, when exposed to sunlight, reflects all colors. The "city," the perfected Soul, has a golden aura and is transparent, "like unto clear glass." This suggests that the Soul's conscious awareness of all its dimensions and lower bodies is clear as the light shines forth through them with no karmic veils of illusion and limitation.

The Precious Stones of the Apocalypse

> *19: And the foundations of the wall of the city were garnished with all manner of precious stones. The first foundation was jasper; the second, sapphire; the third, a chalcedony; the fourth, an emerald;*

> *20: The fifth, sardonyx; the sixth, sardius; the seventh, chrysolite; the eighth, beryl; the ninth, a topaz; the tenth, a chrysoprasus; the eleventh, a jacinth; the twelfth, an amethyst.*

Collectively, the "precious stones" represent wisdom, or the precious sacred qualities of Spirit. These precious stones are not all identified with certainty. According to Pryse, some of the Greek names are dubious, but when interpreted in modern terms, they are likely the following: (1) opal, (2) lapis lazuli, (3) chalcedony, (4) aquamarine, (5) sardonyx, (6) carnelian, (7) topaz, (8) beryl, (9) chrysolith, (10) chrysoprase, (11) hyacinth (zircon), and (12) amethyst. When taken in a circle, they form the prismatic scale and are like the circular rainbows circling the throne of

God (Revelation 4:3). At this point, we will discuss the stones' spiritual, emotional, and physical attributes and the twelve lessons of spiritual evolution that they bring.

Saint John's vision of the twelve stones takes place on the spiritual planes of consciousness, yet each of these gemstones exists in the physical world of matter. Quantum physics may assist us here to understand this condition. The idea that all matter is really another form of energy is the essence of the Einsteinian and quantum worldview. Daskalos was asked to discuss the nature of mind. He spoke of it by analogy to the phenomena of the three states of water. Water can be solid (as ice), in a liquid state, or in a vaporous state. The state of water depends on the speed at which the water molecules are oscillating, with ice the slowest and water vapor the most rapid. Solid mind would correspond to the physical body (the slowest vibrational state of mind), liquid water to the emotional (astral) state of mind, and water vapor to our mental state, our thoughts and thinking processes. When looked at from the perspective of quantum physics, the physical body is actually solid or frozen light. With this understanding, the symbolism of "a new heaven and a new earth" is clearer. The holistic notion that all life is, in reality, unified in God's universal body of light and love—with heaven and earth no longer separated in consciousness, as before, as a result of the apocalyptic trauma to earth and humanity—reflects the union of the bride (Soul) and bridegroom (Spirit). The idea of "a new heaven and a new earth" corresponds to the Age of Aquarius.

1. Opal—New Awakening

In Roman times, opal was associated with good luck and hope. Opal is an iridescent stone that relates to the promises of God. In its white form it relates to purity, righteousness, holiness, and the Soul or the bride of Christ. In general, opal has a gentle, calming, and soothing effect on the emotional body. It purifies the energy field, cleansing and rebalancing the chakras of the etheric body and the chakras connected to the physical body. Spiritually opal helps to calm, clarify, and focus the mind. Emotionally it soothes the emotional body, and physically it can help heal indulgences coming from all types of abuse. Opal helps eliminate fibroids, tissue densities in the body. The elements associated with opal are generally earth and water; therefore, the archangels that govern the energy of opal are Uriel (earth) and Sandalfon and Gabriel (water). The chakra most associated with opal's effects is the crown, or seventh, chakra.

Opal helps awaken and heal the unworthy self that feels separated and disconnected from God. The spiritual essence of opal represents new beginnings. The story of the Samaritan woman that Christ met at the well is an example of the new beginnings of a spiritual life based on the impact of spiritual truth. Opal also reflects the truth that no one is ever neglected by God or Spirit and therefore it is a stone that helps one develop a higher faith, a faith in the higher power of guidance that is available for each of us. Opal helps remove our feeling of separation and unworthiness from the Source and reconnects us to follow the light. When Christ met Saint Philip and said, "Follow me," he was alluding to the same truth—of walking together in trust toward the light of spiritual realization.

MEDITATION

Healing the Unworthy Self

1. Breathe deeply and relax your body.
2. Feel the healing white light flowing up your body, filling you with warmth and good feelings.
3. Visualize yourself walking into a beautiful healing temple.
4. Ask yourself this question: "In what way do I allow feelings of unworthiness to separate me from my ascension into sacred marriage (union) with my Christ Self?"
5. Contact the sensations, feelings, and thoughts of unworthiness within you.
6. Somewhere in the temple is the Christ Self, the one who cares unconditionally for you.
7. Go and stand before him. Reach within yourself and draw out all your unworthy energy and place it in the Christ's hands of light, feeling him dissolve the unworthy self in his healing hands of divine love.
8. See him exchanging with you and placing in your hands a beautiful white opal stone. Feel the fiery light of Archangel Sandalfon and Archangel Gabriel supporting your healing.
9. Feel the great energy of the stone fill your every breath, activating your seventh chakra and filling you downward, soothing you emotionally, clearing and focusing your mind, strengthening your Soul, and cleansing your physical body of abuse and unworthiness.
10. Hear his words to you: "You have been adopted by me. You are very precious and, as my child, you have been given my authority. Follow me that I may teach you how to walk with spiritual dignity and love as I did on earth. I love you just as you are."
11. Feel embraced by him, joining his heart, becoming unified with him.
12. Leave your temple and return from your journey.

2. Lapis Lazuli—Power of Discernment

The ancient Greeks and Romans called this stone "sapphire." The Buddhists recommended lapis as a stone to bring inner peace and freedom from negative thoughts. Lapis activates intellectual abilities and the throat chakra. When lapis is combined with moldavite, it facilitates transformation to one's highest purpose. Lapis activates the higher mind and our psychic abilities. Spiritually, lapis awakens the third eye, enhancing meditative journeys and clearer visualization. Lapis is a stone of precognition and clairvoyance. Emotionally, it helps us identify habit patterns, lessons that may be blocking our spiritual progress. Physically, it helps us identify the karmic roots of disease and habitual thought patterns. Lapis relates primarily to the air element and Archangel Rafael.

The spiritual essence of lapis enhances the power of discernment, the ability to know the difference between light and darkness, in order to let go of darkness and follow one's intuition to greater light. Lapis also facilitates the development of gratitude and working from a continual state of forgiveness and blessings. Lapis helps remind us of where we feel attached to the worldly life and how better to follow the spiritual life in all things.

MEDITATION

Healing the Deceptive Self of Worldly Attachment

1. Breathe deeply and relax your body.
2. Feel the healing white light flowing up your body, filling you with warmth and good feelings.
3. Visualize yourself walking into a beautiful healing temple.
4. Ask yourself this question: "In what way do I allow attachment to comfort, material goods, money, position, image, and/or negative habitual thought patterns in my worldly life to block my spiritual progress, to separate me in confusion and darkness from my ascension into sacred marriage (union) with my Christ Self, inner light, and higher purpose?"
5. Contact your sensations, feelings, and thoughts of attachment and enslavement to outer deceptions.
6. Somewhere in the temple is the Christ Self, the one who cares unconditionally for you.
7. Go and stand before him. Reach within yourself and draw out all this dark worldly energy of deception that you carry and place it in the Christ's hands of light, feeling him dissolve the deceptive self in his healing hands of divine love.
8. See him exchanging with you and placing in your hands a beautiful blue stone of lapis lazuli. Feel Archangel Rafael's healing flames of light supporting you.
9. Feel the great energy of the stone fill your every breath, initially filling your sixth and seventh chakras, helping you identify the habit patterns that block your spiritual progress, awakening your power of visualization and mental discernment, and assisting you to reclaim your sovereignty and release you from all karmic roots of physical disease.
10. Hear the words of the Christ: "Let go of what is familiar and comfortable that holds you back from a deeper surrender to the light of truth within you. Love God first, and all things that are needed will follow."

11. Feel embraced by him, joining his heart, becoming unified with him.
12. Leave your temple and return from your journey.

3. Chalcedony—Developing Faith and Humility in God

Chalcedony is a bluish-white or purple stone. It represents purity, righteousness, and holiness. The name chalcedony may have been derived from the Greek part of a city called Chalcedon. Chalcedony is a stone that was used a great deal in ancient times. In general, it restores calm and balance and soothes one's whole being from the conscious mind to the inner child. It also restores connection to the magical child within and heals the wounded child that adapts itself to the expectations of others so it will be loved. The adapted child is that part of our inner child that took on a certain role in order to receive love, that separated itself from its essential source in Spirit. The magical child is the part of us that remains connected as a bridge to Spirit or the Soul and can be reawakened through healing the adapted child within. Chalcedony supports us in this process.

Chalcedony improves our inner communications and connection to our subconscious. It also facilitates remembrance of past lives, helping us recall past-life memories relevant to our spiritual growth. Chalcedony brings calmness and encourages communication with Spirit. Chalcedony supports releasing deep anger patterns from the energy field and alleviates desperation and anxiety. On a spiritual level, it helps with divine communication and channeling work. Chalcedony can help support us in repairing our etheric energy field, healing tears from traumas of the past and leaks or holes in our aura. Emotionally, this stone is supportive in healing anxiety, fear, irrational anger, and panic and will help dissolve these energies in the energy field. Physically, chalcedony is good for all-round physical health, and it can strengthen our vocal chords and soothe throat infection. Chalcedony's is connected to the water element, and the governing archangel is Gabriel. It is most helpful in healing the fifth and sixth chakras.

The spiritual essence of chalcedony is involved with overcoming pride and doubt and embracing God authority. The Greek root is from the word *chalkos*, which describes a "hollowing out" process, an emptying of self or state of humility. When pride is released, the Holy Spirit can reach into us more deeply. When we face our weaknesses and inabilities, we can open ourselves to surrender to a higher power and receive renewed energy and life. Chalcedony can help us open to seeing how our God power works through us. Humility is the key. Humility opens us to receive all gifts from our Source. When we go into our spiritual challenges with faith, we can overcome low self-value or weaknesses and move forward, reclaiming our innocence and our direct connection to God.

MEDITATION

Healing the False Self (Wounded Adapted Child Holding Pretense, Anger, Fear, and/or Anxiety)

1. Breathe deeply and relax your body.
2. Feel the healing white light flowing up your body, filling you with warmth and good feelings.
3. Visualize you are walking into a beautiful healing temple.
4. Ask yourself these questions: "In what way do I use the idea 'I Am better than others' or pride or self-importance to protect my vulnerability to feeling unloved, and what anger, fear, or anxiety do I hold in secret of being unacceptable or unworthy of love? How did I adapt in childhood to meeting others' expectations in order to be lovable, and what do I do now to prove my self-value in the eyes of others? How has my false self separated me from my ascension into sacred marriage (union) with my Christ Self and the true innocence and purity of my Soul (the magical child within)?"
5. Contact the sensations, feelings, and thoughts of the child within you that adapted itself to be loved that may also carry fear, anger, and anxiety of being found out to be unlovable.
6. Somewhere in the temple is the Christ Self, the one who cares for you unconditionally.
7. Go and stand before him. Reach within yourself and draw out all your fears, anger, anxiety, and pretense about being unacceptable and unlovable and place it in Christ's hands of light, feeling him dissolve the false self (adapted child) in his healing hands of divine love.
8. See him exchanging with you and placing in your hands a beautiful bluish chalcedony stone. Feel Archangel Gabriel's flames of blue light supporting your healing.
9. Feel the great energy of the stone fill your every breath, initially filling your fifth and sixth chakras and flowing wherever needed, calming you emotionally and dissolving your held pride, fear, anger, and anxiety from trauma of the past, in childhood or other lives, opening a channel of communication between you and Spirit, strengthening your body and vocal cords for authentic communication.
10. Hear the Christ's words to you: "Love casts out fear. Every gift comes from the hand of God. Have love and trust in God, and empty yourself to receive in humility all that the Holy Spirit has in store for you."
11. Feel embraced by him, joining his heart, becoming unified with him.
12. Leave your temple and return from your journey.

4. Aquamarine—Healing Grief, Developing Communication Skills

Aquamarine is in the beryl family and is of a blue-greenish color. It was first used in Greece between 300 and 500 BC. Its name means "water of the sea." It was believed to be a treasure of the mermaids. Aquamarine is governed primarily by the water element and Archangel Gabriel. It works particularly in the fourth and fifth chakras. Aquamarine in general has a calming, soothing effect and allows us to communicate our truth more clearly. Aquamarine connects our heart and our throat chakra in such a way to express our truth more authentically. Aquamarine brings a deeper feeling of the heart and is especially good for the clearing of grief and past sorrow.

In women, aquamarine encourages clarity and the courage to express themselves and increase their intuitive abilities. In men, it helps release emotional blocks, emotional numbness, and difficulty in communicating feelings. In both men and women, aquamarine enhances gentle, truthful, compassionate communication. It is a stone of empowerment for both sexes, and it helps connect us to the divine feminine element. Aquamarine also assists with releasing old things and moving energy from the heart to the throat to be expressed. It frees us of old grief. It helps us release emotional attachment to our losses so we can connect positively with our spiritual side and the lessons of those losses. It helps us overcome fear and anger.

Spiritually, aquamarine activates the throat chakra, facilitating communication of truth, and promotes understanding of divergent viewpoints. It helps clear stagnant energy and assists us in releasing old patterns. Emotionally, it helps release old emotional baggage and helps calm anger. Physically, it is a stone that helps counter infection, strep throats, and laryngitis, and it helps with inflammatory diseases. Aquamarine is also good for skin conditions such as hives, rosacea, psoriasis, and eczema. The spiritual essence of aquamarine is to teach us the importance of discovering God's plan in each situation for us, regardless of the challenges we are up against.

MEDITATION
Healing the Grieving Self

1. Breathe deeply and relax your body.
2. Feel the healing white light flowing up your body, filling you with warmth and good feeling.
3. Visualize yourself walking into a beautiful healing temple.
4. Ask yourself this question: "In what way do I allow my unexpressed feelings of grief and loss to separate me from my ascension into sacred marriage (union) with my Christ Self?"

5. Contact your sensations, feelings, and thoughts of unexpressed sorrow and grief of loss within you. Who or what did you lose or feel is missing for you? What do you need to express about it from your heart to reclaim your inner and outer peace?
6. Somewhere in the temple is the Christ Self, the one who cares unconditionally for you.
7. Go and stand before him. Reach within yourself and draw out all your unexpressed sorrow, communicating it to him, and place it in the Christ's hands of light, feeling him dissolve the grieving self in his healing hands of divine love.
8. See him exchanging with you and placing in your hands a beautiful aquamarine stone. Feel the support of Archangel Gabriel's soothing blue-green flames of light with you.
9. Feel the great energy of the stone fill your heart and throat chakras, releasing you from old sorrow and sadness. Feel it calming you, opening you to truthful communication, and combating any inflammation of your skin, throat, or inner organ tissues that may exist in your body.
10. Hear the Christ's words to you. "Whatever winds of change God is bringing you, through seasons of rest and solace, through seasons of new growth and movement, through seasons of surrender and letting go of the past, I Am always with you—my guidance, my love, my light, my protection, my voice of comfort."
11. Feel embraced by him, joining his heart, becoming unified with him.
12. Leave your temple and return from your journey.

5. Sardonyx—Overcoming Laziness, Taking Right Action

Sardonyx is a variety of onyx that contains layers or bands of carnelian. It combines the properties of onyx, carnelian, and chalcedony. It has been known as a "stone of virtue." It was often used in the breastplates of high priests. It relates to the fire element and Archangel Michael and is most effective in chakras one, two, three, and six. Sardonyx has been known since ancient times to support happiness, friendship, and bliss, and it teaches one to love nature, acts as the protector of the youth, and brings good fortune. Sardonyx is especially important in helping us overcome dullness and laziness in spiritual affairs. It helps us activate our chakras to become spiritual warriors and to learn persistence, discipline, and consistency in our efforts to reconnect with our Source and live the spiritual life.

MEDITATION

Healing Laziness and Self-forgetfulness

1. Breathe deeply and relax your body.
2. Feel the healing white light flowing up your body, filling you with warmth and good feelings.
3. Visualize yourself walking into a beautiful healing temple.
4. Ask yourself these questions: "In what way do I allow my laziness, apathy, and lack of discipline to separate me from my ascension into sacred marriage (union) with my Christ Self? What do I substitute for my relationship with God that numbs me out to my real needs?"
5. Contact your sensations, feelings, and thoughts of laziness, apathy, and rationalization for not being disciplined in spiritual matters.
6. Somewhere in temple is the Christ Self, the one who cares unconditionally for you.
7. Go and stand before him. Reach within yourself and draw out all your dullness, apathy, and lack of discipline and place it in the Christ's hands of light, feeling him dissolve the lazy self-forgetting part of you in his healing hands of divine love.
8. See him exchanging with you and placing in your hands a beautiful reddish sardonyx stone. Feel the support of Archangel Michael's fiery light with you.
9. Feel the great energy of the stone fill your every breath, flowing into your first, second, third, and sixth chakras, bringing you strength, activating your physical and emotional bodies with new life force, and stimulating your mind to new activity and spiritual focus.
10. Hear the Christ's words: "God's spiritual will is within you. Open your belly to the living waters of light and awaken the spiritual warrior within you. Follow my footsteps to the light."
11. Feel embraced by him, joining his heart, becoming unified with him.
12. Leave your temple and return from your journey.

6. Carnelian—Developing Courage and Overcoming Challenges

Carnelian is a variety of chalcedony that in ancient times was believed to bring the wearer courage in battle. It will support the qualities of courage and leadership in those wearing it. It opens an influx of life force, the sexual creative energies, and helps us build confidence, courage, passion, and power. This stone increases vitality in our physical chakras, boosting our zest for living and our willingness to take risks. Carnelian is of the fire element and is controlled by Archangel Michael. Chakras one, two, and three are its primary domain. It helps in activating our connection to our Soul and our etheric chakras as well. Spiritually, carnelian assists in taking actions to manifest our highest goals. Emotionally, it helps us overcome fear and develop courage. It helps us embrace change and transformation in life. Physically, carnelian helps bring vitality and energy to our physical body for purification, helping to sanctify the body, a temple of Spirit. It assists in detoxification from alcohol and drugs, helps break hurtful physical habits, and improves overall health. The spiritual essence of carnelian is feeling and connecting with the peace God brings us when we face our greatest challenges of life. So when we place ourselves in our Christ Consciousness or light before us and we remain in peace, we can move mountains. Carnelian represents the spiritual quality of courageous obedience.

MEDITATION

Healing the Fearful Self, Developing Courage, and Facing Your Greatest Challenges

1. Breathe deeply and relax your body.
2. Feel the healing white light flowing up your body, filling you with warmth and good feelings.
3. Visualize yourself walking into a beautiful healing temple.
4. Ask yourself this question: "In what way do I allow my feelings of fear to hold back my courage in dealing with my life challenges and to separate me from my ascension into sacred marriage (union) with my Christ Self, preventing me from receiving the inner guidance I need to navigate my life?"
5. Contact your sensations, feelings, and thoughts of your greatest fears holding you back.
6. Somewhere in the temple is the Christ Self, the one who cares unconditionally for you.
7. Go and stand before him. Reach within yourself and draw out all your fearful, mistrusting energy and lack of spiritual power and place it in the Christ's hands of light, feeling him dissolving the fearful self in his healing hands of divine love.
8. See him exchanging with you and placing in your hands a beautiful orange carnelian stone. Feel Archangel Michael's fiery orange-red flames of light supporting your healing.
9. Feel the great energy of the stone fill your every breath, filling your first, second, and third chakras and activating your confidence, strength, courage, and assertiveness. Feel the stone's energy awakening your urge to take right action in your life situations, empowering you as you face your greatest challenges and drawing more vitality and energy into your physical body.
10. Hear the Christ's words for you: "All giants of fear eventually fall. Trust in my strength; have I ever failed you? I Am as close to you as your breath, as the beating of your heart. I Am always with you."

11. Feel embraced by him, joining his heart, becoming unified with him.
12. Leave your temple and return from your journey.

7. Topaz—Surrendering to Divine Will

Topaz comes in several colors, including gold, blue, and white. Golden topaz helps to enhance our creativity and ability to manifest our desires, and it grounds us. Golden topaz is involved primarily with the third chakra. Golden topaz brings our personal desires into alignment with divine will, and it carries the golden-pink ray of the Christ Consciousness, which helps clear the second and third chakras. This stone helps us build intention and focus our thoughts and energy into action for manifestation. It teaches us the importance of boundaries and clarifies our intentions and emotions. Golden topaz helps us build and maintain our physical and mental boundaries as well. Physically, it particularly stimulates the kidneys and adrenals.

Topaz is of the fire element, whichever color it comes in, and Archangel Michael controls it. In its blue form, topaz enhances the mind and communications involved primarily with the fifth and sixth chakras. It carries the energy of fire of mind and enhances mental processes and verbal skills. It improves our attention span and concentration. It can help magnify our psychic abilities and opens our minds to higher knowledge. White topaz brings mental clarity and spiritual and psychic gifts; in this form, it is involved mostly with the seventh and the eighth chakras and above.

Spiritually, in its golden form, topaz helps us focus our will and desires through our intention and helps bring our highest visions into manifestation. Emotionally, it teaches us emotional boundaries and honoring the space of others and ourselves. Physically, it can help support us when urinary and kidney imbalances are present.

The spiritual essence of topaz is to build a connection between our personal will and the divine will, to overcome our rebellion against God, and to embrace divine will or truth as our way of life. It helps us root out selfishness and rebellion. It helps us overcome entitlement and any sense of superiority, such as, "I am more spiritual," "I am better," "I am older," "I am wiser."

Spiritually it helps us integrate our lessons and gain knowledge from our experiences. It calms our mind in meditation. Emotionally it has a soothing, relaxing effect on the emotional body and helps us open to our deepest feelings. Physically it can be used in conditions of the throat, sore throat, speech impediments, public speaking fears and even hyperactive thyroid. It can also help calm migraines.

MEDITATION
Healing the Rebellious Self

1. Breathe deeply and relax your body.
2. Feel the healing white light flowing up your body, filling you with warmth and good feelings.
3. Visualize yourself walking into a beautiful healing temple.
4. Ask yourself these questions: "In what way am I in rebellion against God's divine will within me for the highest good in my life? How do I fight against Spirit's Divine Plan and purpose for my life? How do I separate myself from my ascension into sacred marriage (union) with my Christ Self?"
5. Contact your sensations, feelings, and thoughts of rebellion within you.
6. Somewhere in the temple is the Christ Self, the one who cares unconditionally for you.
7. Go and stand before him. Reach within yourself and draw out all your destructive, rebellious energy and place it in the Christ's hands of light, feeling him dissolving the rebellious self in his healing hands of divine love.
8. See him exchanging with you and placing in your hands a beautiful golden topaz stone. Feel Archangel Michael's golden–pink flames of light supporting your healing.
9. Feel the great energy of the stone fill your every breath, flowing into your second and third chakras and aligning your personal will-desires with God's divine will and purpose for your life. Feel the inflowing energy clarifying your intent and building healthier emotional, mental, and physical boundaries in your relationships. Allow the healing light to support any healing you might need for urinary and kidney imbalances.
10. Hear the Christ's words for you: "Let all your resistance and struggle flow freely away and draw closer to me, my beloved. Embrace the I Am within. The wheel of God grinds slowly but exceedingly well, polishing the Soul that you are."
11. Feel embraced by him, joining his heart, becoming unified with him.
12. Leave your temple and return from your journey.

8. Beryl—Accepting Spiritual Authority and Clarity

The eighth stone is clear beryl, also known as goshenite. In its blue form, it is aquamarine, and in its green form, emerald. This stone is related to the air element, Archangel Rafael, and especially the sixth and seventh chakras and all the etheric chakras eight through fourteen above the head. Beryl clears and activates the crown chakra for meditation. It opens a portal for Spirit and stimulates logical thinking. It is a stone of persistence, assisting us in our determination to complete things. It helps build loyalty, fidelity, and faithfulness in relationships and brings clarity and truthfulness. Beryl helps us detach ourselves, to become dispassionate when we need to. In the form of emerald, beryl will bring loving and forgiving qualities into one's heart.

Goshenite, the clear form of beryl, is a stone of very high frequency. It is spiritually uplifting and brings inspiration and a release from concerns. It is a powerful dream stone and encourages lucid dreaming. It can calm the lower mind and stimulate the higher mind. Spiritually, its function is to enhance dream work and meditation, clearing the mind to be a pure channel for higher consciousness. It helps us emotionally to feel uplifted. Physically, it supports the healing of headaches, sinusitis, insomnia, and brain imbalances. This stone's spiritual essence represents new beginnings and the embracing of God within us. It opens us to experience spiritual empowerment and intimacy with God Source through which we receive spiritual resurrection—the stage of our spiritual development in which we can experience that God's power within us is taking over. This stone also helps us protect ourselves against spiritual pride and awaken all the gifts and abilities and give total glory to God for those gifts and abilities that we are given, and to know that we are utterly dependent upon our source for everything.

MEDITATION

Healing Spiritual Pride (False Ego Authority), Developing Deeper Intimacy, and Awakening the Spirit-Soul's True Authority

1. Breathe deeply and relax your body.
2. Feel the healing white light flowing up your body, filling you with warmth and good feelings.
3. Visualize yourself walking into a beautiful healing temple.
4. Ask yourself these questions: "In what way do I allow my egotistical self-importance to keep me from a deeper intimacy and dependence on my God Source? How do I glorify myself rather than the higher power within me that is the source of all my divine gifts? How do I separate myself from my ascension into sacred marriage (union) with my Christ Self?"
5. Contact your sensations, feelings, and thoughts of self-importance within you.
6. Somewhere in the temple is the Christ Self, the one who cares unconditionally for you.
7. Go and stand before him. Reach within yourself and draw out all your spiritual pride and place it in the Christ's hands of light, feeling him dissolve the self-importance and inflated ego energies in his healing hands of divine love.
8. See him exchanging with you and placing in your hands a beautiful clear beryl stone. Feel the healing light of Archangel Rafael supporting you.
9. Feel the great energy of the stone fill your every breath, filling your sixth and seventh chakras and the etheric doubles of the physical, emotional, and mental bodies. Feel the emotional upliftment, inspiration, the new mental vision, and the physical healing of any brain imbalances within you.

10. Hear the words of the Christ for you: "Give glory and gratitude to God for all the gifts and abilities you have been given. Guard yourself against spiritual pride and thoughts of self-importance."
11. Feel embraced by him, joining his heart, becoming unified with him.
12. Leave your temple and return from your journey.

9. Chrysolith—Developing Prosperity and Well-Being

The ninth stone is chrysolith, which is also called peridot. It comes from the Greek word *peridona,* meaning "giving plenty" or "gold and stone." This stone was often viewed as a symbol of the sun and believed to confer the energy of royalty. It was worn as a protection against evil spirits and as a stone essentially of prosperity and well-being. Chrysolith activates and harmonizes the third and fourth chakras, creating an integration of love and will. It helps us develop the courage to act out of our heart's desires. It is a stone of spiritual and financial abundance and attracts our visions to earth. It can be used to bless one's work, whatever it might be. The stone helps bring the physical dimension in alignment with one's inner truth. It gives a sense of self-worth to those that are particularly plagued by guilt, and it helps us take self-responsibility.

Peridot is a powerful generator of wealth, health, and joy, and assists us to expand and receive from the universe. Spiritually, it helps us honor the source of all abundance. Emotionally, it helps us remove and dissolve blockages to receiving. Chrysolith helps us learn to receive grace and to be grateful. Physically, it helps alleviate heaviness of heart and all heart-related imbalances. It strengthens the blood and counters anemia and poor oxygenation. It is also helpful with alcohol and inhalant addictions. Chrysolith represents the spiritual essence of developing complete obedience to God. The stone is represented primarily by the earth element, and archangels Sandalfon and Uriel help govern it. It is involved primarily in the third and fourth chakras and their linkage.

MEDITATION

Overcoming Poverty Consciousness and Developing Prosperity and Well-Being

1. Breathe deeply and relax your body.
2. Feel the healing white light filling you with warmth and good feelings.
3. Visualize yourself walking into a beautiful healing temple.
4. Ask yourself these questions: "In what way do I allow my belief in limitation and/or my inability to receive materially and spiritually to block my power to manifest prosperity and well-being in all areas of my life? How does my belief in limitation separate me from my ascension into sacred marriage (union) with my Christ Self?"

5. Contact any sensations, feelings, and thoughts of material and spiritual limitation that you may hold.
6. Somewhere in the temple is the Christ Self, the one who cares unconditionally for you.
7. Go and stand before him. Reach within yourself and draw out all your self-limiting beliefs and energies about manifestation and place them in the Christ's hands of light, feeling him dissolve the limited, impoverished self in his healing hands of divine love.
8. See him exchanging with you and placing in your hands a beautiful green peridot stone. Feel Archangel Sandalfon in a burning pillar of light and Archangel Uriel in a silver-white flame of light supporting the healing.
9. Feel the great energy of the stone fill your every breath, filling and linking your third and fourth chakras, activating the harmony of your will and heart to realize your deepest visions and dreams for prosperity in all areas of your life. Feel the energy of abundance in wealth, health, joy, and well-being, and open to receive it all in your heart. Open yourself to allow this energy to fortify your blood and enhance oxygenation in your body. Feel yourself releasing any guilt you hold that is keeping you from receiving the unconditional abundance that God wishes for your life."
10. Hear the words of the Christ for you: "Stay strong in your obedience and love for God, whatever you may be asked to endure, knowing that all doubt and unbelief will be lifted from you."
11. Feel embraced by him, joining his heart, becoming unified with him.
12. Leave your temple and return from your journey.

10. Chrysoprase—Connecting with Divine Love and Mother Earth

The tenth stone is chrysoprase. Chrysoprase is a green chalcedony used as a gemstone in ancient Greece. It activates the third and fourth chakras, and is governed by Archangel Gabriel and the water element. It helps us cultivate deep heart connection with the spirit of Mother Earth and other earth spirits. It helps us remain centered in the heart at all times and gives us the courage to face difficult situations with resolve and truth. It enhances our forgiveness of past relationships that have ended. It activates our personal will in the solar plexus and blends it with our heart and our higher will. It brings hope to the darkest regions of our shadow self and expands the heart, allowing one to receive infinite love and abundance from the universe. This stone helps us receive the hidden treasures of Spirit and gives us full renewal, abundance, prosperity, and honesty.

Spiritually, chrysoprase assists us in connecting with the abundant energy and love of the Divine. It stimulates the heart chakra and expands our ability to feel and express love. Emotionally, it helps us to release attachment to fear-based emotions and belief systems. It assists us to heal from abuse and helps break the cycle of abuse transgenerationally. It also helps us to understand our transgenerational or ancestral karmas. Physically, chrysoprase supports our general healing and cellular regeneration. It has been called the stone of youth.

MEDITATION

Healing Isolation and Despair, Awakening Deep Heart Connection to Mother Earth, and Compassion

1. Breathe deeply and relax your body.
2. Feel the healing white light flowing up your body, filling you with warmth and good feelings.
3. Visualize yourself walking into a beautiful healing temple.
4. Ask yourself this question: "In what way do I allow feelings of despair about life and /or a closed heart of unforgiveness to separate me from my ascension into sacred marriage (union) with my Christ Self?"
5. Contact your sensations, feelings, and thoughts of unforgiveness and despair about life within.
6. Somewhere in the temple is the Christ Self, the one who cares unconditionally for you.
7. Go and stand before him. Reach within yourself and draw out all of your unforgiveness and despair for whatever has happened in your life that holds you back from opening your heart to divine love. Place it all in the Christ's hands of light, feeling him dissolve the despair and/or unforgiven feelings you hold.
8. See him exchanging with you and placing in your hands a beautiful green chrysoprase stone. Feel the gentle healing light of Archangel Gabriel supporting your healing.
9. Feel the great energy of the stone in every breath, filling your third and fourth chakras with compassion and unconditional love for yourself and who or what has yet to be forgiven. Feel the energy of hope and renewed purpose and meaning for your life. Feel the abundant love of the universe entering your heart and deepening your commitment to life, freeing you from the prison of emotional isolation. Breathe and receive rejuvenation, regeneration, and healing for your body.
10. Hear the words of the Christ for you: "My light is your light, my healing hands your healing hands, my love your love, my body and blood your etheric vitality. Step into my heart and experience my love for all of life."
11. Feel embraced by him, joining his heart, becoming unified with him.
12. Leave your temple and return from your journey.

11. Hyacinth (Zircon)—Actualizing Spiritual Ideals and Purpose

The eleventh stone is hyacinth, which is also known as zircon, particularly the red variety. It is a stone of authority. According to ancient Greek myth, a young man named Hyacinth was killed by a disc thrown during a competition by Apollo, the god of light. The drops of blood of the young man, which fell to the ground and turned into hyacinth flowers, soon hardened into jewels. Hyacinth, or zircon, is involved primarily with the water, air, and fire elements and therefore is under the control of archangels Gabriel, Rafael, and Michael. The stone affects all of the chakras in a positive way. It helps us overcome being ungrounded. It helps us ground and actualize our ideals in the physical world. Hyacinth (Zircon) is a stone of high intensity and precise focus. It stimulates all sluggish energies in our chakras and meridians. It transmutes spiritual energies into the physical world. It brings energy and strength of purpose to those who are overwhelmed by conflict between their inner desires to change the world and the fear that their dreams are impossible to realize.

Hyacinth (Zircon) has been used in the past as a talisman of spiritual protection and acts as a "shield of light" around the wearer. It also supports us in breaking co-dependent patterns. Hyacinth (Zircon) activates all chakras, grounds us, stimulates the crown chakra and modulates the flow of the chi through the meridian system. It also lends protective energy to people who are in out-of-body travel. Hyacinth (Zircon) assists us in maintaining spiritual consciousness while doing mundane tasks, and stimulates the physical body to detoxify itself. It aids one in becoming a vehicle of Spirit while maintaining one's earth connection. Emotionally, it brings reconciliation with being a spiritual being in a physical body, and it helps balance these polarities. Physically, the stone helps balance the adrenal glands and supports the adrenals when they are overworked and overstressed. It is also useful for clearing toxins from the body.

MEDITATION

Integrating and Aligning All Chakra Energies, and Living Your Spiritual Purpose in Harmony with Life

1. Breathe deeply and relax your body.
2. Feel the healing white light flowing up your body, filling you with warmth and good feelings.
3. Visualize yourself walking into a beautiful healing temple.
4. Ask yourself these questions: "How do I separate my spiritual ideals and desires from the physical world and life I live? What keeps me from finding wholeness, alignment, and harmony between my inner and outer life? What keeps me from living my spiritual purpose and finding my perfect alignment with God

physically, emotionally, mentally, and spiritually? How does this all separate me from my ascension into sacred marriage (union) with my Christ Self?"

5. Contact your sensations, feelings, and thoughts that keep you separated from living a full spiritual life here on earth.
6. Somewhere in the temple is the Christ Self, the one who cares for you unconditionally.
7. Go and stand before him. Reach within yourself and draw out all your ungrounded and scattered energy that keeps you unfocused and unaligned with your spiritual purpose for being in the world and place it all in the Christ's hands of light, feeling him dissolve the separated and scattered self in his healing hands of divine love.
8. See him exchanging with you and placing in your hands a beautiful red-purple hyacinth (zircon) stone. Feel the red flames of Archangel Michael, the violet flames of Archangel Rafael, and the blue flames of Archangel Gabriel joining to support the healing.
9. Feel the great energy of the stone fill your every breath, filling and aligning your crown chakra to your root chakra, filling all your chakras, bridging heaven and earth within you. Feel the energy surrounding you like a shield of light for protection, assisting you to feel more stable emotionally and physically, clearing toxins from your body, and supporting your adrenal glands.
10. Hear the Christ's words to you: "Reawaken your love and passion for God, and let your light and purpose for spiritual living shine brightly for all to see and feel, being an example of a life lived in gratitude, love, and service to God in the world."
11. Feel embraced by him, joining his heart, becoming unified with him.
12. Leave your temple and return from your journey.

12. Amethyst—Spiritual Purification and Awakening Higher Truth

The twelfth stone is amethyst, a member of the quartz family that has been used for thousands of years. Even 25,000 years ago, Neolithic people were familiar with this stone. It was often used in crowns, rings, and scepters. Amethyst was said to have been the ninth stone in the breastplate of the high priest of Israel, and one of the ten stones upon which the names of the tribes of Israel were engraved. The Greek word for amethyst, *amethystus*, means "not drunken or intoxicated." The myth about amethyst is that the god Bacchus was angry because of an insult, and he decreed that the first person he met would be eaten by his tigers. The unfortunate person happened to be Amethyst, who was on her way to worship at the shrine of Diana. When the tigers sprang, Diana transformed the girl into a transparent crystal. In remorse, Bacchus poured the juice of his grapes over the stone as an offering, thus giving the gem its purple color.

Amethyst relates mostly to the air element and to Archangel Rafael. It helps activate the sixth, seventh, eighth, and higher chakras above the head. The Greeks believed that amethyst would prevent intoxication, calm anger, and relieve frustrated passions (vices). It has been used for spiritual protection, for purification, and for addictions. It stimulates the crown chakra and aids us in meditation. It helps clear the energy field from attachments and acts as an energy shield. The violet flame associated with amethyst clears our karmic burdens. It keeps our healing space clear. Amethyst stimulates the mind, intuition, and psychic abilities. It is a natural stone for psychic and intuitive work. It helps us get a clear comprehension of the root causes of our life experiences. It also helps us release emotionally based decisions in our life and see things from the level of higher truth.

Spiritually, amethyst facilitates meditation and communication with one's inner guides. It clears the third eye and crown chakras. Emotionally, it helps those who are prone to playing the role of victim to recognize their empowerment and their ability to fulfill their spiritual purpose in their physical lives. Physically, amethyst helps counter habitual behaviors and thought patterns, leading to clarity of mind, and helps release addiction to alcohol, drugs, and other mind-altering agents. It helps balance the brain and nervous system.

This stone's spiritual essence is represented by the number 12, which symbolizes perfection and completion—the reaping of the rich harvest of our eternal rewards in our connection with Spirit.

MEDITATION

Clearing Karmic Burdens, Purification, and Opening the Higher Chakras for Realizing the Truth

1. Breathe deeply and relax your body.
2. Feel the healing white light flowing up your body, filling you with warmth and good feeling.
3. Visualize yourself walking into a beautiful healing temple.
4. Ask yourself this question: "What karmic burdens do I carry that I can release to the light that separate me from my ascension into sacred marriage (union) with my Christ Self?"
5. Contact your sensations, feelings, and thoughts that arise when you ask to be shown what you are carrying that feels the most difficult for you to change throughout your life experience, *i.e.,* the aspect of your life that you feel most unempowered to change.
6. Somewhere in the temple is the Christ Self, the one who cares unconditionally for you.

7. Go and stand before him. Reach within yourself and draw out all this untransformed energy into a ball and place it with the spirit of true humility of your heart into the Christ's hands of violet light, feeling him dissolve it in his healing hands of divine love.
8. See him exchanging with you and placing in your hands a beautiful violet amethyst stone. Feel Archangel Rafael in a great violet cleansing flame of light and, next to him, the Ascended Master Saint Germain joining the Christ in this healing process, supporting you.
9. Feel the great energy of the stone and the violet flame of Saint Germain and Archangel Rafael filling your every breath, burning away all karmic burdens you are now ready to transform within you. Feel the violet light opening your sixth, seventh, and eighth chakras and cleansing the etheric doubles of your physical, emotional, and mental bodies; stimulating your intuition; eliminating all emotion-based, impulsive decision-making; and clearing all addictive tendencies within your physical body.
10. Hear the Christ's words for you: "If you ask anything in my name, in the true spirit of love, I will do it." "He who believes in me, the works that I do he will do also; and greater works than these he will do, because I go to my Father" (John 14:12-14). "Embrace your perfection as my holy bride."
11. Feel embraced by him, joining his heart, becoming unified with him.
12. Leave your temple and return from your journey.

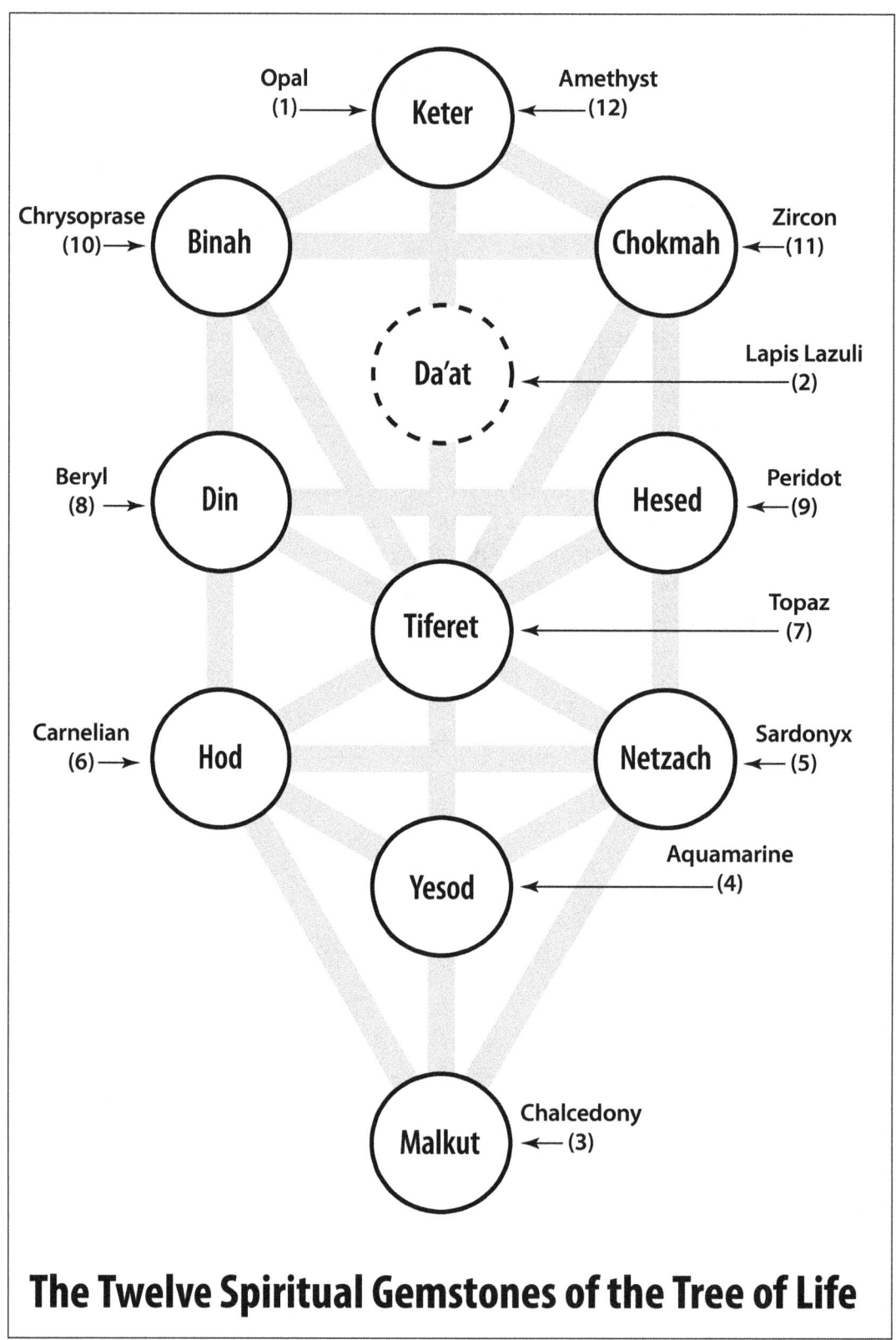

The Twelve Spiritual Gemstones of the Tree of Life

Volume II, Diagram 10

The Unfolding of the Seventh Initiation — Awakening Divine Love

> *21: And the twelve gates were twelve pearls; every several gate was of one pearl: and the street of the city was pure gold, as it were transparent glass.*

The "twelve pearls" represent the perfected personalities of all the twelve astrological types. The "city"—the Soul—emanates an aura, or light, of "pure gold" and holds no distortions or impurities, for "it were transparent glass."

> *22: And I saw no temple therein: for the Lord God Almighty and the Lamb are the temple of it.*

In the Soul's connection with Spirit ("the Lamb") and "the Lord God Almighty," there is no external source of authority or power. There is only that which is, the "I Am"—the pure state of spiritual consciousness. This state of the initiate's process is approaching the seventh initiation of spiritual realization—"We are many, yet we are one."

> *23: And the city had no need of the sun, neither of the moon, to shine in it: for the glory of God did lighten it, and the Lamb is the light thereof.*

At this stage, which coincides with the seventh initiation, no external teacher or teaching exists for the spiritually realized Soul, in unity with its source in Keter. "The Lamb," the initiate's Christ Consciousness "is the light thereof." As in Revelation 6:12, "the sun" is taken as an external teacher; "the moon" is an external teaching found in books. Here, the self-realized Soul has "no need" of teacher or teachings; it is a law unto itself that follows only its inner guidance and movement into the world. It is cause, not effect, of internal or external circumstances. As Meher Baba taught, in the sixth plane of consciousness, the Soul can see God external to itself in everything and everyone, yet not within itself. In the seventh plane of consciousness, the Soul experiences and understands itself as God's Source of divine love; this is the seventh initiation and connection with Keter.

> *24: And the nations of them which are saved shall walk in the light of it: and the kings of the earth do bring their glory and honour into it.*

"The nations" represent all parts of the personality in transformation. The "kings of the earth," the thoughts of the personality, are all guided by the light of divine will and now "do bring their glory and honor into it."

> *25: And the gates of it shall not be shut at all by day: for there shall be no night there.*

The Soul's wakefulness is present day and night in self-realization, for the Soul itself never sleeps. The physical body may sleep at night, but the Soul is awake all the time. The Soul does not rely on cycles for its activity. It is eternally awake and present at all times and beyond time.

> *26: And they shall bring the glory and honour of the nations into it.*

Divine will infuses the personality, "the nations," with light and guidance continuously.

> *27: And there shall in no wise enter into it any thing that defileth, neither whatsoever worketh abomination, or maketh a lie: but they which are written in the Lamb's book of life.*

Only the highest ideals and virtues shall enter the personality of the initiate, for the Christ Consciousness ("the Lamb") is in rulership. In Gnostic Christianity, the "book of life" is carried by Archangel Tzafkiel—the archangel of Binah or the Divine Mother. The Divine Mother sanctifies all divine ideas, divine purpose, and gifts for the initiate. This holy book of life becomes an integrated part of the initiate's unfolding life on earth and the source of supreme inner guidance.

MEDITATION JOURNEY

Close your eyes. Breathe deeply. Put your attention on your feet. And feel the healing white light flowing up your body. Feel it moving all the way up to your heart, over your shoulders, down your arms, to your hands and fingers, into your neck, your head, you face. And once again go to the entrance of your temple. Step in now and come to an altar in the center. And on the altar you see the Bible open to the very last page. This is not the end of the world. This is the end of an age and the beginning of a new one, and the book that gives the manual, the instructions, is written in your heart. Not in anything outside you. It is in you. And in this book is the whole message of Saint John's Revelation. For the word *apocalypse* means "that which is secret or hidden within." This is the book of your heart, your awakened Soul. And your temple, your New Jerusalem, is what you are. No one can tell how it must look or what is in it. As long as you create it from the divine love of your heart, it is a holy temple.

So as you stand at the altar, see a great column of white and golden light coming down to connect with you. Feel the Christ and Saint Mary lifting you up into this light—higher, freer, lighter, higher, lighter and freer, freer and lighter, higher and freer—lifting you up to a very high mountain. And Saint John shows you the city in his vision, and this activates in your heart your own vision for your city of Spirit. You see that the whole outer wall, the upper wall of the city, is in gold, a clear translucent gold, like crystal.

Let yourself enter the gate of the city, and as you do, inside you see a great throne where the transcendent Christ sits, the Lamb. The brightness of the sun coming out of his body is immense and blinding, and filled with divine love. From the throne, flows out a very crystal-clear river. And inside the city, many Souls in their golden auras, their solar bodies, move about, singing the prayers of God, the one God, the one life, and the one love of the universes. On either side of the river are the two great trunks of the Tree of Life. The trunks merge and intertwine above the river. Step into the clear river and touch the trunks of the tree, both trunks. The branches bear twelve different kinds of fruits—all the powers and virtues of the Soul. Touch each fruit and receive its energy—the fruit of love; the fruit of peace; the fruit of humility; the fruit of hope and honesty; the fruit of balance, contentment, and gratitude; the fruit of abundance and non-attachment and neutrality; the fruit of courage; the fruit of satisfaction and contentment; the fruit of innocence and purity; the fruit of illumination and service to all humanity; the fruit of sacred responsibility to the earth and to humanity and the heavens; the fruit of transformation of all things to God and Oneness.

The great river spirit, the Kundalini force, flows up your spine. Feel this energy upliftment. And now touch the leaves of the tree. Feel the spirit of service toward humanity and beauty, the beauty of life. And now approach the throne of the Lamb. As you approach, the light grows brighter and brighter. You sit at the feet of the Lamb, and the light grows even brighter, the love growing stronger and stronger. You are the light. You are divine love. Feel yourself being embraced by the Lamb, the divine marriage of your Soul to the Spirit, as you say, "I Am the light. I Am love. I Am peace and humility. I Am hope. I Am balance. I Am neutrality and acceptance. I Am courage. I Am a worker of God. I Am the purity and innocence of the Lamb. I Am. I Am. I Am."

And within your heart the Lamb places your own book, your own temple. And it is for you to build your own mandala and your own temple within, a mandala that reflects the marriage of your Soul to Spirit. And from the heavens above the holy city, feel the divine light of the unseen God, the invisible God, the mystery, pouring down into the city, transforming everything into light. "I Am. I Am. I Am." Slowly, slowly feel yourself leaving the great city of the New Jerusalem, giving thanks for this journey you have completed to awaken your spiritual energies, giving thanks for the cleansing of yourself and of the earth.

Slowly step back into the ray of golden-white light that lifted you up and come back down to the altar and temple where you started your journey. Feel yourself surrounded by the protective light of the temple. Now step up to the altar and, closing the Bible, say, "It is done. My life starts anew today, a new me, a new journey, a new beginning. And the guidance I need is written in my heart, in the Christ Light within me. Amen." Breathe deeply. And now let yourself step out of the temple, dissolving it behind you. And begin to become aware of your physical body. Rub your hands, massage your face and eyes, and return.

Chapter 22 of Revelation

From Spiritual Realization to God-Realization and Beyond

In Chapter 22, we have arrived into the consciousness of spiritual realization in Atzilut (Absolute Infinite Beingness)—the pure expression of God's divine will-pleasure and plan for humanity, free of separation from its source, flowing freely as the river from the throne of the Lamb. The ongoing journey into the consciousness of God-Realization takes place in Adam Kadmon (Absolute Infinite Be-ness). Daskalos described the state of Be-ness as the aspect of God that lies beyond the reach of human and archangelic comprehension. It is the ultimate source, that fathomless and inarticulate depth of the Divine beyond expression. In Saint John's New Jerusalem, this would be unity with the Throne and the Lamb.

In Atzilut, the spiritual awareness of the initiate expresses itself through nine qualities of Spirit-Soul essence, which are each representative of nine expressions of the fully transformed Enneagram personality types.

At the fourth stage of spiritual development (Integrated Soul), all these essences are available to all the sephiroth types (Enneagram personality points) as an expression of their wholeness and individuation in Spirit. The New Jerusalem acts as a healed Kabbalah, or mandala of integration and wholeness—also represented by the circular symbol of the Enneagram. *(See Enneagram symbol, Appendix I and II, Volume I).*

The great river flowing from the throne (spiritual consciousness), the emanation of primal light and sound of Atzilut, is eloquently expressed through the teachings of Jesus Christ's parables on the qualities of essence. It is likely that these sayings were known to Saint John by his close association with Jesus and are instructive as a complementary biblical addition to our book. They are stories of divinity in spontaneous action, expressing the qualities of the New Jerusalem.

The Nine Qualities of the Soul's Essence

> *1: And he shewed me a pure river of water of life, clear as crystal, proceeding out of the throne of God and of the Lamb.*

The "pure river" is the spiritual stream of energy, light, and sound—the purified middle pillar of the Kabbalah, the Tree of Life—flowing from God's heart of divine love ("proceeding out of the throne of God") and through the Christ Consciousness ("the Lamb") of the initiate. The pure river expresses the nine qualities of essence of the self-realized Soul in Atzilut: Beingness, power, emptiness, absorption, joy, love, peace, purity, and kindness. Essence can be defined as Soul qualities that were hidden by the personality and later revealed upon the Soul's awakening in self-realization.

➤ *(See Volume II, Diagram 6, p. 74)*

1. Beingness

According to Daskalos, Absolute Infinite Beingness—all beings within one Being—is the divine common selfhood. Therefore, Beingness in the Malkut Type (Enneagram Point 9), would suggest that the completion of God's Divine Plan begins and ends in Malkut, for in Malkut all subtle energies and dimensions are palpable. Since Point 9 is the container and completion of all points and traits, then Beingness would contain all nine holy essences. Passivity and following the agenda of others is the Malkut Type's earlier struggle with separation-consciousness. In unity, there is consciousness of the oneness of self with all beings. This can only be understood mentally as the holy idea of love and, emotionally and behaviorally, as the virtue of right action.

The Parable of the Lost Sheep

How think ye? if a man have an hundred sheep, and one of them be gone astray, doth he not leave the ninety and nine, and goeth into the mountains, and seeketh that which is gone astray?

And if so be that he find it, verily I say unto you, he rejoiceth more of that sheep, than of the ninety and nine which went not astray.

Even so it is not the will of your Father which is in heaven, that one of these little ones should perish.

Matthew 18:12-14

MEDITATION

Meditation Practice for Beingness

Imagine walking into a garden with the Christ awaiting you there. He is the shepherd in unity and love with his flock of sheep. Look at them and attune to the flock. How often do you give yourself up to belong or be loved? When did you do it as a child, going away from your Beingness, your authentic self, your unity with the Christ Consciousness? Somewhere out there is the lost sheep. It is you. Go to this lost sheep, your neglected inner child, and look into its eyes. Say "I see your light. I feel your love. I see your inner beauty and richness." Touch the heart of your child as the Christ touches the back of your heart, filling you with the golden light of divine love. Embrace and unite with your authentic Beingness, your magical child. Feel your root chakra awakening in a rose-red light. And as you breathe, feel it flooding your whole Being.

2. Power

The next quality of essence is power in the form of transpersonal or cosmic power. In the earlier stages of spiritual development, the Yesod Type (Enneagram Point 8) struggles with issues of personal power—domination, force, and control. This comes from the experience of separation. In oneness, there is unity with the Shakti, or cosmic power, which can be understood mentally as the holy idea of truth and experienced emotionally and behaviorally as the virtue of innocence.

The Parable of the Good Shepherd

Verily, verily, I say unto you, He that entereth not by the door into the sheepfold, but climbeth up some other way, the same is a thief and a robber.

But he that entereth in by the door is the shepherd of the sheep.

To him the porter openeth; and the sheep hear his voice: and he calleth his own sheep by name, and leadeth them out.

And when he putteth forth his own sheep, he goeth before them, and the sheep follow him: for they know his voice.

And a stranger will they not follow, but will flee from him: for they know not the voice of strangers.

This parable spake Jesus unto them: but they understood not what things they were which he spake unto them.

Then said Jesus unto them again, Verily, verily, I say unto you, I am the door of the sheep.

All that ever came before me are thieves and robbers: but the sheep did not hear them.

I am the door: by me if any man enter in, he shall be saved, and shall go in and out, and find pasture.

The thief cometh not, but for to steal, and to kill, and to destroy: I am come that they might have life, and that they might have it more abundantly.

I am the good shepherd: the good shepherd giveth his life for the sheep.

But he that is an hireling, and not the shepherd, whose own the sheep are not, seeth the wolf coming, and leaveth the sheep, and fleeth: and the wolf catcheth them, and scattereth the sheep.

The hireling fleeth, because he is an hireling, and careth not for the sheep.

I am the good shepherd, and know my sheep, and am known of mine.

As the Father knoweth me, even so know I the Father: and I lay down my life for the sheep.

And other sheep I have, which are not of this fold: them also I must bring, and they shall hear my voice; and there shall be one fold, and one shepherd.

John 10:1-16

MEDITATION
Meditation Practice for Power

Imagine a beautiful garden before you. As you enter, see the Christ joining you. Feel him activating your second chakra with a bright orange light. The light floods up your spine, filling you with the chi (Shakti) energy. What have you been addicted to that takes you away from your chi energy? Bring your addictive self into the garden. Feel the Christ supporting you by activating the golden light of your heart as you let the combined orange and golden light within you flood the second and fourth chakras of your addicted self with the light of true power. Unite with your lost power. Now invite into the garden the people in your life you've seen as either inferior or superior to you, for whatever reason. See the Christ fill their second chakras with true power. How do they transform? Connect to them all in this new energy. And experience the truth and innocence of your Being that can only see equality like the young child. Oneness is your truth. Witness the innocence in their eyes and the true power within all.

3. Emptiness

The third quality of essence is emptiness. This is the living pure divine intelligence that is the truth of one's Being; it has no qualities, forms, or color; it gives rise to all things. It is empty of attachment to form, and contains the divine energy and intelligence necessary to guide the creative process. The Netzach Type (Enneagram Point 6), in the earlier stages of spiritual development, struggles in separation consciousness with issues of doubt, mistrust, and fear. In unity, there is oneness with the essence of pure divine intelligence, which is empty of separation, doubt, and fear. This oneness of consciousness is understood mentally as the holy idea of trust, felt emotionally as the virtue of courage, and expressed behaviorally as courageous action.

The Parable of Walking on Water

Immediately Jesus made His disciples get into the boat and go before Him to the other side, while He sent the multitudes away.

And when He had sent the multitudes away, He went up on the mountain by Himself to pray. Now when evening came, He was alone there.

But the boat was now in the middle of the sea, tossed by the waves, for the wind was contrary.

Now in the fourth watch of the night Jesus went to them, walking on the sea.

And when the disciples saw Him walking on the sea, they were troubled, saying, "It is a ghost!" And they cried out for fear.

But immediately Jesus spoke to them, saying, "Be of good cheer! It is I; do not be afraid.

And Peter answered Him and said, Lord, if it is You, command me to come to You on the water.

So He said, Come. And when Peter had come down out of the boat, he walked on the water to go to Jesus.

But when he saw that the wind was boisterous, he was afraid; and beginning to sink he cried out, saying, Lord, save me!

And immediately Jesus stretched out His hand and caught him, and said to him, O you of little faith, why did you doubt?

And when they got into the boat, the wind ceased.

Then those who were in the boat came and worshiped Him, saying, Truly You are the Son of God.

Matthew 14:22-33

MEDITATION

Meditation Practice for Emptiness

Breathe deeply and relax your body. Close your eyes and visualize a situation in your life that causes you fear or confusion, where you need clarity and guidance. See the Christ at a distance from you and your challenge standing before you. Feel the Christ filling your solar plexus with yellow-golden light, and feel the light flowing up into your heart. Now hear his guidance as he shares how you can maneuver across the barriers of doubt and mistrust you feel. What understanding, what insight do you gain? How do you step forward with courage, recommitting yourself to your life and new movement with the essence of pure divine intelligence that is empty of separation, doubt, and fear. Your emptiness carries the guidance of divine intelligence that you need to navigate through everything in your life.

4. Absorption

The fourth quality of essence of the Soul's expression of Atzilut is absorption. When the full consciousness is merged with the Divine, it expresses as the condition of bliss or divine splendor, a state of happiness in and of itself. The Hod Type (Enneagram Point 7) in separation consciousness struggles with issues of avoidance, excessive ego planning, gluttony, and the search for bliss through outer activities. In unity consciousness, there is oneness with the essence of absorption—the consciousness of absorption in divine bliss—which is understood mentally as the holy idea of holy work and expressed emotionally and behaviorally as the virtue of sobriety.

The Parable of the Prodigal Son

And he said, A certain man had two sons:

And the younger of them said to his father, Father, give me the portion of goods that falleth to me. And he divided unto them his living.

And not many days after the younger son gathered all together, and took his journey into a far country, and there wasted his substance with riotous living.

And when he had spent all, there arose a mighty famine in that land; and he began to be in want.

And he went and joined himself to a citizen of that country; and he sent him into his fields to feed swine.

And he would fain have filled his belly with the husks that the swine did eat: and no man gave unto him.

(Continued)

And when he came to himself, he said, How many hired servants of my father's have bread enough and to spare, and I perish with hunger!

I will arise and go to my father, and will say unto him, Father, I have sinned against heaven, and before thee,

And am no more worthy to be called thy son: make me as one of thy hired servants.

And he arose, and came to his father. But when he was yet a great way off, his father saw him, and had compassion, and ran, and fell on his neck, and kissed him.

And the son said unto him, Father, I have sinned against heaven, and in thy sight, and am no more worthy to be called thy son.

But the father said to his servants, Bring forth the best robe, and put it on him; and put a ring on his hand, and shoes on his feet:

And bring hither the fatted calf, and kill it; and let us eat, and be merry:

For this my son was dead, and is alive again; he was lost, and is found. And they began to be merry.

Now his elder son was in the field: and as he came and drew nigh to the house, he heard musick and dancing.

And he called one of the servants, and asked what these things meant.

And he said unto him, Thy brother is come; and thy father hath killed the fatted calf, because he hath received him safe and sound.

And he was angry, and would not go in: therefore came his father out, and intreated him.

And he answering said to his father, Lo, these many years do I serve thee, neither transgressed I at any time thy commandment: and yet thou never gavest me a kid, that I might make merry with my friends:

But as soon as this thy son was come, which hath devoured thy living with harlots, thou hast killed for him the fatted calf.

And he said unto him, Son, thou art ever with me, and all that I have is thine.

It was meet that we should make merry, and be glad: for this thy brother was dead, and is alive again; and was lost, and is found.

Luke 15:11-32

MEDITATION

Meditation Practice for Absorption

Imagine yourself at the gate of a bridge going over a river. At the other end of the bridge appears a bright golden rose-colored light with the Christ standing there with open arms. As you prepare to cross the bridge, look back at what you have been obsessed with in your life that takes you away from being absorbed in your divine light of bliss. Ask the questions, "Who am I? Am I this body? Am I my emotions, or am I my thoughts?" Surrender all that holds you back from your inner bliss. Let it go into the river and float away. Now, cross the bridge and feel and see the golden-rose light of the Christ getting brighter. Absorb yourself in the light and the feeling of bliss it brings. Walk deeper into the light and the arms of Christ, knowing there is no end to plunging into this bliss.

5. Joy

The fifth quality of essence is joy. When the individual's consciousness is united with the divine throne, or heart, of God (the Source), the awareness is of joy and celebration. In separation consciousness, the Tiferet Type (Enneagram Point 4) struggles with the outer search for happiness, which ends in melancholy and envy of what is missing. In unity, there is oneness with the consciousness or essence of joy, which is understood mentally as the holy idea of origin or Source and experienced emotionally and behaviorally as the virtue of balance.

The Parable of the Lost Coin

Or what woman, having ten silver coins, if she loses one coin, does not light a lamp, sweep the house, and search carefully until she finds it?

And when she has found it, she calls her friends and neighbors together, saying, Rejoice with me, for I have found the piece which I lost!

Likewise, I say to you, there is joy in the presence of the angels of God over one sinner who repents.

Luke 15:8-10

MEDITATION

Meditation Practice for Joy

Imagine yourself walking in a marketplace along a road or walkway. On either side of the street are the various things, people, ideas, jobs, etc., that you have sought to bring you happiness and joy. Review your life and how you've searched to find happiness in the world, only to be disappointed when things didn't work out or when the happiness and desire faded into emptiness, boredom, or even pain. What is really missing for you? Come to the end of the marketplace. In front of you is a vast space of darkness. Gently feel behind you the great Archangel Rafael filling your heart with light. Feel and see the sun emerging within you in golden light and a rose blooming in your heart. Feel your fullness, contentment, and joy growing. Feel the dark space before you filling with light. Now, turn and fill the marketplace with this inner light and enjoy all before you without attachment.

6. Love

The sixth quality of essence is love. To love is to be aware of being in the heart of all beings and experiencing the grace, sacredness, and greatness of all gifts that are manifested and expressed through the common selfhood of all beings. This is the true nature of the Hesed Type (Enneagram Point 3) in unity consciousness. The Hesed Type in separation consciousness struggles with issues of vanity and deceit about its true identity, becoming identified with the trappings of performance and efficiency through exaggerated self-importance. In unity, there is oneness with the consciousness or essence of love, which is understood mentally as the holy idea of compassion. Emotionally and behaviorally, love is experienced and expressed through the virtues of veracity, honesty, and hope.

The Parable of the Man with the Two Sons

But what think ye? A certain man had two sons; and he came to the first, and said, Son, go work today in my vineyard.

He answered and said, I will not: but afterward he repented, and went.

And he came to the second, and said likewise. And he answered and said, I go, sir: and went not.

Whether of them twain did the will of his father? They say unto him, The first. Jesus saith unto them, Verily I say unto you, That the publicans and the harlots go into the kingdom of God before you.

For John came unto you in the way of righteousness, and ye believed him not: but the publicans and the harlots believed him: and ye, when ye had seen it, repented not afterward, that ye might believe him.

Matthew 21:28-32

The Parable of the Mustard Seed

Another parable put he forth unto them, saying, The kingdom of heaven is like to a grain of mustard seed, which a man took, and sowed in his field:

Which indeed is the least of all seeds: but when it is grown, it is the greatest among herbs, and becometh a tree, so that the birds of the air come and lodge in the branches thereof.

Matthew 13:31-32

MEDITATION

Meditation Practice for Love

Imagine yourself standing at the side of Christ as a long line of people appears to be healed by him. Imagine in this group those that you love and care for appearing to receive his blessings and healing touch. Feel the power of his compassion as you merge with his healing hands, his heart, his light and compassion. He is in their hearts and in yours. He only sees and feels love as love is the true reality—the common selfhood. Now see standing in line those who you have judged in your life. Hold to his heart and experience their hearts beyond your mind's criticisms. Breathe in their darkness into your spiritual heart and let your spiritual light fill them in the spirit of the Christ. Let others who appear in need of healing to receive it as well.

7. Peace

The seventh quality of essence is peace. Underneath all activity and manifested expressions of life is the still point of oneness and unity that works through, and is a part of, everything. This omniscience of the Divine brings the consciousness or essence of divine peace and eternal stillness to the Din Type (Enneagram Point 5). The Din Type in separation consciousness struggles with the issue of attempting to create peace through withdrawal from life and their physical and emotional surroundings. Fear, withdrawal, and greed for time, energy, space, and belongings predominate. In unity consciousness, there is the essence of peace, which is understood mentally as the holy idea of omniscience and experienced emotionally and behaviorally through the virtue of non-attachment.

The Parable of the Treasure in the Field

Again, the kingdom of heaven is like unto treasure hid in a field; the which when a man hath found, he hideth, and for joy thereof goeth and selleth all that he hath, and buyeth that field.

Matthew 13:44

The Parable of the Pearl of Great Price

Again, the kingdom of heaven is like unto a merchant man, seeking goodly pearls:

Who, when he had found one pearl of great price, went and sold all that he had, and bought it.

Matthew 13:45-46

MEDITATION

Meditation Practice for Peace

Breathe deeply. Go within. Feel the consciousness you carry now—your energy, emotions, beliefs, and attitudes. What old beliefs, feelings, and attitudes within yourself are you still trying to fit into like an old worn-out coat—those old beliefs, emotions, and behaviors that can no longer hold your new consciousness or serve you or others? Let go of that old coat. Now imagine you are swimming in the ocean on a warm, beautiful day. Each wave that you ride toward shore is a cycle of your life. Each wave contains the consciousness of that time. Now feel the wave that represents you now. Plunge deeply into it, to the stillness beneath. Experience the peace that exists below all cycles, all waves, and all activity.

8. Purity

The eighth quality of essence is purity. Purity here refers to transpersonal purity, the oneness behind all duality that rests at the ocean depths, beneath all differences. The Chokmah Type (Enneagram Point 1) in separation consciousness struggles with the issue of anger and resentment at the impurity of the world and its ever-changing nature. Once the Chokmah Type enters the depths within and engages its own divine energy, the essence of purity is understood mentally as the holy idea of perfection; it is experienced emotionally and expressed behaviorally as the virtue of serenity.

The Parable of the Transfiguration

And after six days Jesus taketh Peter, James, and John his brother, and bringeth them up into an high mountain apart,

And was transfigured before them: and his face did shine as the sun, and his raiment was white as the light.

And, behold, there appeared unto them Moses and Elias talking with him.

Then answered Peter, and said unto Jesus, Lord, it is good for us to be here: if thou wilt, let us make here three tabernacles; one for thee, and one for Moses, and one for Elias.

While he yet spake, behold, a bright cloud overshadowed them: and behold a voice out of the cloud, which said, This is my beloved Son, in whom I am well pleased; hear ye him.

And when the disciples heard it, they fell on their face, and were sore afraid.

And Jesus came and touched them, and said, Arise, and be not afraid.

And when they had lifted up their eyes, they saw no man, save Jesus only.

Matthew 17:1-8

MEDITATION

Meditation Practice for Purity

Imagine yourself viewing your life and the frustrations and even anger you hold about the ever-changing conditions that never seem to go right. What expectations about life fail you and make you angry? What could be perfect but never is? If only? Take this frustration and disappointment with you to a very high mountain. There you join the disciples John, Peter, and James. They too experience difficulties and challenges in life. They are gazing at the Christ before them at the top of the mountain. He transforms into a great white light. Go to the Christ and let him breathe into his heart and light your negative emotions and sentiments. Feel and see him return to you the transfigured light of purity. Continue to breathe out to him your darkness and receive more and more light until you experience your purity. Look down the mountain at your ever-changing life below and recognize the perfection behind all the change.

9. Kindness

The ninth quality of essence is kindness, a quality of free spontaneous caring, affection, and giving that is unconditional. In the expression of kindness, there is no need for reward. God is love and demonstrates divine kindness to all who are open and receptive to it. In the earlier stages of spiritual development, the Binah Type (Enneagram Point 2) struggles in separation consciousness with the imitation of kindness, with pride, and uses flattery to seduce others, making themselves indispensable in caring for the needs of others. In unity, there is oneness with the consciousness or essence of kindness, which is understood mentally as the holy idea of freedom and experienced emotionally and expressed behaviorally through the virtue of humility.

The Parable of the Good Samaritan

And, behold, a certain lawyer stood up, and tempted him, saying, Master, what shall I do to inherit eternal life?

He said unto him, What is written in the law? how readest thou?

And he answering said, Thou shalt love the Lord thy God with all thy heart, and with all thy soul, and with all thy strength, and with all thy mind; and thy neighbour as thyself.

And he said unto him, Thou hast answered right: this do, and thou shalt live.

But he, willing to justify himself, said unto Jesus, And who is my neighbour?

And Jesus answering said, A certain man went down from Jerusalem to Jericho, and fell among thieves, which stripped him of his raiment, and wounded him, and departed, leaving him half dead.

And by chance there came down a certain priest that way: and when he saw him, he passed by on the other side.

And likewise a Levite, when he was at the place, came and looked on him, and passed by on the other side.

But a certain Samaritan, as he journeyed, came where he was: and when he saw him, he had compassion on him,

And went to him, and bound up his wounds, pouring in oil and wine, and set him on his own beast, and brought him to an inn, and took care of him.

And on the morrow when he departed, he took out two pence, and gave them to the host, and said unto him, Take care of him; and whatsoever thou spendest more, when I come again, I will repay thee.

Which now of these three, thinkest thou, was neighbour unto him that fell among the thieves?

And he said, He that shewed mercy on him. Then said Jesus unto him, Go, and do thou likewise.

Luke 10:25-37

MEDITATION

Meditation Practice for Kindness

Go into a garden. Breathe deeply. Fill yourself with white healing light. Go back in your recent memories to those times when you faced a situation with someone who had a real need. First look at situations where you took action selflessly. Now look at situations where the person had a real need and you did not take any action. What prevented you from doing so? Now feel the Christ at your side. Look again at these situations and observe how he takes action for them. Placing yourself in his heart, look at people in your life and ask yourself in what ways you can take action to support their real needs with genuine kindness.

The Twelve Fruits of the Tree of Life

> *2: In the midst of the street of it, and on either side of the river, was there the tree of life, which bare twelve manner of fruits, and yielded her fruit every month: and the leaves of the tree were for the healing of the nations.*

The twin pillars of the Kabbalah—the left pillar of consequence and the right pillar of blessings—are referenced here as being "on either side of the river" (the "river" being the middle pillar of the Tree of Life). The one river that flows through the holy city is the reintegrated consciousness. Before, this "river" was the four rivers that went out of Eden; the fourth, the Euphrates (symbolizing the spiritual energies), is the only one mentioned in the Revelation. Its course flows east, which symbolizes the spiritual element. The twelve fruits of the "tree of life" are the perfected capacities or powers of the initiate, and its leaves "for the healing of nations" are the unfolding of spiritual life and service. The twelve fruits can also be understood as the twelve steps of spiritual unfoldment aligning with the twelve precious stones that form the foundation of the New Jerusalem, the healed Kabbalah of wholeness.

To "bare twelve manner of fruits" refers to the initiate's maturation on the journey through these twelve milestones of spiritual unfoldment. The first fruit represents the awakening of the spiritual life and new beginnings. The second fruit represents the parting from subconscious darkness and receiving forgiveness, separating into light, and letting go of love for the world. The third fruit represents growing into the truth through sincerity and humility, overcoming pride. The fourth fruit, developing strength against the storms in life, involves breaking down what is no longer needed and developing faith in higher authority. The fifth fruit represents overcoming adversity, great obstacles of suffering, and loss, followed by acceptance and surrender, a deeper faith, and single-mindedness about God. The sixth fruit represents developing courageous obedience in the face of overwhelming forces of ignorance) by remaining steadfast in Christ Consciousness. The seventh fruit represents wrestling with God, rebellion against God, and rooting out entitlement and ego-desires for glory. The eighth fruit represents experiencing a new beginning where human desire and attachments are losing their hold, accepting God's power, and awakening our spiritual authority. The ninth fruit represents spiritual maturity, developing depth of love and devotion to God regardless of hardships and seeming injustices. The tenth fruit represents becoming restored as a citizen of Spirit walking in alignment with Spirit's Divine Plan and purpose, experiencing the flow of interdimensionality, healing, and miracles. The eleventh fruit moves us through the deeper tests of spiritual refinement and purging in our spiritual maturation process, with service to God foremost; whether we live or die is not important, as only God's life in us has real value. The twelfth fruit represents receiving heavenly rewards, experiencing victory in God, and fully realizing God's Divine Plan for our lives.

> *3: And there shall be no more curse: but the throne of God and of the Lamb shall be in it; and his servants shall serve him:*

The consciousness of separation from Source is abolished ("and there shall be no more curse") The Sephiroth of the Kabbalah are now united ("the throne of God and of the Lamb shall be in it"). The fragmentation described as the Fall of Adam and Eve in the biblical story of Genesis is now being healed. The post-traumatic stress held by the regional maritime civilization of 12,000 to 14,000 BC—the time of the great cataclysms affecting Lemuria and Atlantis—is in the process of being healed within the initiate and all those who have chosen this path of self-realization.

> *4: And they shall see his face; and his name shall be in their foreheads.*

The initiate will see God's "face" of wisdom, power, and love in everything and will put no one before their Source in Spirit. That "his name shall be in their foreheads" refers in Kabbalah to the supernal triad of Chokmah (the presence of God), Binah (the nature of God), and Keter (the consciousness of God), all centered in the brow and crown chakras.

> *5: And there shall be no night there; and they need no candle, neither light of the sun; for the Lord God giveth them light: and they shall reign for ever and ever.*

The Soul never sleeps. The supernal consciousness is beyond polarity of cycles of light and darkness. No outer light source, exoteric guidance, intellectual understanding, or outer instruction is needed. The source of all is the source of light itself and the Soul is eternal, not temporal. From the Soul's light emanates intuition, inner guidance, and the holy ideas.

> *6: And he said unto me, These sayings are faithful and true: and the Lord God of the holy prophets sent his angel to shew unto his servants the things which must shortly be done.*

This message is real, "faithful and true," as it has been sent by "his angel," a messenger of God.

> *7: Behold, I come quickly: blessed is he that keepeth the sayings of the prophecy of this book.*

The transmission of truth through the inner faculties is available for those who keep the instructions of this book of life in their hearts.

> *8: And I John saw these things, and heard them. And when I had heard and seen, I fell down to worship before the feet of the angel which shewed me these things.*

John attempts to praise the messenger who showed these things to him.

> *9: Then saith he unto me, See thou do it not: for I am thy fellow servant, and of thy brethren the prophets, and of them which keep the sayings of this book: worship God.*

The angel is telling John not to make an idol or guru out of him, but instead remain humble and praise only God. Daskalos would often say that he was not a guru, that he preferred to be seen as and called a "brother guide." Similarly, the angel tells John, "See thou do it not: for I am thy fellow servant, and of thy brethren the prophets, and of them which keep the sayings of this book; worship God" — praise only God, the Source, as "thy brethren the prophets" do.

> *10: And he saith unto me, Seal not the sayings of the prophecy of this book: for the time is at hand.*

The Soul, or inner self, has now opened to receive this constant flow and renewal of spiritual energy, light, and consciousness.

> *11: He that is unjust, let him be unjust still: and he which is filthy, let him be filthy still: and he that is righteous, let him be righteous still: and he that is holy, let him be holy still.*

Allow everyone to be in their own consciousness in their learning process, whatever their condition. This is spiritual free will and honoring of the law of non-interference. Those of lighter consciousness, through co-vibration, will gather together to receive support and share it.

> *12: And, behold, I come quickly; and my reward is with me, to give every man according as his work shall be.*

Emphasis is placed on the idea that divine help is always being given to the initiate.

> *13: I am Alpha and Omega, the beginning and the end, the first and the last.*

The voice of reassurance is identified as coming from the God Source.

> **14:** *Blessed are they that do his commandments, that they may have right to the tree of life, and may enter in through the gates into the city.*

Support and blessings flow to those who honor the laws of life, and they will have access to the inner secret teachings of the Kabbalah and the spiritual journey to the Source itself.

> **15:** *For without are dogs, and sorcerers, and whoremongers, and murderers, and idolaters, and whosoever loveth and maketh a lie.*

The external world of illusionary or separation consciousness carries all the negative elementals of false devotion ("dogs") and "sorcerers" (confusion), "whoremongers" (lust), "murderers" (anger and violence), and "idolaters" (greed).

> **16:** *I Jesus have sent mine angel to testify unto you these things in the churches. I am the root and the offspring of David, and the bright and morning star.*

Jesus Christ, spiritual guide of this divine journey, has taught you ("sent my angel to testify unto you") about the chakras ("these things in the churches"). He is your spiritual heritage and lineage ("the root and offspring of David") and your illumination ("and the bright and morning star"). The morning star, Venus, is here symbolic of divine love.

> **17:** *And the Spirit and the bride say, Come. And let him that heareth say, Come. And let him that is athirst come. And whosoever will, let him take the water of life freely.*

This unification is the consciousness, presence, and nature of Keter, Chokmah, and Binah, respectively. It is available to all, for it is the Soul's birthright as a son or daughter of God. Spiritual love reaches out to those who are receptive ("that heareth") and gives of itself unconditionally to all life.

> **18:** *For I testify unto every man that heareth the words of the prophecy of this book, If any man shall add unto these things, God shall add unto him the plagues that are written in this book:*

Don't change the instructions of this book ("add unto these things"). Follow them as consistently as possible, according to your own understanding. Be consistent and true to your authentic self. If you are not, the unconscious state of the living of your life will bring you "the whips of destiny."

> *19: And if any man shall take away from the words of the book of this prophecy, God shall take away his part out of the book of life, and out of the holy city, and from the things which are written in this book.*

If you neglect to apply any of these instructions ("take away from the words of the book of this prophecy"), your access to the higher planes of awareness will atrophy. You must continue transforming and living the light and love of your Being to stay in touch with it.

> *20: He which testifieth these things saith, Surely I come quickly. Amen. Even so, come, Lord Jesus.*

The "I Am" consciousness is available to all of us; those who are able to unveil their minds from passions, vices, and addictions of the personality, awaken quickly.

> *21: **The grace of our Lord Jesus Christ be with you all. Amen.***

The grace of Christ Consciousness will always be with you all. "Amen."

Annotated Bibliography

Addison, Rabbi Howard A. (2006). The Enneagram and Kabbalah: Reading Your Soul. Jewish Lights Publishing. (Referenced: Chapters 5-14, Kindle Edition.)

> *A groundbreaking book correlating two ancient wisdom traditions and containing supportive biblical stories. I highly suggest this book to anyone wanting to broaden their understanding of Enneagram and Kabbalah.*

Alexander, Eben, III (2012). *Proof of Heaven: A Neurosurgeon's Near-Death Experience and Journey into the Afterlife.* Simon & Schuster.

Allan, D. S., and J. B. Delair (2007). *Cataclysm! Compelling Evidence of a Cosmic Catastrophe in 9500 B.C.* Bear & Company. (As referenced in Clow, *Awakening the Planetary Mind*, Kindle edition.)

Atwater, L. H. D. (2005). *Beyond the Indigo Children: The New Children and the Coming of the Fifth World.* Bear & Company. (Referenced: Chapter 12: Soaring Intelligence, pp. 118-128.)

> *This book is well-researched and gives me hope for our future generations. It also demonstrates the responsibility we have for our future generations to insure their transition into the new world.*

Atteshlis, Stylianos (1992). *The Esoteric Practice: Christian Meditations and Exercises.* The Stoa Series, revised English edition. (Referenced: Part 1: The Esoteric Teachings (Individuated Selfhood), pp. 34-38.)

> *Wonderful guidebook to spiritual healing and Esoteric Christian meditation and introspection practices.*

Atteshlis, Stylianos (better known as Daskalos). Lectures and personal interviews (1991-1994) on the subject of spirituality and mental health. Strovolos, Cyprus.

> *Inspiring commentaries and personal stories that opened new avenues of spiritual instruction from a Master healer and Christian mystic teacher.*

Atteshlis, Stylianos (1998). *The Symbol of Life (Das Symbol Des Lebens).* The Stoa Series.

Atteshlis, Stylianos. *A System for the Research of Truth: An Esoteric Christian Approach.* The Stoa Series. (Referenced: Booklet—*Prayer of Daskalos.*)

Atteshlis, Stylianos (2001). *Joshua Immanuel The Christ: His Life on Earth and His Teaching.* The Stoa Series. (Referenced: Stories on the Beatitudes: Chapter 19, p. 111; Chapter 18, pp. 105-106; Chapter 18, pp. 99-100; Chapter 19, pp. 108-109; Chapter 22, pp. 135-136; Chapter 18, pp. 101-102; Chapter 13, pp. 72-73; Chapter 16, pp. 84-85; Chapter 32, pp. 184-185; Chapter 8, p. 44.)

> *A personal account of Daskalos from past-life recall of his journey with Jesus Christ. This book has inspired and healed my own relationship to the Christ story. The stories touch the heart deeply with profound understanding and awaken the Soul to deeper reflection on the truth. A great catalyst for personal healing of all woundings of the heart and soul.*

Atteshlis, Stylianos (1991). The Parables and Other Stories. Imprinta. Text in the biblical parables cited in this book were taken from The New English Bible (Oxford and Cambridge University Press, 1961).

> *I highly suggest that anyone interested in gaining a deeper understanding of the parables of Jesus to read this book and gain a deeper perspective on their hidden meanings.*

Baba, Meher (1973). *God Speaks: Sufism Reoriented.* (Referenced: Part Five: The Planes, pp. 41-54.)

> *One of the great spiritual classics on the various God Worlds and the dimensions of heaven.*

Bailey, Alice A. (1951). *Esoteric Astrology: A Treatise on the Seven Rays, Volume III.* Lucis Trust. (As referenced in Lansdowne, *The Revelation of Saint John.*)

Bauval, Robert, and Adrian Gilbert (1993). *The Orion Mystery: Unlocking the Secrets of the Pyramids.* Three Rivers Press. (Referenced: Chapter 6, Giza and the Belt of Orion; Chapter 7, the star correlation theory.)

> *A fascinating book on how objective research and great intuition and inner guidance reveal the hidden secrets of lost history of antiquity.*

Clow, Barbara Hand, with Gerry Clow (2004). *Alchemy of the Nine Dimensions: Decoding the Vertical Axis, Crop Circles, and the Mayan Calendar.* Hampton Roads Publishing Company, Inc. (Referenced: Part One, Chapters 1-9, pp. 3-153. Nine Dimensions. Specific correlations on galactic dimensional connections to the chakras. The seventh dimension, pp. 99-100.)

> *A brilliant and insightful must-read for anyone who is interested in the changing times in which we live. Wonderful synthesis of science and shamanic realities.*

Clow, Barbara Hand (2011). *Awakening the Planetary Mind: Beyond the Trauma of the Past to a New Era of Creativity.* Bear & Company. (Referenced: Chapter 2, The Great Cataclysm and the Fall, Hamlets Mill and the Precession of the Equinoxes; Chapter 3, The Orion Correlation and the Riddle of the Sphinx, the Giza Plateau as a Cosmic Clock, Maat and the Djed Pillar.)

> *This book brings compelling evidence to us that post-traumatic stress is even greater in scope than only on the level of personal impact. As a psychiatrist interested in shamanism, ancestral trauma, and transcultural and transpersonal psychology, this book opened new doors of understanding for me and what we as humanity must now face and heal in our collective shadow.*

Daskalos. See books by Stylianos Atteshlis (better known as Daskalos).

Demetry, Nicholas C., and Edwin L. Clonts (2007). *The Healing Power of Archangels: For Support and Direction in these Apocalyptic Times.* Verlagsgruppe Random House. From the original manuscript "Apocalypse of Peace" by Edwin Clonts and Nicholas C. Demetry (copyright 2007, Kosel-Verlag, Munchen, Germany). (Referenced: Chapters 6-14, pp. 113-171; Chapter 1: A Psychological View of the Apocalypse, pp. 11-18.)

> *A good book to prepare readers for the collective changes of 2012 and beyond.*

Demetry, Nicholas C. (2010). *Divine Partnership: Unity beyond Duality.* Etherikos Press. (Referenced: Co-dependent roles and qualities, pp. 18-25; chakra functions and elementals, pp. 64-84.)

> *A great read on the seen and unseen dynamics of relationships and how to begin healing yourself and your partnerships.*

Demetry, Nicholas C., and Edwin L. Clonts (2001). *Awakening Love: Universal Mission: Spiritual Healing in Psychology and Medicine.* Blue Dolphin Publishing. Volume II, Appendix 1 is adapted from Chapter VI, The Universal Journey of Transformation, pp. 75-88. Volume II, Appendix 2 is from Chapter IX, Private Interview with Daskalos on Love and Nonattachment, pp. 171-175.

> *Excellent reference on spiritually healing the personality and awakening love.*

Dunn, Christopher (2011). *The Giza Power Plant: Technologies of Ancient Egypt,* Kindle edition. Bear & Company.

Edinger, Edward F. (1999). *Archetype of the Apocalypse: A Jungian Study of the Book of Revelation.* Open Court. (Referenced: Editor's preface by George R. Elder, Ph.D., p. xvii; The Grand Final Catastrophe, pp. 1-7.)

> *A great work of Jungian psychology applying the understanding of archetypes to the Book of Revelation.*

Emoto, Masaru (2011). *The Secret Life of Water,* Kindle edition. Atria Books.

> *Fascinating exploration of the water element blending spiritual and scientific thought.*

Flamma, Thomas (1981). *Metaphysics: A Bridge to Eckankar.* IWP Publishing. (Referenced: Chapter 4, p. 90.)

> *A spiritual understanding of the field of metaphysics to prepare the student for further studies. Excellent understanding of the journey of Soul.*

Hay, Louise L. (2004). *You Can Heal Your Life.* Hay House, Inc. (Referenced: Chapter 15: The List, pp. 145-207.)

> *A great classic on mind-body healing. A must-read for anyone dealing with health and illness issues.*

Hawkins, David R. (2013). *Power vs. Force: The Hidden Determinants of Human Behavior.* Kindle edition. Hay House, Inc.

> *Info on states of consciousness and life-force energy. Includes a logarithmic ranking of levels of consciousness and helpful self-testing methods. A wonderful pioneering work in the field of consciousness research.*

Grove, Daisy E. (2005). *The Apocalypse and Initiation.* The Theosophical Publishing House, Adyar. (Referenced: Chapter 3: Messages to the Churches, pp. 22-37; Part 2: The Drama of Apocalypse, pp. 65-131.)

> *A very fine work that assists the reader to begin a deeper understanding of the complex symbology of the Book of Revelation.*

Jaxon-Bear, Eli (2011). *From Fixation to Freedom: The Enneagram of Liberation.* Leela Foundation, Digital Format. (Referenced: Part 3: Qualities of Essence and The Black Hole: Bliss and Despair.)

> *One of my favorite books on the Enneagram. A perfect complement to the Advaita practices of Ramana Maharshi. Anyone who loves the teachings of Hari Poonjaji, as I do, will find this book a valuable addition to their understanding of personality and its relationship to the Self.*

Joseph, Frank (2006). *The Lost Civilization of Lemuria: The Rise and Fall of the World's Oldest Culture.* Bear & Company. (Referenced: Afterword: The Real Meaning of Lemuria.)

> *A well-researched book on the ancient motherland of Lemuria. This book offers compelling evidence for the existence of Lemuria and offers fresh understanding of humanity's origins and the traumatic impact of global change to an ancient people.*

Jung, Carl Gustav (2014). *The Collected Works of C. G. Jung: Complete Digital Edition.* Princeton University Press, eds. Gerhard Adler, Michael Fordham, Herbert Read, translated from the German by R. F. C. Hull.

Lansdowne, Zachary F. (2006). *The Revelation of Saint John: The Path to Soul Initiation.* Weiser Books. (Referenced: Chapters 1-22 on various commentaries on the interpretation of Revelation.)

> *This is a wonderful book that makes an understanding of the Book of Revelation accessible to the student of spirituality and theology. It is well-researched with numerous biblical references and theological origins of the Revelation material of St. John.*

Liebert, Elizabeth (1992). *Changing Life Patterns: Adult Development in Spiritual Direction.* Paulist Press.

> *Wonderful and insightful study of spiritual development.*

Maharshi, Sri Ramana (2010). *Words of Grace. Who Am I? Self-Inquiry, Spiritual Instruction.* Sri Ramanasramam. (Referenced: Self-Inquiry, pp. 17-35.)

> *The wisdom of Sri Ramana's practice of self-inquiry shines brightly in this booklet on practices for self-realization.*

Maitri, Sandra (2000). *The Spiritual Dimension of the Enneagram: Nine Faces of the Soul.* Jeremy P. Tarcher/Putnam. (Referenced: pp. 43-44, 48, 70, 91-93, 115-116, 134-135, 161, 182, 202-203, 224.)

> *An in-depth study of the psychospiritual dimensions of the Enneagram with a wonderfully insightful clarity of the existential childhood origins of point structure.*

Malachi, Tau (2005). *Gnosis of the Cosmic Christ: A Gnostic Christian Kabbalah.* Llwellyn Publications. (Referenced: Chapter 4, Angels of Grace and the Divine Gift; Chapter 5, Spiritual Practices for Divine Knowledge; Chapter 6, The Wisdom of Creation, Spiritual Practices for Hokmah; Chapter 7, The Faces of the *Shekinah,* Holy Thrones and Dominions; Chapter 8, The Speaking Silences; Chapter 9, The Purifying Fire of God, The Adversary of God and Humanity; Chapter 10, The Messengers of God; Chapter 11, The Divine Muse, Principalities, Dominions and Authorities; Chapter 12, Sons of Light and Sons of Darkness; Chapter 13, The Great Ofan of the Faithful/The Shoeangel, The Order of the Ashim/Souls of Fire.)

> *An amazing book of light and brilliance on the Gnostic teachings of Jesus that transmits to the reader the richness of the Gnostic Christian tradition. A book that will be at the forefront of this topic for many years to come.*

Men, Hunbatz (2010) *The 8 Calendars of the Maya: The Pleiadian Cycle and the Key to Destiny.* Bear & Company. (Referenced: p. 97.)

> *This book, written by a great Mayan elder of wisdom, widens our understanding of the complexity of the Mayan Calendar system.*

Newton, Michael (1994). *Journey of Souls: Case Studies of Life Between Lives.* Kindle edition. Llewellyn Publications.

Pales, Emil (2009). *Seven Archangels: Rhythms of Inspiration in the History of Culture and Nature.* Sophia, Bratislava. (Referenced: pp. 17, 22, 26, 36-37, 40, 49, 63-64, 78-80, 91-93, 103-105.)

> *A brilliant work that masterfully weaves years of painstaking mathematical research with clear intuition to demonstrate the cycles of the Holy Spirit's activity in evolution and proves without a doubt that science and spirituality are unified in the spirit of truth.*

Palmer, Helen, and David Daniels—Enneagram Professional Training Program (1990-1991).

> *A great thanks and deepest gratitude for the high-caliber professional training that gave me the foundation to explore the Enneagram and broaden my understanding of the dynamics of personality and type. The work has given me a valuable tool for psychiatric practice and teaching of spiritual growth groups.*

Pryse, James Morgan (1910). *Apocalypse Unsealed.* Kessinger Publishing. (Referenced: pp. 27, 39, 87, 90, 93, 131, 187, 204-207, 213-214.)

> *An amazing study of the origins of the Book of Revelation in Greek and Jewish thought. This book offers a rich interpretation of the symbolism of Revelation and helps the reader bridge a very cryptic text into a clear and reasonable interpretation and contemporary understanding.*

Smith, Marshall L. (2008). *Spiritual Anatomy Book 2: The Cause and Healing of Disease.* Dimensional Brotherhood Publishers. (Referenced: pp. 205-225.)

> *A wonderful work bringing to the reader of Revelation new and revealing information on its meaning and purpose for humanity.*

Trask, Mary (2009). *The 12 Gemstones of Revelation: Unlocking the Significance of the Gemstone Phenomena.* Destiny Image Publishers (Referenced: pp. 26, 38, 49, 63-66, 70, 84-85, 100, 110-111, 119, 119, 131, 139, 151.)

> *A very moving and inspiring book of faith and understanding of the stages on the path to Christ Consciousness and spiritual surrender.*

Taschen (2010). *The Book of Symbols: Reflections on Archetypal Images.* Taschen GmbH. (Referenced: Color: Yellow, p. 644.)

> *A great resource book on the archetypal meaning of symbols.*

Van Auken, John (2005). *Edgar Cayce on the Revelation: A Study Guide for Spiritualizing Body and Mind.* Sterling.

Velikovsky, Immanuel (1952). *Ages in Chaos.* Doubleday. (As referenced in Clow, *Awakening the Planetary Mind,* Kindle edition.)

Endnotes

1. Daskalos ("teacher" in Greek) is the name by which Dr. Stylianos Atteshlis is best known. He is therefore referred to as Daskalos throughout this book, and all discussions and cited material are taken from his personal teachings and books (by Stylianos Atteshlis in the Annotated Bibliography).

2. George Lamsa, *Holy Bible of the Peshitta.* Where quotations are taken from the Peshitta, this is so indicated following the biblical citation in the text.

3. Edward F. Edinger, *Archetype of the Apocalypse.* All discussions in text reference this book (see Annotated Bibliography).

4. Nicholas C. Demetry and Edwin L. Clonts, *Awakening Love.*

5. Tau Malachi, *Gnosis of the Cosmic Christ,* Kindle Edition.

6. Tau Malachi, *Gnosis of the Cosmic Christ,* Kindle Edition.

7. James Morgan Pryse, *Apocalypse Unsealed,* p. 162.

8. Stylianos Atteshlis [Daskalos], *Joshua Immanuel The Christ: His Life on Earth and His Teaching,* p. 111.

9. Atteshlis [Daskalos], pp. 105-106.

10. Meher Baba, *God Speaks,* p. 45.

11. Atteshlis [Daskalos], pp. 135-136.

12. Atteshlis [Daskalos], pp. 99-100.

13. Atteshlis [Daskalos], pp. 108-109.

14. Atteshlis [Daskalos], pp. 72-73.

15. Atteshlis [Daskalos], pp. 84-85.

16. Atteshlis [Daskalos], pp. 183-185.

17. Atteshlis [Daskalos], pp. 101-102

18. Tau Malachi, *Gnosis of the Cosmic Christ,* Kindle Edition.

19. Atteshlis [Daskalos], p. 44.

20. Elizabeth Liebert, Changing Life Patterns: Adult Development in Spiritual Direction, from *The Ennegram and Kabbalah,* Rabbi Howard A. Addison, Kindle Edition

21. Pryse, p. 178.

22 Atteshlis [Daskalos], p. 143.

23 The Apocrypha of Philip is perhaps most famous as an early source for the popular theory that Jesus was married to Mary Magdalene. The Ancient Greek manuscript describes Jesus as Mary's *koinonos,* or "companion," which may imply an intimate sexual relationship or a friend or companion in faith.

24 Atteshlis [Daskalos], p. 143.

25 Daisy E. Grove, *The Apocalypse and Initiation,* p. 115.

26 David R. Hawkins, *Power vs. Force,* pp. 68-69. The levels depicted in text (Volume I, Chapter 4) are adapted from Hawkins' complete "Map of Consciousness."

27 Pryse, p. 199.

28 Hawkins, pp. 68-69.

29 Hawkins, pp. 68-69.

30 The collective shadow is explored in great detail in *The Collected Works of C. G. Jung: Complete Digital Edition.*

31 Zachary F. Lansdowne, *The Revelation of Saint John,* p. 181.

32 Elizabeth Liebert, Changing Life Patterns: Adult Development in Spiritual Direction, from *The Ennegram and Kabbalah,* Rabbi Howard A. Addison, Kindle Edition

33 Pryse, p. 213

Appendix 1

A UNIVERSAL JOURNEY OF TRANSFORMATION
The Parable of the Prodigal Son

A certain man had two sons: and the younger of them said to his father, "Father, give me the portion of goods that falleth to me." And he divided unto them his living.

And not many days after the younger son gathered all together, and took his journey into a far country, and there wasted his substance with riotous living.

And when he had spent all, there arose a mighty famine in that land; and he began to be in want. And he went and joined himself to a citizen of that country; and he sent him into his fields to feed swine. And he would fain have filled his belly with the husks that the swine did eat: and no man gave unto him.

And when he came to himself, he said, "How many hired servants of my father's have bread enough and to spare, and I perish with hunger! I will arise and go to my father, and will say unto him, 'Father, I have sinned against heaven, and before thee, and am no more worthy to be called thy son: make me as one of thy hired servants.'"

And he arose, and came to his father. But when he was yet a great way off, his father saw him, and had compassion, and ran, and fell on his neck, and kissed him. And the son said unto him, "Father, I have sinned against heaven, and in thy sight, and am no more worthy to be called thy son."

But the father said to his servants, "Bring forth the best robe, and put it on him; and put a ring on his hand, and shoes on his feet: and bring hither the fatted calf, and kill it; and let us eat, and be merry: For this my son was dead, and is alive again; he was lost, and is found." And they began to be merry. (Luke 15:11-24)

The Parable of the Prodigal Son is one of the most frequently told parables of Jesus, because it reveals so much about the forgiving and merciful nature of God. It can also serve as an allegory of the universal journey of transformation from the depths of separation to the heights of ascension via the various stages of consciousness. The process of separation and the return to love will be presented step by step according to the parable.

> **A certain man had two sons: And the younger of them said to his father, "Father, give me the portion of goods that falleth to me." And he divided unto them his living.**

These opening lines illustrate the state of grace that exists in the awareness of the presence of God. This is the same state that existed for Adam and Eve prior to the "Fall" described in Genesis.

> **And not many days after the younger son gathered all together, and took his journey into a far country, and there wasted his substance with riotous living.**

These lines illustrate that entrance into the illusory state of ego separation, the "Fall," where the awareness of the presence of God is lost.

The Parable of the Prodigal Son reminds us, and Daskalos taught, that we most commonly create elementals subconsciously in response to material cravings. These desire-thoughts, or "unclean spirits," serve our desires by creating the conditions for satisfaction at the expense of happiness. In so doing, these negative elementals bind the present-day personality to the material plane as its slave, creating the conditions for suffering. The Parable illustrates the primal material enslavement of addiction consciousness and how this enslavement dissipates our life "substance"—what Daskalos calls our "etheric vitality."

While every form of egotism is rooted in some form of enslavement to the material plane, egotism often takes subtler and more clever forms than that of simple material substance or pleasure addiction. The ego enslaved by egotism is such a trickster that it can successfully manipulate situations where it technically should have no business at all. In fact, the enslaved ego often prefers those realms where it can enter incognito, because it can most reliably preserve itself when it can't be seen for the "devil" it is. Prime examples of such ego subterfuge are found in religion and psychotherapy.

Personalities caught up in religious egotism, or religiosity, typically view themselves in moralistic terms that may assume either the inflated or deflated aspect of a given negative elemental. On one hand, religious egotism likes to clothe itself in strengths and see itself as good, very good. This is that quality of self-righteousness which Jesus encountered so often among the Pharisees and other religious leaders of his day. As Jesus himself was the object of so much adoration as a spiritual teacher, he understood that he likewise had to stay vigilant against the snare of this inflated elemental called self-righteousness. The following story illustrates his concern:

> **And a certain ruler asked him (Jesus), saying, "Good Master, what shall I do to inherit eternal life?"**
> **And Jesus said unto him, "Why callest thou me good? none is good, save one, that is, God." (Luke 18:18-19)**

While it might appear that Jesus was rebuking this ruler, on closer consideration it is evident that this statement was meant as much for himself as it was meant to steer the ruler away from the snare of religiosity. Jesus went on to answer the man's question.

The authors once asked Daskalos what form of egotism he considered to be the most dangerous. He immediately responded, "a demon disguised as an angel of light." Pride is the most noteworthy of these demons and was the downfall of the mighty angel Lucifer, according to semitic traditions. Self-righteous pride could not exist without a "deflated" twin, an inverted form of pride called guilt. Guilt, as used in this context, is not that healthy, transient sense of remorse that's needed to change an attitude or behavior. Guilt is that deflated elemental of religiosity which says, "I am a miserable sinner and I deserve hell." Jesus was equally free from the influences of guilt and self-righteousness. One of his closest associates, Mary Magdalene, was an ex-prostitute. Prostitutes were considered among the worst of "miserable sinners" in that day. Jesus was constantly under attack from the religious leaders for keeping company with "publicans and sinners." His manner of relating to even the overt "sinners" as a brother in spirit did much to dispel guilt as he went about the work of healing.

Guilt keeps a person locked into the mistakes and attitudes of the past, making effective change now all but impossible. While religious egotism puffs itself up and shrinks itself incessantly like the puffer fish, it remains oblivious to the true grandeur and genuine holiness of the Christ Self within. Religion must help de-energize the tenacious twin elementals of self-righteousness and guilt if it is to inspire genuine change in the personality.

Egotism infiltrates psychotherapy in much the same manner as it does religion. Egotism's goal is always to validate the existence of the false, separated self and its unfulfilled desires, even at the expense of suffering and hardship of the personality. It does so in psychotherapy by substituting one self-image for another, puffing up one elemental and deflating another. It takes seeming strengths and congratulates itself for being "good," then wrings its hands about the deflated elementals that make it "bad." All the while the enslaved ego is thoroughly satisfied with itself, because it has kept these elementals vitalized by all the attention to them and thus preserved itself. The enslaved ego may keep "puffing" in psychotherapy for years, fascinated by endless self-analysis and satisfied that it's preventing any genuine change, if this is what the personality wants. The present-day personality can be very clever indeed as it clings to its illusions and distances itself from healing!

Psychotherapy faces a common and difficult challenge from the wiles of egotism when it deals with the emotional consequences of early childhood trauma. Therapy attempts to bring these traumatic memories into conscious awareness for healing. If the therapy is strictly ego-based, it may unwittingly perpetuate a sense of victimization and powerlessness that arises from the immature world view of the wounded "inner child." According to the eminent Jungian psychologist James Hillman, this is the error that frequently sabotages inner child work.[1]

Hillman espouses the idea that each child has an "acorn" within, the seed of a soul mission which is fostered by the child's particular circumstances and in turn influences the child's life deeply. From this perspective, trauma and difficulty may have a much deeper meaning than an ego-based or developmental psychologist can appreciate. Hillman cites several examples of adult greatness that were preceded by corresponding childhood difficulty or trauma, such as the life of Winston Churchill. Churchill as a boy had a lot of trouble with language—reading, writing, speech, spelling. Hillman postulates that these childhood difficulties arose from his soul knowledge that he would one day have to save the Western world through his communication abilities, and that it was simply too much for a child to handle.[2]

Hillman goes so far as to assert, "In your pathology is your salvation."[3] This same theme has been expressed in different ways throughout this book. Each form of psychopathology casts a particular shadow of separation in particular domains of the psyche. These shadows, while experienced as suffering, give the soul its unique mission of incarnation to bring love and light to fear and darkness. The soul, under the unfathomable guidance of the Spirit-ego-self, finds a way to encounter the challenges it needs in order to achieve its particular mission of greatness. Many of our soul challenges arise from the physical, emotional, mental, and social traumas of childhood. Hillman says, "Wounds and scars are the stuff of character. The word character means, at root, 'marked or etched with sharp lines,' like initiation cuts."[4] It is through the encounter with hardship and trauma that the soul has the opportunity to gain strength and resilience.

As adults we do far better to accept our soul challenges gracefully than to forever feel sorry for ourselves. This is not to justify any harm done consciously to a child or to an adult. As Paul said, "Be not deceived; God is not mocked: for whatsoever a man soweth, that shall he also reap." (Galatians 6:7) Spirit can, however, take our best efforts, even the abysmal failures of ignorance and separation, and turn it all to the good. There is no greater joy for the soul than to participate in such a divine adventure. The Prodigal Son is now about to experience the consequences of his ignorant choice for separation and begin the journey back to love.

And when he had spent all, there arose a mighty famine in that land; and he began to be in want.

The Prodigal Son, having wasted the "substance" he was so freely given through addiction consciousness, has cut himself off from the Source of all vitality and has no way to replenish it. In this "land of famine," the state of separation, he is now in want. He is separated at the first chakra domain, which governs those issues around self-preservation, physical survival and security. His life is ruled by that subconscious elemental which says, "I am not worthy to exist." He will look outside himself to this barren land for help.

And he went and joined himself to a citizen of that country; and he sent him into his fields to feed swine.

In the land of separation and scarcity, the Prodigal Son now enters the second chakra domain of the subconscious mind, that of personal relationships. He is looking for validation of himself as a personal entity, but again does so outside of himself and out of a sense of lack. He and the citizen of that country join in a mutual state of fear and a sense of vulnerability. Neither really trusts the other, but they use each other in such a way as to maintain mutually the state of egotism. The core elemental, "I am vulnerable to others," and its associated elementals are the "swine" that the Prodigal Son feeds and his associate maintains. In a relationship driven by subconscious forces, both partners feel dissatisfied and sold short, because neither can ever fill the other's inner void.

And he would fain have filled his belly with the husks that the swine did eat: and no man gave unto him.

The Prodigal Son is now feeling the utter helplessness in the world that results from third chakra separation. His life is a struggle. He's achieved nothing of worth in the world and has no recognition or respect. Meanwhile the subconscious "swine," which maintain his powerless relationship to the world, feed fat off his life force. They accomplish nothing other than the preservation of their own existence. They manage to keep the Prodigal Son convinced that little as he is, he is nothing at all in the world without them. They know that their own power would be lost should his personality gain any true power. The Prodigal Son now in third chakra separation makes a desperate attempt at social validation, yet "no man gave unto him" any respect or acknowledgment. His control plan is a failure. All the while, he continues to submissively feed his "inner swine."

The present-day personality of the Prodigal Son has made its home among the veil of negative elementals in the first three chakra domains that comprise the subconscious mind. The higher faculties of the mind do nothing but serve the swine that now dominate the subconscious. These "unclean spirits," created to serve the material cravings of the personality, now betray the Prodigal Son by binding and nailing his hands and feet to the material world. He bleeds and suffers as on a crucifix, unable to see the light of his own Christ Self that would so readily save him in this, his dark night of the soul. This is the state of crucifixion prior to salvation and healing.

> **And when he came to himself, he said, "How many hired servants of my father's have bread enough and to spare, and I perish with hunger! I will arise and go to my father, and will say unto him, 'Father, I have sinned against heaven, and before thee, and am no more worthy to be called thy son: make me as one of thy hired servants."**

Eventually, the Prodigal Son suffers enough to recognize the original wound of separation. He admits that he has been starved nearly to death by the subconscious elementals of addiction consciousness that he feeds. He has decided that he would prefer to serve his father humbly as a hired hand, if it comes to that, than to continue feeding these swine; he will accept his Father's free gift of salvation and take charge of his destiny. The Prodigal Son is now in the fourth chakra domain, the first level of conscious awareness, and the way is open for healing and transformation. The "unclean spirits" of the subconscious, which make his heart suffer, are losing their grip on his conscious mind. In time, these swine will weaken into a dormant state from his conscious neglect of them. He will replace them with virtues on the journey home.

It appears necessary for virtually all of us, like the Prodigal Son, to discover through our own unique experiences that the illusions of egotism simply do not work. While theoretically possible, it is exceedingly rare for any person to "come to himself" without the stimulus of a certain amount of pain and suffering. The time this process takes and the intensity of the associated suffering vary greatly from one soul to another. Buddhist philosophy actually rests on the premise that suffering exists as a universal fact of human experience. This is the "First Noble Truth" of Buddhism.

This suffering need not go on forever, regardless of what the external circumstances of one's life may be. At some point we gain the capacity to choose how we want to live. As Daskalos says, we may live consciously in love, light, and joy or we may continue to live subconsciously in darkness, driven by the "whips of destiny." With the acceptance of salvation, there is created in the heart an immediate expansion of consciousness and a longing to return to the Source of life. The awakening personality finds ways to look consciously at the elementals of separation it has created in the lower centers. It then dis-identifies with them through a process that says, "I created you, but I am not you. I don't need you any more." It creates virtue, or positive elementals, in their place. However we go about the process, it is the intention to "arise and go to my Father" that is key.

> **And he arose, and came to his father. But when he was yet a great way off, his father saw him, and had compassion, and ran, and fell on his neck, and kissed him. And the son said unto him, "Father, I have sinned against heaven, and in thy sight, and am no more worthy to be called thy son."**

The Prodigal Son has now ascended to the fifth chakra domain, that realm of consciousness where devotional love extends itself to others and the personality expresses its truth fearlessly. It might be considered the realm of conscious relationship, where communication flows freely and truthfully out of a conscious heart connection. The father runs a great distance to meet the son and embraces him, expressing that "joy in heaven over one sinner that repenteth, more than over ninety and nine just persons, which need no repentance." (Luke 15:7) The son, feeling unworthy of this compassion, expresses the remorse he feels for having been such a foolish ingrate. He is really asking for forgiveness.

These few lines from the parable reveal the essential ingredients in psychotherapy, and in any successful relationship, for that matter. Progress will flow from even the most ego-based systems of therapy if the therapist genuinely cares about the client and the client is genuinely motivated to express his or her truth and change his or her mind about "Who I am." Effective psychotherapy, or repentance, brings "unclean spirits" and the "sins" they provoke into the conscious and compassionate embrace of the therapist. Each of these "demons," if examined closely, will reveal in hiding some angelic virtue that is waiting for an opportunity to emerge and find expression in the personality. Within the father's embrace, a son of rebellious disloyalty and ingratitude is transformed into a son of unsurpassed devotion and loving appreciation.

> **But the father said to his servants, "Bring forth the best robe, and put it on him; and put a ring on his hand, and shoes on his feet: and bring hither the fatted calf, and kill it; and let us eat, and be merry: For this my son was dead, and is alive again; he was lost, and is found.**

With continued devotion to love and truth, and their extension in service, consciousness expands into that state which Daskalos calls Self-consciousness. This is that perception of the self as Spirit-ego-self, or Christ Self. With the perception of self as Spirit comes the perception of others as Spirit; this is that sixth chakra realm of expansion called forgiveness of which Jesus and Shankara spoke so passionately. It is the domain of final resignation to the truth, which the Prodigal Son now enters. Self-consciousness still holds onto a dualistic me-you perception, but marks the early stages of true personality transformation.

The Prodigal Son has achieved the forgiveness he seeks. The father sees beneath his son's surface human flaws to the reality of his true nature. He honors his son as he would a divine being, as he pours forth the spirit of that beautiful Indian greeting, "Namaste!" ("to the divine in you"). The Prodigal Son is safely on the path to enlightenment.

And they began to be merry.

With wholehearted devotion to love and truth and the achievement of consistent forgiveness toward all beings, the personality finally breaks into the state which Daskalos calls Self-superconsciousness. This is the realm of unified consciousness, or atonement, in which the personality knows itself to be in a state of at-one-ment with All-That-Is, yet maintains an individual identity. At first this state of enlightenment may be achieved in fleeting glimpses only. When enlightenment does become stabilized, still higher and higher levels of unified awareness and truth comprehension are left to be achieved. These enigmatic realms of divine potential lie within the seventh chakra domain and above. Daskalos also refers to this final God-knowing experience as theosis.

This is the realm the Prodigal Son has now entered, a mystical state of oneness and merriment in the light of Christ. Atonement marks the beginning of true universe citizenship and an eternal "cosmic career" of co-creation with God. It is the crowning achievement of the soul. Unconditional love reigns supreme in the personality and nothing is unforgiven. Eternity itself cannot exhaust the limitless potential of the Christ Self.

The Symbolic Journey of Transformation

The levels of consciousness may be summarized on this diagram of the present-day personality, still "crucified" and awaiting healing of its separation from God in awareness:

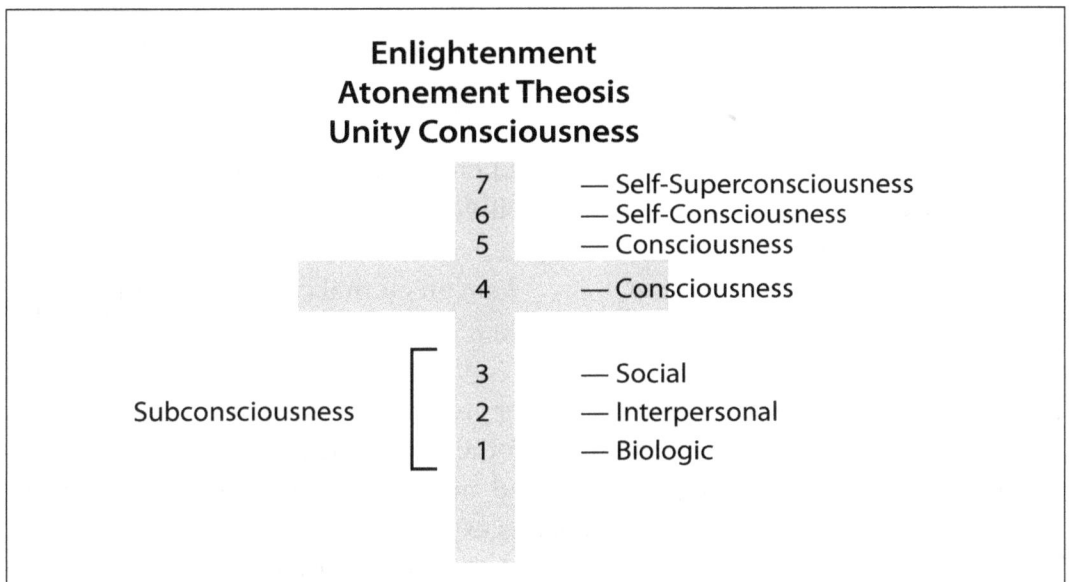

Volume II, Diagram 11

The process of healing begins the moment we "come to ourselves" and invite the presence of the Christ Self into awareness through faith. This is salvation, the entrance into the state of conscious self-determination by an act of will. As we "arise and go to the father," we make our own decisions intelligently under the inspiration of the Christ Self rather than subconsciously, under the domination of negative elementals of the lower chakra domains. As we dis-identify with these "unclean spirits," they begin to weaken and lose their grasp on our minds. In their place we create virtues at every chakra domain to purify the mind, as below:

Negative Elementals of Separation	**Corresponding Virtues of Healing**
Root Chakra (#1)—"I'm unworthy to exist."	"I have infinite worth as a Child of God."
Sacral Chakra (#2)—"I'm vulnerable in relationships."	"I trust every other Child of God."

Solar Plexus Chakra (#3)—"I'm helpless."	"I can do all things through Christ which strengtheneth me." *(Philippians 4:13)*
Heart Chakra (#4)—"I suffer."	"As love incarnate, I care for my neighbor and all creation as my Self."
Throat Chakra (#5)—"I must lie to get what I want."	"I express my truth freely and fearlessly."
Brow Chakra (#6)—"I perceive only imperfection."	"I perceive the perfection of Spirit within all beings."
Crown Chakra (#7)—"Life has no higher purpose."	"I am an eternal co-creator with God."

The mind becomes progressively clearer and more refined, serving as a mirror to reflect one's own Spirit Self and that of others into our awareness. Forgiveness naturally unfolds as we identify more and more with Spirit and less with our elemental creations of mind. Consciousness expands.

Once all things have been forgiven and the personality breaks into the realm of atonement, the conditions of mind that created the suffering of the present-day personality no longer exist. The cross may now return "to the dust from which it came." (Genesis 3:19) The permanent personality, one with its own soul, resurrects from the dust of the present-day personality and knows itself to be at one with all creation in the light of Christ. The soul has reunited consciously in the Garden which it never really left, but with the experiential knowledge of itself as the incarnation of love. This Garden is symbolically represented by The New Jerusalem in Saint John's Book of Revelation.

Notes

1 James Hillman & Michael Ventura, We've Had a Hundred Years of Psychotherapy and the World's Getting Worse, New York: Harper San Francisco, 1992, p. 6.

2 Ibid., pp. 17-21.

3 Ibid., p. 152.

4 Ibid., p. 29.

Appendix 2

Private Interview with Daskalos on Love and Nonattachment

Nick Daskalos, you have talked a lot about love. What is the difference between unconditional love and the conditional love that most people struggle with?

Daskalos First of all we must understand that love is love. And I call it unconditional love. And this unconditional love should be directed as a reflection of the love of God coming to us, and the means of reflection is our heart. He is asking us not to contaminate his love which is reflected from our heart. So, this is first of all his love, and we don't have the right to color it. Our hearts should be the crystal clear mirror to reflect his love which is the unconditional love.

Towards whom do we reflect this love? We say in the prayer before starting our lesson, "to reflect your love towards you." To love him unconditionally does not mean to ask him in ignorance for that and that and that, to give it to us. His mercy is such as Joshua (Jesus) told us, "Ask and it will be given to you, knock and it will be opened to you, to one who is asking it will be given." It is the greatest expression of mercy from God the Father. He might say:

> You unaware creatures, I have given you everything. A perfect body, which is perfect and can remain perfect provided you don't ruin it by your irreverent way of living. I have given you everything so that in this body, you may live in it happily. You're destroying it. What else can you ask of me? Favors, temporary things which are passing? I have given you

everything! The body, the sun, all these things. Everything that I have created that you need to keep your gross material body alive and in good health. Food, water, everything. I have given to you within your body your lungs to breathe my vitality and myself in them. You are breathing, and taking in food and liquids and everything else I have given to you, so you can keep your material body in perfect health. I have given to you now apart from your body, on your body your senses, sight. You can see and enjoy the sun, and everything in nature that I have created. I enjoy them through them and through you. Why don't you enjoy them? For I have not done them for you but you can enjoy everything with your senses. Now everything is mine. I have created it, from my own self, from my own mind super-substance. And you are in the body, which is not yours. It is mine. He which eats my flesh, the logos supersubstance, is making it his flesh. What is my blood? In your bodies is my blood. So what do you expect me to give you? More? So do you give me at least thanks if not your love to me? Even thanks do you give me? No. Who is giving thanks to God?

Nick Where is the gratitude?

Daskalos "And all the time you ask for what? For what I have created? You live on the planet. I have given you the opportunity to enjoy it by seeing it? And instead you take the attitude of insolence toward me. To call it yours? My house, my property, mine, mine, mine, all mine. What were you going to ask of me as God which isn't mine and that you call it yours. I gave it to you! Before asking, I give you everything. What else? So, if you see what human beings are asking from God, it is imaginary and ignorant because everything is given already. And you don't even thank me and recognize that I am, and I am existing. So in giving a reflection of my unconditional love to me from you, you have not succeeded.

Now what is conditional love? We will study that. You have created in your personality, time and place petty self, in the body you are living, in my body that I have given you to live and that I sustain, a demon in reality. Why? Hating my other life reflections, my fellow man? Hating them, you hate me. I am in them. This is what Joshua has taught. Whatever you do, good or bad to any human being around me, you are doing it to me! All of you are in my oneness. You are injuring me, or you are just doing something good to me. Yet, we don't see that.

What do you call conditional love apart from love given to God? What do we ask from human beings and what are we giving other human beings, to our wives, to our husbands, to our children, to our parents? What is it? Study it. Satisfaction of our stupid egoism? Do you love the others as they are or as you think they should be? Why, who gave you that right? Each fellow is on the scale of his evolution. So what is love towards human beings? To a wife, to a husband, to children, to parents, to friends? All around us. What you call conditional love for me is just ingratitude to God and to the human beings. What is conditional love? Kneel before me and satisfy my desires, sexual or not sexual. If you serve this interest of mine, you love me. Otherwise you don't love me, and therefore, why should I love you? The conditional love you mention for me, what can call it? Insolence is a very mild word. Insolence to God, because in every human being is God.

So, the first principle of Christianity which Joshua had taught, love the Lord your God in you. Your being self, your spirit being self, with what I have given you to love it, loving me! Because I am in you also. You're in my oneness. With all the heart I have given you, with all the soul I have granted you, with all your intelligence, your mind. I gave you the right to use my mind supersubstance. It's clear what Joshua has given. And love your fellow man—all your fellow human beings—your fellow man not less than you love yourself.

Nick Daskalos, as well as you have shared it and embodied that love, too, very few people at this time on the planet really know perfect love. Does one have to reach into theosis in oneself to really know love?

Daskalos Definitely.

Nick Can it be achieved in different ways, not only through practice in daily life, but through exosomatosis and reaching in and beyond? Or can people do it through loving service to others?

Daskalos Now Joshua has spoken clearly. If you are living in darkness, in a dark place, can you avoid stumbling? And he said, "If the light is in you, what will be the darkness for you then?" When we ask something from God, does he hear us? Definitely, before even the idea comes in your head and the thought, he knows it, that it is coming in your head. And if we ask him for something, see his great tolerance. For material things? He will give it! Definitely, he will give it, and he will give what is good for you. Because no father will give a snake when his child is asking him for a fish to satisfy his hunger. He will give it. And whatever is asked in his name, his name means becoming such as you have inside you, the Christhood, he will give it!

People are still asking for material things. Things are illusions, chimera, coming and going. Why ask God for that? God has given you everything. The material body, a father, a mother, loving, your heart, your mind, everything you need to keep your body alive, the holy archangels working in your body. They sustain it and keep it alive. What else can I ask? Even the kingdom of the heaven is within. I don't ask for anything! I have it, it's in me, I know it, I found it. Why should I ask for something that I have already found? Let us rather say, "Thank you for having it!"

Nick Ah, that's the attitude. That's the correct way!

Daskalos Ask for something I have already in me? Or thank you for having it! So, what shall I ask? "My Beloved, forgive me for not loving you, for minimizing you in the dimensions of my heart, putting you there. Forgive me for not being able to give you more love, but allow me only to love you, that's enough for me. I don't ask for anything else. Everything is given to me." What do I ask from my beloved one? Offering him a little of the unconditional love and not asking for anything, because in loving and asking, it's not unconditional love.

Nick Love is the only reality.

Daskalos The kingdom of heaven is in the spirit-soul-ego-self. Now, human beings are asking for a house, a car, a bicycle, a radio, etc. What are all these things? Illusions. What do I mean, illusions? These illusions are depriving me of everything good, because I'm concentrated only on what I call mine. For example, in reality all flowers in the world in the gardens of all people are mine! I see them, and from presentations I have them within the kingdom of the heavens within me as representations. I can see them, love them, enjoy them. Those things (objects) will decay after a time, because the Law in the gross material world is the rapid change of everything. Having it in me in the kingdom of the heavens, I must have my treasures permanently. Seeing a flower, loving it, I can close my eyes, not materialize it but substantializing it in me, seeing it in the light of the heaven, I can bring it forward any moment I like in my memory. Who can take it away from me?

Nick So one lacks nothing, there is no lack, and so there should be no attachment—only nonattachment!

Daskalos Definitely. Yes, you transform gross matter into something more real—the forms, the colors, the shapes. For the mind is more real than its expressions. Yes, "nonattachment." Loving each thing separately, I attach myself. But loving everything is "dis-attachment" (dis-identification), so "dis-attachment" is needed even in the kingdom of the heaven in us. Because one of the kingdoms of the heavens within us is the Psychical body and the Psychical plane. The noetical body and the noetical plane. Why should I attach myself and not be in the whole, i.e., expansion, superconsciousness, many places and many conditions at the same time? I go beyond the illusions of time. I enter in your omnipresence, Beloved, and I can love you everywhere. In everything I can love you. By expansion I don't lose you, my Beloved. I'm gaining more of you! More of love, more of your even human appearance as Joshua. But I can find you in everything I love.

This is unconditional love for me.

—Strovolos, Cyprus
March 30, 1994

Appendix 3

The Ascension Ladder

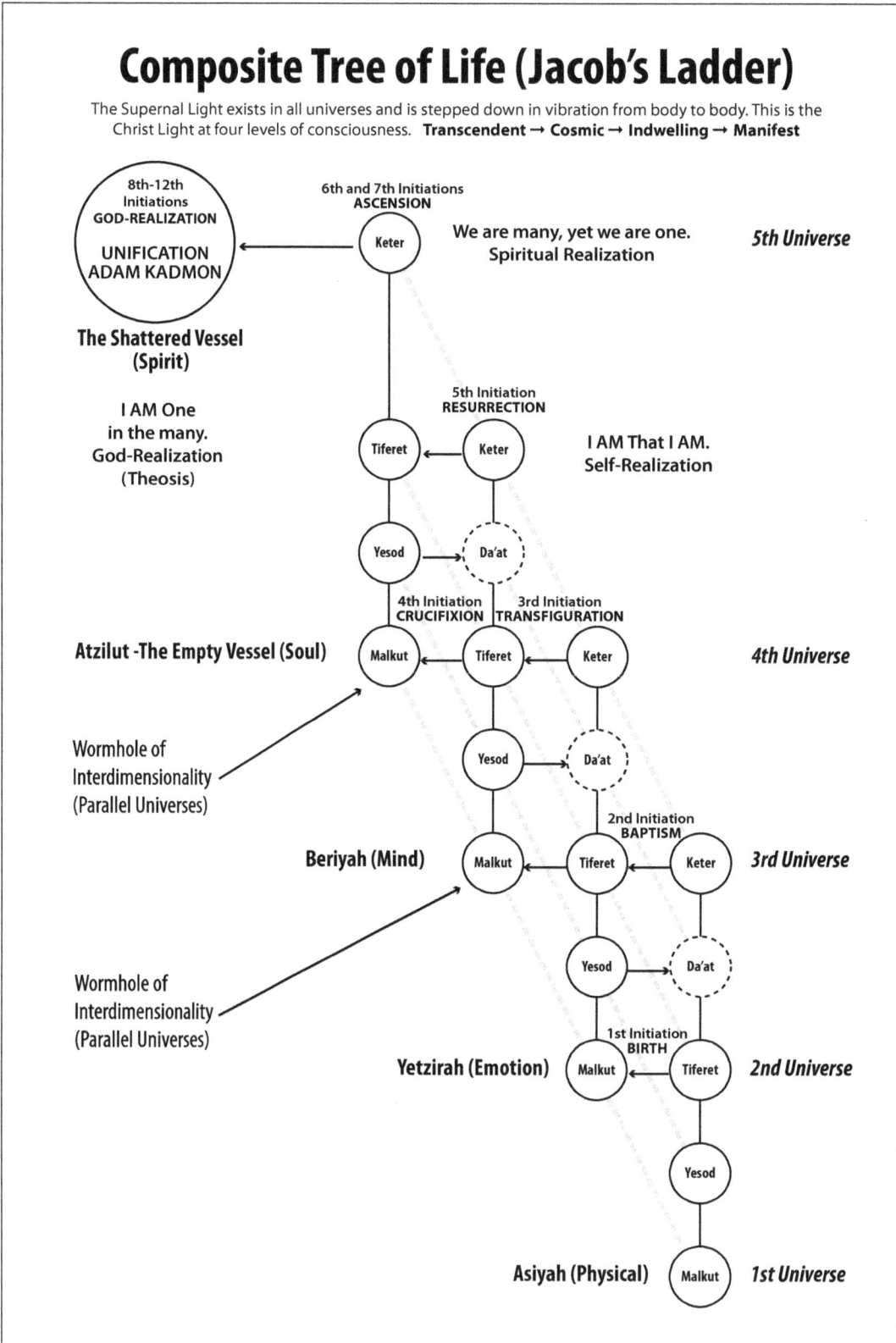

Volume II, Diagram 12

Jacob's Dream by William Blake (c. 1805, British Museum, London)

Genesis 28:12, New International Version

> 12 He had a dream in which he saw a stairway resting on the earth, with its top reaching to heaven, and the angels of God were ascending and descending on it.

John 1:49-51, New International Version

> 49 Then Nathanael declared, "Rabbi, you are the Son of God; you are the King of Israel."

> 50 Jesus said, "you believe I told you I saw you under the fig tree. You will see greater things than that."

> 51 He then added. "Very truly I tell you, you will see 'heaven open, and the angels of God ascending and descending on ' the Son of Man."

"And I saw a new heaven and a new earth: for the first heaven and the first earth were passed away; and there was no more sea."

—REVELATION 21:1 KJV

"A man will meet you carrying an earthen pitcher of water; follow him into the house where he goes in."

—LUKE 22:10

www.ingramcontent.com/pod-product-compliance
Lightning Source LLC
Chambersburg PA
CBHW081916170426
43200CB00014B/2748